The Curious Researcher

S0-AZT-563

The Curious Researcher

A Guide to Writing Research Papers

NINTH EDITION

Bruce Ballenger
Boise State University

 Pearson

330 Hudson Street, NY NY 10013

This work is solely for the use of instructors and administrators for the purpose of teaching courses and assessing student learning. Unauthorized dissemination, publication or sale of the work, in whole or in part (including posting on the internet) will destroy the integrity of the work and is strictly prohibited.

VP & Portfolio Manager: Eric Stano
Development Editor: Ginny Blanford
Marketing Manager: Nick Bolte
Program Manager: Emily Biberger
Project Manager: Alverne Ball, Integra

Cover Designer: Anuj Shrestha, Pentagram
Manufacturing Buyer: Roy L. Pickering, Jr.
Printer and Binder: LSC Communications/ Crawfordsville
Cover Printer: Phoenix Color/Hagerstown

Acknowledgments of third-party content appear on pages xviii–xix, which constitute an extension of this copyright page.

PEARSON, ALWAYS LEARNING, and REVEL are exclusive trademarks in the United States and/or other countries owned by Pearson Education, Inc., or its affiliates.

Unless otherwise indicated herein, any third-party trademarks that may appear in this work are the property of their respective owners and any references to third-party trademarks, logos, or other trade dress are for demonstrative or descriptive purposes only. Such references are not intended to imply any sponsorship, endorsement, authorization, or promotion of Pearson's products by the owners of such marks, or any relationship between the owner and Pearson Education, Inc., or its affiliates, authors, licensees, or distributors.

Copyright © 2018, 2015, 2012 by Pearson Education, Inc. All Rights Reserved. Printed in the United States of America. This publication is protected by copyright, and permission should be obtained from the publisher prior to any prohibited reproduction, storage in a retrieval system, or transmission in any form or by any means, electronic, mechanical, photocopying, recording, or otherwise. For information regarding permissions, request forms and the appropriate contacts within the Pearson Education Global Rights & Permissions Department, please visit www.pearsoned.com/permissions/.

Library of Congress Cataloging-in-Publication Data
Names: Ballenger, Bruce P.
Title: The curious researcher: a guide to writing research
    papers/Bruce Ballenger.
Description: Ninth edition. | Hoboken, New Jersey: Pearson Education, 2017.
Identifiers: LCCN 2016042267 | ISBN 9780134498263 (softcover)
Subjects: LCSH: Report writing—Handbooks, manuals, etc. |
    Research—Handbooks, manuals, etc.
Classification: LCC LB2369.B246 2017 | DDC 808/.02—dc23
    LC record available at https://lccn.loc.gov/2016042267

1   16

Student Edition
ISBN 10:   0-134-49826-7
ISBN 13: 978-0-134-49826-3

Instructor's Review Copy
ISBN 10:   0-134-49954-9
ISBN 13: 978-0-134-49954-3

A la Carte
ISBN 10:   0-134-49953-0
ISBN 13: 978-0-134-49953-6

www.pearsonhighered.com

For Rebecca, who reminds me to ask, Why?

Contents

3   The Third Week   79

Thematic Table of Contents

Preface

Features of the New Edition

Writing a textbook is like discovering an aunt you never knew you had. She arrives unexpectedly one summer and stands at your door beaming and expectant. Naturally, you welcome her in. How charming she is, and as you get to know her, you get to know yourself. This is her gift to you. At some point, many months later, you see her luggage by the door, and with a certain sadness, you send her off. "Come again," you yell as she ambles away. "Come again anytime. I'll miss you!" And you do. Your fondness for this newly discovered relative grows as you learn that other people who aren't even blood related like her too.

If a textbook is successful, the aunt returns again and again, and you get to know her well. Though you may wish, especially in the beginning, that she wouldn't visit so often, after a few weeks there are new conversations and new discoveries. That's the way it has always been for me with *The Curious Researcher*, and the ninth edition is no different. Here are some of the new features of the book that make me feel that way:

- **New content on presenting research in alternative genres.** Since the early editions of *The Curious Researcher*, how students compose research projects has changed. Though they may often still write papers, research is also presented in other genres, many of which are multimodal. In this edition, a recurring feature on "Presenting Research in Alternative Genres" helps students to reimagine their projects as a slide presentation, infographic, photographic essay, or poster. They will find tips for choosing, planning, designing, and reflecting on a relevant genre for their research project.

- **Latest approaches on how to think about sources.** While genres for student research have evolved, approaches for how researchers look at sources have, too. Inspired by the recent *Framework for Information Literacy for Higher Education*, a dramatic new report from the group that represents university librarians, this edition encourages students to see sources in a more rhetorical context. The question "what is a good source?" is no longer simply that it is scholarly. Instead, students are encouraged to consider their audience, genre, and purpose.

- **Updated MLA citation conventions.** With the publication of the latest *MLA Handbook* came a revolution in how to document sources in the humanities. In the new edition of *The Curious Researcher*, students will find a straight-forward and lively discussion of these changes that will help them adapt to the new style, including lots of examples.

- **More help on crafting search terms.** Now more than ever, care in choosing search terms and phrases for library databases and Web searches makes a huge difference in the quality of results. This edition includes some new ways of thinking about how to come up with the best language.

- **New sections on narrative and argumentative logic.** From the beginning, *The Curious Researcher* advocated the exploratory research essay as a useful alternative to the argumentative research paper. The new edition looks at each option more closely, examining how essay and argument draw on different reasoning strategies, information that will help students choose which is most appropriate for their project.

- **New thematic table of contents.** For users who want to tailor their use of the book to meet the needs of a particular course or the particular challenges of their students, this edition features a table of contents organized around five key categories: research skills, research strategies, writing process, inquiry, and genre.

Placing Inquiry at the Heart of the Course

For many of my college writing students, there are two kinds of school writing—"creative" writing and "academic" writing—and the two have very little in common. Creative writing is typically any personal writing assignment—a personal narrative, a reader response, or a freewriting exercise—and academic writing is almost anything that involves research. I've spent quite a few years now trying to understand this perceived gap between creative and academic writing, a distinction that I have found troubling because it short-circuits the connection I have been trying to build between the personal and the academic, especially the idea that students' own subjectivities are not only relevant to academic work but are also an inescapable part of it. I also know from my own experience as an academic that research writing is a creative enterprise. *Why don't my students see that?* I've wondered.

The answer, in part, lies with the traditional research paper assignment itself. Despite our best intentions, students often see the assignment as a closed process: come up with a thesis quickly, hunt down evidence to support it, and wrap it up—all the while focusing less on learning something

than on getting it right: the right number of pages, the right citations, the right margins. This isn't the way academics approach research at all, of course. We do research because we believe there is something to discover that we don't already know. How might I help my students understand that?

The answer is to teach inquiry, which is "the heart of the [academic] enterprise." Reviewing the state of undergraduate learning, the Boyer Commission lamented the largely passive experience that students have during their first year. They sit in lectures, regurgitate information in exams, and if they do write, students often do so without much passion. Rarely do they get a chance to genuinely inquire into questions that interest them where the motive is discovery. How strange this is, especially because we often imagine the first year as an introduction to thinking and learning as college students. Shouldn't they get at least some experience with genuine inquiry, which is so central to higher education? The Boyer Commission concurred. The freshman year, the report concluded, should provide "new stimulation for intellectual growth and a firm grounding in inquiry-based learning."

The Curious Researcher answers that call. Research-based assignments, especially in the first-year writing class, present an ideal opportunity to encourage inquiry-based learning and the kinds of thinking it demands. In the many years I've taught inquiry, I've found that students—though sometimes confused at first—embrace the opportunity to exercise their curiosity. In some ways, new generations of college students are better prepared for inquiry-based approaches because they have lots of practice following trails on the Web as they explore questions that interest them. They know discovery. They just don't experience it much in school. This book provides students with a more systematic approach to exploration, one that draws on intellectual practices and skills that will help them search, think, and write well. *The Curious Researcher* also tries to inspire students to ask those questions that will shape their thinking well after they leave school. But how does it do that?

Teaching the Spirit of Inquiry

Over the years, I've refined *The Curious Researcher's* approach to teaching inquiry, but it still rests on these premises:

1. **Students should have the experience of investigating a topic in an open-ended way, at least initially.** Whether their research projects are ultimately exploratory or argumentative, students should experience the power of suspending judgment. This goes completely against their instincts, which are to nail things down as quickly as possible. However, discovery depends on entertaining contradictions, tolerating ambiguities, and simply wondering about what you read and hear.

2. **Inquiry seeds argument.** Most research writing in college is argumentative. Yet in most cases, we develop arguments inductively, through inquiry. We discover our thesis either by exploring the evidence or by testing our thesis against the evidence, including evidence that is inconvenient or contrary to what we already think.

3. **One of the most useful—and difficult— things to teach and to learn is the power of questions.** Inquiry-based approaches rest on wonder. These investigations often begin with questions of fact—*What is known about the health effects of tanning booths?*—that later flower into a question, say, of policy—*What should be done to minimize the risks of tanning booths?* The power of questions fuels the critical mind and drives the research.

4. **Writing as a way of thinking is a vital tool in discovery and learning.** What students in any major can learn in a writing class is how to put language into the service of inquiry.

As any composition instructor knows, writing isn't just a means of getting down what you already know. It's much more interesting than that. Writing can help writers *discover* what they think. In an inquiry-based classroom, this is invaluable, and we need to teach students how to use writing not only to report the results of their research but also to think about what they're discovering *as* they do research.

Ways of Using This Book

Because procrastination ails many student researchers, this book is uniquely designed to move them through the research process, step-by-step and week by week, for five weeks—the typical period allotted for the research paper assignment. The structure of the book is flexible, however; students should be encouraged to compress the sequence if their research assignment will take less time or ignore the sequence altogether and use the book to help them solve specific problems as they arise.

Naturally, the book is organized narratively, beginning with some of the issues students will initially encounter as they begin a research assignment, things like confronting their assumptions about research and finding a topic, and then taking them through the process of acquiring the knowledge about it to create a composition. Students who follow the five-week sequence usually find that they like the way *The Curious Researcher* doesn't deluge them with information, unlike so many other research texts. Instead, *The Curious Researcher* doles information out week by week, when it is most needed. I've also been told by instructors who use the book for online classes that its structure is particularly well suited for teaching research writing in that environment, especially because each chapter contains exercises that help students work on their own to push their projects along.

Alternatives to the Five-Week Plan

The narrative structure is just one way your students might experience the book. Imagine the content falling into the following categories:

- **Skills.** Discrete practices and techniques that students might begin to master (e.g., paraphrasing, documentation, annotated bibliography, understanding databases, crafting interview questions, avoiding plagiarism, integrating quotes)

- **Strategies.** Approaches to gathering, evaluating, and organizing information (e.g., evaluating sources, developing working knowledge, notetaking as conversation with sources, choosing appropriate databases)

- **Genre.** Consideration of how forms and conventions of research are shaped by users and situations (e.g., considering alternative genres, reading academic articles, citation conventions, types of research papers, etc.)

- **Writing Process.** Methods of composing, including invention exercises, and how they respond to rhetorical situations (e.g., brainstorming topics, drafting lead paragraphs, revision, structuring the draft, writing for readers, model student essays, etc.)

- **Inquiry.** Intellectual practices and ways of knowing that encourage exploration and discovery (e.g., unlearning, narrative and argumentative logic, qualities of strong inquiry questions, etc.)

Because writing courses that feature research assignments vary widely, you might consider which of these five categories best support the class you're teaching. The new edition includes an alternative table of contents on page xii that is organized around each of these categories and will help you decide what content might work for your class.

REVEL™

Educational Technology Designed for the Way Today's Students Read, Think, and Learn

When students are engaged deeply, they learn more effectively and perform better in their courses. This simple fact inspired the creation of REVEL: an interactive learning environment designed for the way today's students read, think, and learn.

REVEL enlivens course content with media interactives and assessments—integrated directly within the authors' narrative—that provide opportunities for students to read, practice, and study in one continuous experience. This immersive educational technology replaces the textbook and is designed to measurably boost students' understanding, retention, and preparedness.

Learn more about REVEL

http://www.pearsonhighered.com/revel/

Acknowledgments

I began working on the first edition of this book back in 1991, and in the many years since then, I've been fortunate to have great students who tutored me on what worked and what didn't. Over the years, these have included many more students than I can name here, but I'd like to single out a few who have been particularly helpful: Andrea Oyarzabal, Amanda Stewart, and Rachel Gallina. My daughter, Becca Ballenger, to whom I dedicated the first edition of this book, is now a part-time collaborator. She's always been a wonderful daughter, and now she's turned into a wonderful writer, too.

A special thanks to Sara Robertson, reference librarian at Portland Community College. Sara reviewed the book to make sure the coverage of information literacy and library resources reflected the latest thinking in her field. She was also instrumental in encouraging me to develop a new approach in Chapter 2 on how to evaluate sources rhetorically, which is one of the best new additions to the text.

The strong support from the Pearson team is key to this book's success. My editor at Pearson, Ginny Blanford, cheerfully spurred me on, offering valuable insights about how to make the book work better. Her expertise on the new MLA guidelines was a godsend. My former editor, Joe Opiela, took a risk on *The Curious Researcher* back in the early nineties, and for that I'm forever grateful. I also appreciate the enormous contribution that Randee Falk made to the book's evolution in the last few editions. My new friends at Ohlinger Publishing Services—Cynthia Cox and Emily Biberger—skillfully shepherded the book through editing and production.

A number of my colleagues have been unflagging in their support of *The Curious Researcher* over the years. Thanks to Carrie Seymour, a colleague at Boise State, who led me to the fine work of one of her students, which is now featured as a model essay in Appendix A. I'd also like to thank Deborah Coxwell-Teague, at Florida State University, and Nancy DeJoy, at Michigan State University. Both have been enthusiastic boosters of the book over the years. There are many others I've met traveling to campuses around the country who have been generous in their support and have

said very kind things to me about the book. These visits are great learning opportunities for me, and they've been instrumental to an evolution in my thinking about how to teach writing and inquiry to all kinds of students in many different contexts. Thanks to all of you.

Most of all, I'm grateful to my wife, Karen, and my two daughters, Becca and Julia, for always leaving the light on to guide me home.

I would like to thank those individuals who have reviewed my book. Reviewers for the eighth edition include the following: Kathleen J. Cassity, Hawaii Pacific University; Sydney Darby, Chemeketa Community College; Holly DeGrow, Mt. Hood Community College; Tom Hertweck, University of Nevada–Reno; Nels P. Highberg, University of Hartford; Elizabeth Imafuji, Anderson University; and Shevaun Watson, University of Wisconsin–Eau Claire. I would also like to extend my thanks to the reviewers of this edition: Shanti Bruce, Ph.D., Nova Southeastern University; Julia Combs, Southern State University; Jordan Curtis, Bryant & Stratton College, Syracuse; Michael Delahoyde, Washington State University; Martha Silano, Bellevue College; Dr. Ann Spurlock, Mississippi State University; and Jennifer Wetham, Clark College.

Bruce Ballenger

About the Author

Bruce Ballenger, a professor of English at Boise State University, teaches courses in composition, composition theory, the essay tradition, and creative nonfiction. He's the author of seven books, including the three texts in the Curious series: *The Curious Researcher*, *The Curious Reader*, and *The Curious Writer*, all from Pearson Education. His book *Crafting Truth: Short Studies in Creative Nonfiction*, is also from the same publisher. Ballenger lives in Boise, Idaho.

About the Author

Introduction
Thinking about— and Rethinking—the Research Paper

 ## Learning Objectives

In this chapter, you'll learn to...

- Recognize the differences between reporting information and using it to explore a question or make an argument.
- Reevaluate your assumptions about the research paper genre and ways of knowing.
- Distinguish between a research *essay* and a conventional research *paper*, and describe the similarities and differences between them.
  - Analyze what a research assignment is asking you to do, and apply that to how you approach tone, structure, narration, and evidence.

Unlike most textbooks, this one begins with your writing, not mine. Open a fresh page in your notebook, computer, or tablet and spend 10 minutes doing the following exercise.

Learning and Unlearning 101

By the time we get to college, most of us have written research papers, beginning as early as the eighth grade. Whenever we've done something for a long time—even if we don't think we're good at it—we have assumptions about how it's *supposed* to be done. For example,

> "Whenever you can, use big words in your school writing to sound smart."

> "The best research is in books."

Exercise 1

THIS I BELIEVE

Most of us were taught to think before we write, to have it all figured out in our heads before we compose. This exercise asks you to think *through* writing rather than *before,* letting the words on the page lead you to what you want to say. With practice, that's surprisingly easy using a technique called *fastwriting*. Basically, you just write down whatever comes into your head, not worrying about whether you're being eloquent, grammatically correct, or even very smart. If the writing stalls, write about that; or write about what you've already written until you find a new trail to follow. Just keep your fingers or pen moving.

STEP 1: Following is a series of statements about the research paper assignment. Choose one that you believe is true or one that you believe is false. Then, in your notebook or on your computer—wherever you can write faster—write for 3 minutes without stopping about the belief you chose. Why do you think it's true or false? Where did you get these ideas? Is there a logic behind your beliefs? What might that be? Whenever you feel moved to do so, tell a story.

- You have to know your thesis before you start.
- You have to be objective.
- You can't use the pronoun *I.*
- You can use your own experiences and observations as evidence.

- You can use your own writing voice.
- There is always a structure you must follow.
- You're supposed to use your own opinions.

STEP 2: Now consider the truth of the following statements. These statements have less to do with research papers than with how you see facts, information, and knowledge and how they're created. Choose one of these statements* to launch another 3-minute fastwrite. Don't worry if you end up thinking about more than one statement in your writing. Start by writing about whether you agree or disagree with the statement, and then explore why. Continually look for concrete connections between what you think about these statements and what you've seen or experienced in your own life.

- There is a big difference between facts and opinions.
- Pretty much everything you read in textbooks is true.
- People are entitled to their own opinions, and no one opinion is better than another.
- There's a big difference between a *fact* in the sciences and a *fact* in the humanities.
- When two experts disagree, one of them has to be wrong.

Dig a little deeper, and you'll discover that these assumptions are often based on beliefs about how things work in the world. For example, the importance of using "big words" and relying on "book facts" both arise from beliefs about authority in academic writing—where it comes from, who has it, and who doesn't. This might seem like overthinking things, but it *really matters* what implicit beliefs are at work whenever someone is trying to learn to do new things. Our assumptions, frankly, are often misleading, incomplete, or downright unhelpful. But how do you know that? By flushing those birds from the underbrush and taking a good look at them from time to time. That was the

---

*Part of this list is from Marlene Schommer, "Effects of Beliefs about the Nature of Knowledge on Comprehension." *Journal of Educational Psychology,* vol. 82, 1990, pp. 498–504.

purpose of Exercise 1. The first part of Exercise 1 focused on a few beliefs you might have about writing academic research papers. Maybe you had a discussion in class about it. From my own research on common beliefs about research writing, I once discovered that one of the most common assumptions first-year college students share is this one: You have to know your thesis before you start a research paper—which obviously implies the belief that discovery is not the point of research.

The second part of Exercise 1 might have gotten you thinking about some beliefs and attitudes you hadn't thought much about—what a "fact" is, the nature and value of "opinions," and how you view experts and authorities.

Both sets of assumptions—one about the research paper genre and the other about how we come to know things—have a huge effect on how you approach the assignment. No doubt many beliefs have some truth to them. Other beliefs, however, may need to be *unlearned* if you're going to take your research writing to the next level. Keep these beliefs out in the open, where you can see and evaluate them to determine if you have some unlearning to do.

Using This Book

The Exercises

Throughout *The Curious Researcher*, you'll be asked to do exercises that either help you prepare your research paper or actually help you write it. You'll need a research notebook in which you'll do the exercises and perhaps compile your notes for the paper. Any notebook will do, as long as there are sufficient pages and left margins. Your instructor may ask you to hand in the work you do in response to the exercises, so it might be useful to use a notebook with detachable pages. You may also choose to do these exercises on a computer rather than in a notebook. If you do, just make sure that it feels good to write fast and write badly.

Write badly? Well, not on purpose. But if the notebook is going to be useful, it has to be a place where you don't mind lowering your standards, getting writing down even if it's awkward and unfocused. The notebook is where you have conversations with yourself, and what's important is not the beauty of a sentence or airtight reasoning but breathlessly chasing after language that threatens to run away from you. Many of the exercises in this book, including the one that started it, invite you to write badly because in doing so, you can use writing to discover what you think.

The Five-Week Plan

If you're excited about your research project, that's great. You probably already know that it can be interesting work. But if you're dreading the work ahead of you, then your instinct might be to procrastinate, to put it off until the week it's due.

That would be a mistake, of course. It's likely that the paper won't be very good. Because procrastination is the enemy, this book was designed to help you budget your time and move through the research and writing process in five weeks. But there's another reason, too, that you should think about how your research project will develop over time: You will start out not knowing much about your topic, and how much you know impacts how much you can do. You will not, for example, be able to come up with a strong research question until you have some working knowledge of your topic. Behind the five-week plan is the idea that research is developmental—your abilities will develop over time.

It may take you a little longer, or you may be able to finish your paper a little more quickly. But at least initially, use the book sequentially, unless your instructor gives you other advice.

Alternatives to the Five-Week Plan

Though *The Curious Researcher* is structured by weeks, you can easily ignore that plan and use the book to solve problems as they arise. (See the alternate Contents on page 000.) Use it when you need to find or narrow a topic, refine a thesis, do advanced searching on the Internet, organize your paper, take useful notes, and so on. The overviews of Modern Language Association (MLA) and American Psychological Association (APA) research paper conventions in Appendixes A and B, respectively, provide complete guides to both formats and make it easier to find answers to your specific technical questions at any point in the process of writing your paper.

Understanding Your Assignment

One of the things I hear most often from my students who have research assignments in other classes is that the instructor "doesn't want my opinion in the paper." Frankly, I'm often skeptical of this. College writing assignments typically are about what or how you think. But because research papers involve considerable time collecting and considering the ideas of others, it's easy to assume that you're supposed to be a bystander.

What these instructors are at pains to point out is that, contrary to what you might believe, they are actively interested in what you think. They want students to *do* something with the information they collect.

Discovering Your Purpose

In high school, I wrote a research "paper" on existentialism for my philosophy class. I understood the task as skimming a book or two on the topic, reading the entry on "existentialism" in the *Encyclopaedia Britannica,* putting notes on some notecards, and writing down everything I learned. That took about six pages. Did I start with a question? No. Was I expressing an opinion of some kind about existentialism? Not really. Did I organize the information with some idea about existentialism that I wanted to relay to readers? Nope. Was I motivated by a question about the philosophy that I hoped to explore? Certainly not. What I wrote was a research *report*, and that is a quite different assignment than almost any research paper you'll be asked to write in college.

If college research assignments don't simply report information on a topic, what do they do? They are organized around what you think—what you believe is important to say about your topic—and there are three ways you can arrive at these ideas:

1. *You can know* what you think from the start and write a paper that begins with a thesis and provides evidence that proves it.
2. You can *have a hunch* about what you think and test that hunch against the evidence you collect.
3. You can begin by *not knowing* what you think—only that you have questions that really interest you about a topic.

Academic inquiry rarely begins with item 1. After all, if you already know the answer, why would you do the research? It's much more likely that what inspires research would be a hunch or a question or both. The motive, as I've said before, is discovery. *The Curious Researcher* promotes a method of discovery that probably isn't familiar to you: essaying.

Writing to Find Out and Writing to Prove

Essay is a term used so widely to describe school writing that it often doesn't seem to carry much particular meaning. But I have something particular in mind.

The term *essai* was coined by Michel Montaigne, a sixteenth-century Frenchman; in French, it means "to attempt" or "to try." For Montaigne and the essayists who follow his tradition, the essay is less an opportunity to *prove* something than an attempt to *find out*. An essay, at least initially, is often exploratory rather than argumentative, testing the truth of an idea or attempting to discover what might be true. (Montaigne even once had coins minted that said *Que sais-je?*—"What do I know?") The essay is often openly subjective and frequently takes a conversational, even intimate, form.

Now, this probably sounds nothing like any research paper you've ever written. Certainly, the dominant mode of the academic research paper is impersonal and argumentative. The purpose is to prove something rather than find something out. But if you consider writing a *research essay* instead of the usual *research paper*, four things might happen.

- **You'll discover that your choice of possible topics suddenly expands.** If you're not limited to arguing a position on a topic, then you can explore any topic that you find puzzling in interesting ways, and you can risk asking questions that might complicate your point of view.
- **You'll find that you'll approach your topics differently.** You'll be more open to conflicting points of view and perhaps more willing to change your

mind about what you think. As one of my students once told me, this is a more honest kind of objectivity.

- **You'll see a stronger connection between this assignment and the writing you've done all semester.** Research is something all writers do, not a separate activity or genre that exists only on demand. You may discover that research can be a revision strategy for improving essays you wrote previously in the semester.

- **You'll find that you can't hide.** The research report often encourages the writer to play a passive role; the research essay doesn't easily tolerate passivity. You'll probably find this both liberating and frustrating. Although you may likely welcome the chance to incorporate your opinions, you may find it difficult to add your voice to those of your sources.

My argument in *The Curious Researcher* is that this more exploratory, possibly less formal researched piece is the best way to introduce you to the spirit of inquiry that drives most academic research. The habits of mind that come from essaying, along with the research and writing skills that essaying develops, should help you whenever you're asked to write a paper that involves research. Put another way, exploration *seeds* argument, and although the argumentative research paper is more common than the exploratory essay, exploration is fundamental to all academic inquiry. Why not take the opportunity to experience what exploration is like?

Analyzing a Research Assignment

Will you be asked to write exploratory research essays in other classes? Probably not often (see "Creative Research Papers?" on p. 000). Although you can apply the research skills and reasoning strategies you gain from essaying your research question to most any research assignment, it's important to know how to *read* what a research paper assignment is asking you to do. Apparently, this analysis can pose a huge problem for students. In one study, for example, 92 percent

 Presenting Research in Alternative Genres

Beginning in the 1920s, it was just the College Research Paper, and this mostly meant one thing: a multipage typed document that uses outside sources. This is still a common format for researched writing, and no doubt will be for many years to come. But as we consume more and more information in digital formats—things like Web pages and infographics—and in other modes—especially sound and images—there are new ways to present research that go beyond the printed page. Throughout *The Curious Researcher,* I'll offer suggestions about how to present your research in alternative genres and tips about how novices can learn the basics of multimedia formats. In particular, we'll look at some alternative genres that are particularly well-suited for research projects, including infographics, posters, slide presentations, and photographic essays. Watch for these features in every chapter.

of students said that the most frustrating part of doing research is figuring out what their professor wants.*

Instructors aren't trying to be obtuse. They want you to understand the assignment, and most have made an effort to be clear. Although there's not much you can do about *how* the assignment is conceived or described, you can be savvy at analyzing the assignment's purpose and guidelines.

One thing that you'll almost always see in a research assignment is that it must contain a thesis. That's true of an exploratory research essay, too. But what may not be immediately obvious is where that thesis is supposed to come from, and *when*. An inquiry-based assignment like the one you'll do in *The Curious Researcher* begins with a question. The thesis often comes pretty late to the party. But that isn't always the case in research papers that focus on argument.

A Thesis: Where and When?

The language that research assignments use to emphasize argument is quite often explicit: "You are to write a research paper in which you make an argument related to some aspect of life in Southeast Asia." Not much ambiguity there. Similarly, some assignments ask that you "take a position" on a topic. Argumentative research papers are most often organized around a thesis, and some assignment descriptions go to great lengths to explain what makes a strong thesis (usually, sufficiently narrow, addressing a significant question, and explicitly stated).

What may not be obvious, however, is how much latitude you have in letting your research revise your thesis or even dramatically change your initial point of view. Most often, instructors *expect* the research to change your thinking, and they often use the term *working thesis* to describe your initial position. These are the more open-ended assignments that might specify that the crafting of a final thesis can occur late rather than early in the research process.

More rarely, an assignment will imply a closed approach: First identify a thesis, and then seek evidence from your research that will support it. This is the conventional thesis-support model in which the expectation is that you will use your thesis, and not your research question, to dictate not just the structure of your paper but also the goal of your research. These kinds of assignments tend not to mention that a thesis might be revised and are silent on how it arises from a research question or problem. Always ask your instructor whether your reading of the assignment as more closed-ended is accurate. The key questions are these:

- Should I know my thesis before I start?
- If not, should I have at least a hunch (hypothesis) that I'm expected to test through the research?
- Or should I begin with a research question and search for my thesis as part of my investigation?

*Head, Alison, "Beyond Google: How Do Students Conduct Academic Research?" *First Monday*, vol. 12, no. 8, 6 August 2007, no pages.

In the inquiry-based approach of *The Curious Researcher*, researchers typically begin with a question, and as you work through the book, you'll learn the methods of discovery that will help you *to discover* a thesis. Both exploratory research essays and argumentative research papers will have a thesis. But where? Typically, argumentative writing puts the thesis front and center, sometimes in the first or second paragraph. There writers are explicit about their purpose: "I will argue that the proposal to ban Sharia law in Idaho is a solution looking for a problem." On the other hand, exploratory essays often first emphasize the research question. Writers then follow their thinking at it evolves through encounters with evidence, arriving at a conclusion *at the end of the essay*.

Audience

For whom are you writing? So much hinges on the answer to this question: the tone of the paper, how specialized its language might be, the emphasis you give on providing background information on the research question, and the degree to which you stress reader interest. Despite the importance of audience, research paper assignments frequently fail to mention it at all. This omission can often mean that you are writing for your instructor. But it actually might surprise you how often this isn't intended to be the case. Particularly if your assignment includes peer review of drafts or class presentations, you may be writing for a more general audience. Sometimes this is explicit: "Your paper should be able to be understood by a broader audience than scholars in your field. You will have to explain concepts and not expect your audience to understand in-house jargon." If the audience for your paper isn't clear, ask your instructor this simple question: *Who is the audience for this assignment—readers like the instructor who are knowledgeable about the topic and/or readers who are not?*

Structure

In a few pages you'll encounter a research *essay*, "Theories of Intelligence," which models the exploratory approach *The Curious Researcher* celebrates. It's casual in tone, has a strong individual voice, and is structured to explore a question—*to find out* rather than *to prove*. It certainly has a thesis, but it is a delayed thesis, appearing not in the beginning but toward the end of the essay. The essay is organized around the writer's questions, not around making a point and logically providing evidence to support it. It does, however, have some formal qualities, including careful citation and attribution, the marshalling of appropriate evidence to explore the topic, and a sensible organization (hopefully!) that moves from question to answers. Later in this book, you'll be introduced to a three-act structure for organizing an essay like that (see page 000).

Research paper assignments in other classes are likely to put considerably more emphasis on a structure based on logic and reasoning. Put another way, these papers differ from an exploratory essay like "Theories of Intelligence" in that they report the *products* of the process of thinking about and researching the question, rather than describe the *process* of thinking and researching the question. The chief product, of course, is your thesis. The thesis—rather than the question—provides the organizing principle for your paper (see page 000). Instead of three acts, an argumentative research paper is structured a little more deductively. Every section loops back to the thesis, directly or indirectly, either providing reasons and evidence it is true, or providing context for understanding where that central claim comes from and why it's significant.

Narrator

"Call me Ishmael." These are, of course, the famous first words of Melville's classic *Moby Dick*, and they signal the arrival of the narrator of the tale. Though we usually associate narration with stories, I think nearly *all* writing has a narrator, a seen or unseen guide who leads us through the material, focusing our attention on this and not that, making inferences, asking questions, offering insights. Even the most formal academic writing is narrated in this way, though in the absence of that slender "I," the narrator's presence can seem ghostly. Academic researchers work within *discourse communities* that may limit their movements somewhat but do not ever bind their feet. *Discourse community* is a term academics use to describe certain identifiable ways in which people with expertise talk to each other, ask questions, or evaluate evidence they consider convincing. We all belong to discourse communities; any time you have a feeling that there are certain things that might be said and certain ways to say them, you're probably thinking of a particular discourse community.

One of the conventions of many academic discourse communities is that you don't use the first person. You may think that this is to make sure the writing is "objective," but that isn't really it at all. Scientists try to manage the influence of bias through careful methodologies, but no one thinks that writing is ever objective. It can't be because language is an inherently social commodity, influenced by changing conventions, cultural practices, and writers' own experiences with it. No, the missing "I" in some academic research isn't about objectivity but focusing readers' attention on the data, not the narrator.

On the other hand, some research is explicitly narrated in the first person. There are a lot of reasons for this. In the exploratory essay, for example, the focus is on how writers *think through* an inquiry question. In some qualitative research like ethnography, writers may be not only observers but participants, and examining their biases is an essential part of validating their research. The rhetorical situation plays a role, too. If you're writing for a general audience (or peers), first person is often more natural and more persuasive. In other words, whether you are an explicit narrator or an implicit one is a *choice*, not a requirement for academic writing. The exploratory research essays I emphasize in *The Curious Writer* are almost always in first person, but some assignments focused on argument may not be. Make sure you clarify the preferred method of narration with your instructor.

Types of Evidence

Whatever the genre, writers write with information. But what kind? There are essentially four sources of information for nonfiction writing:

1. Memory and experience;
2. Observation;
3. Reading; and
4. Interview.

A particular type of writing may emphasize one source over another. For example, literary analysis obviously leans heavily on reading. The information largely comes from the text you're studying. A personal essay is often built largely from memory. The research essay, however, is a genre that typically fires on all four cylinders, powered by all four sources of information. For example, for an essay exploring the behavior of sports fans, you may observe the behavior of students at a football game, read critiques of unruly soccer fans at the World Cup or theories about group behavior, and remember your own experience as a fan of the Chicago Cubs (God help you!) when you were growing up.

What makes research writing "authoritative" or convincing is less whether you sound objective than whether you are able to find *varied* and *credible* sources of information to explore your research question. Credible to whom? That depends on your audience. The more specialized the audience (the more expertise they have on your topic), the more demanding their standards for evidence.

In popular writing—say, articles in *Wired* or *Discover* or op-ed pieces in the newspaper—the types of evidence that writers use to convince readers are quite varied. Personal experience and observation, for instance, are often excellent ways to support a point. But as you begin writing research papers in academic disciplines, you need to pay attention to what your instructor considers *appropriate* evidence in that field and for that particular assignment. Scientific papers, for example, often rely on experimental data. Literature papers lean most heavily on evidence culled from the literary text you're writing about. Papers in anthropology might rely on field observations.

Sometimes assignments explicitly talk about appropriate evidence for your paper. More often they do not. Generally speaking, research papers that are assigned in lower-division courses won't require you to conduct experiments or generate field notes. They will likely ask you to draw evidence from already published, or secondary, sources on your topic. But this isn't always the case. A history paper, for example, might require that you study primary texts, perhaps letters by historical figures, political documents, or archived newspapers. This is something you need to know, so whenever you receive a research assignment ask what types of evidence you should emphasize: primary or secondary? And is personal experience and observation relevant?

Thinking Like an Academic Writer and Researcher

Whatever the details of your research assignment, one of the best things you will learn—and transfer into other writing situations—is how to *think* like an academic writer. These are some of the habits of mind you'll practice in the pages that follow:

1. Academic inquiry begins with questions, not answers.
2. Because genuine inquiry must be sustained over time, it's essential that researchers suspend judgment and even tolerate some confusion. You do research not because you know what you think already but because you want to discover what you think.
3. Insight is the result of *conversation* in which the writer assumes at least two seemingly contrary roles: believer and doubter, generator and judge.
4. Writers take responsibility for their ideas, accepting both the credit for and the consequences of putting forth those ideas for dialogue and debate.

To cultivate this kind of thinking you have to think about how you think. I know that sounds weird. But the research on how learners transfer knowledge is unambiguous on this point: the power of metacognitive thinking. What this means is that learners actually take the time to reflect on *how* they approached a task, how they thought about it, and what worked and what didn't. You can do this informally, of course, like in the shower. But I encourage you to make time to *reflect through writing* both when you're doing something new and after you've done it. Your instructor may ask you to keep a reflection journal as your work on your research project, or post to a class blog, or draft a cover essay at the end of this project or in your final portfolio that highlights this metacognitive thinking. It's not busy work. It really does help you to apply what you learn.

"It's Just My Opinion"

In the end, *you* will become an authority of sorts on your research topic. I know that's hard to believe. One of the things my students often complain about is their struggle to put their opinions in their papers: "I've got all these facts, and sometimes I don't know what to say other than whether I disagree or agree with them." What these students often *seem* to say is that they don't really trust their own authority enough to do much more than state briefly what they feel: "Facts are facts. How can you argue with them?"

Perhaps more than any other college assignment, research projects challenge our knowledge beliefs. These can reach pretty deeply: things like how we feel about the value of our ideas, our relationship to authority, and most profoundly, whether we think that knowledge is fixed and certain or is something that is constantly shifting. Step 2 of Exercise 1, which began this Introduction, may have started you thinking about these questions. Are facts unassailable? Or are they simply claims that can be evaluated like any others? Is the struggle to evaluate conflicting claims an obstacle to doing research, or the point of it? Are experts supposed to know all the answers? What makes one opinion more valid than another? What makes *your* opinion valid?

I hope you write a great essay in the next five or so weeks. But I also hope that the process you follow in doing so inspires you to reflect on how you—and perhaps all of us—come to know what seems to be true. I hope you find yourself doing something you may not have done much before: thinking about thinking.

Facts Don't Kill

When my students comment on a reading and say, "It kinda reads like a research paper," everybody knows what that means: It's dry and it's boring. Most of my students believe that the minute you start having to use facts in your writing, the prose wilts and dies like an unwatered begonia. It's an understandable attitude. There are many examples of dry and wooden informational writing, and among them, unfortunately, may be some textbooks you are asked to read.

But factual writing doesn't have to be dull. You may not consider my essay, "Theories of Intelligence" (see the following exercise), a research paper. It may be unlike any research paper you've imagined. It's personal. It tells stories. Its thesis is at the end rather than at the beginning. And yet, it is prompted by

Exercise 2

REFLECTING ON "THEORIES OF INTELLIGENCE"

The following essay may challenge your "genre knowledge." That is, it may defy your expectations about what a "research paper" should be like. Before you read it, then, spend a little time jotting down the five or six features of an academic research paper, at least as you understand it. For example,

- What should it sound like?
- How should it be structured?
- How should it use information, and what kinds of information?
- What are appropriate topics for academic research?
- What kind of presence should the writer have?
- What makes a research paper authoritative?

Jot down your list of research paper conventions, and then read "Theories of Intelligence," paying attention to the presence or absence of those features. Here are the questions I hope you discuss or write about:

1. If this isn't a research paper, what is it?
2. What conventions does it share, and which doesn't it share, with academic research, at least as you understand it?
3. More generally, what (or who) determines conventions of a genre like the college research paper in the first place? Do they matter? Why are there genres anyway?

a question—Why is it that for so many years I felt dumb despite evidence to the contrary?—and it uses cited research to explore the answers. "Theories of Intelligence" may not be a model for the kind of research essay you will write—your instructor will give you guidelines on that—but I hope it is a useful model for the kind of thinking you can do about any topic when you start with questions rather than answers.

Theories of Intelligence

by Bruce Ballenger

At age 55, I've finally decided I'm not as dumb as I thought. This might seem a strange confession from a professor of English, a man who has spent 25 years making his living with his intellect, working all those years in an environment where being "smart" was a quality valued above all others. This revelation—that I'm not as dumb as I thought—is a relief, of course. More and more, I can sit in a meeting of my colleagues and feel okay when I'm unmoved to speak. It pains me less when I can't quite follow someone's argument or sort out the arcane details of a curriculum proposal. Now, more than ever before, I can stand in front of my classes and say, without shame, "That's a good question. I don't really know the answer."

It's quite possible—no, likely—that I'm not nearly as smart as many of the people around me; but I've learned, at last, not to care. Self-acceptance may simply be one of the few blessings of late middle age. I was watching the news the other day and learned of a report on happiness that suggests the midlife crisis is a universal phenomenon. The study, with the straightforward title "Is Well-Being U-Shaped over the Life Cycle?", reviewed data from two million people in 72 countries, and it concluded that American men are most miserable at around age 52, perhaps because they have the sobering realization that life did not unfold the way they hoped it would. Happiness slowly returns when they "adapt to their strengths and weaknesses, and . . . quell their infeasible aspirations" (Blanchflower and Oswald 20). It's a great relief for me to know that things should be looking up.

I've considered this idea—that I'm really not that smart but have finally accepted my limitations—but I'm coming around to the belief that I'm probably smarter than I thought I was—that I was *always* smarter than I thought I was. I'm pretty sure this is true for most people and, frankly, the ones who have always known they were really smart—and who behave as if they are quite sure of this—are not the kind of people I usually like very much. Yet even the self-consciously smart people deserve our sympathy because being intelligent really, really matters to most of us. We can live with being unattractive, but no one wants to feel dumb. One of the most popular videos on YouTube is a clip from the Miss Teen USA contest when, during the interview segment of the program, Caitlin Upton, the contestant from South Carolina, was asked this question: "Recent polls have shown that a fifth of Americans can't locate the U.S. on a world map. Why do you think this is?" Her response was, sadly, completely incoherent, and the relentless, often unkind ridicule Upton endured prompted her appearance on the *Today Show* a few days later. "I was overwhelmed," she said. "I made a mistake. Everyone makes mistakes. I'm human" ("Miss Teen on Today"). I'm ashamed to admit that I joined the throngs who gleefully watched the clip and enjoyed Upton's humiliation;

at the time, I told myself that my response wasn't personal—it just confirmed my belief that beauty pageants are socially bankrupt. But I know that the real reason I enjoyed it was the relief that it wasn't me up there.

The YouTube clip is now painful for me to watch, not only because the humor in humiliation wears off quickly but also because I recognize in Caitlin Upton a phenomenon I see in myself: We believe that our own intelligence is a script that others author and we cannot revise. Researchers tell us that children typically have one of two theories of intelligence. Some believe that intelligence is an "uncontrollable trait," a thing they are stuck with like eye color or big ears. Others, particularly older children, believe that intelligence is "malleable," something they can alter through effort and hard work (Kinlaw and Kutz-Costes 296). I have never met any of these children, but apparently they're out there.

It is a nearly inescapable fact of American childhood that we are branded as smart or somewhat smart or not too smart or even dumb. For many of us who lack faith in our own intelligence, this branding begins in school, a sad fact that researchers say is especially true of African American kids (Aronson, Fried, and Good 113). I am white, but I can trace my own experience with this by following the scent of old resentments back to memories of school that never lose their bitter taste—even when I try to sweeten them with humor. There was the time in the second grade when I was sent to the back of the room to sit alone in a corner because I couldn't remember all the months of the year. And later, in the eighth grade, I moved from green to orange in the SRA reading packet but never moved again. In those days orangeness was a sign of mediocrity. The shame of never busting through orange to blue, the color Jeff Brickman, Mark Levy, and Betsy Cochran achieved with ease, convinced me that reading and writing were just not my thing, a feeling that was reinforced by my teacher, Mrs. O'Neal, who spattered my essays with red marks. From then on I hated school and, ironically, especially English (a feeling I freely shared on the inside covers of my class yearbooks). I spent my high school days languishing in "Level 3" English and science classes, where I joined the working-class Italian American students from Highwood and the kids from the army base at Fort Sheridan. We found solidarity in hating Shakespeare, lab reports, and the five-paragraph theme. And we pretended to find solidarity in being dumb, though I think most of us were secretly ashamed.

In my junior year, I dated Jan, one of the "smart" kids who moved in a small herd, migrating from one AP class to another. I was awed by her intelligence, and in the twisted logic of an adolescent male, this awe translated into indifference. I pretended I didn't really care about her. Eventually, however, I found Jan's persistent kindness moving and began to write her bad poetry that she copied and bound into a book that she gave me for my birthday. For a time, I entertained the idea that I wasn't unintelligent. Not smart, exactly—not like Jan—but maybe I could hold my own in the AP crowd. Yet what I did not understand back then was that whatever small gains I was making in school could easily be undone at home.

There was never any question that I would go to college. My parents expected it, and so did I. But I knew that I was not destined to go anywhere Jan and her friends were headed—University of Michigan, Brown, Tufts, Beloit, Kalamazoo. I applied to one school, Drake, with rolling admissions, and when I was accepted early, I excused myself from the endless senior chatter about colleges. I pretended I just didn't care. "You're selling yourself short," my father said, disappointed that I wouldn't pursue more schools. My brother—who was two years older—attended my father's alma mater, the University of Rochester, a school with high academic standards. Dad never encouraged me to apply there, confirming what I had already suspected—that I was a dimmer bulb.

My father was an intelligent man, a Rhodes scholar with an interest in British literature who worked for both Chicago and New York newspapers before the booze took him down. Nothing pleased him more than an argument. When I went to college in the early seventies it was an easier time for students to believe in values and ideas without being wounded by the charge that they were being "naïve." My idealism made me an easy target, and when the vodka kicked in, my father would pick up the scent of some belief I held with uninformed fervor and go after it. Even drunk, Dad knew what he was talking about, and with a cold, ruthless logic he would pick apart whatever passion I brought to the dinner table. I felt young, stupid, and hopelessly inadequate. Dad was not a cruel man; what I know now is that his head may have been full, but his heart was empty. His intellect was one of the last things he clung to as drink became the only way to dull some unspeakable pain; in the end, of course, even intellect succumbs.

There were moments after these arguments when I sat seething and my father would turn to me, wagging his finger. "The most important thing you can be, Bruce," he said, "is an intellectual. Live the life of the mind." Oddly enough, I have become an academic, and, had he lived, my father would likely have approved. Yet the ache I feel about Dad these days is that he didn't possess the kind of knowing that might have saved him had he only valued it. One of the things my Dad's alcoholism taught me was how weak-kneed his kind of intelligence could be against the sucker punches of self-loathing. "Your Dad was just too smart for his own good," my mother would say. "Just too smart for his own good."

Theories of intelligence have evolved considerably since I was a child, a time when everyone was taking IQ tests. In the early eighties, Howard Gardener's "multiple intelligences" came as a relief to many of us whose scores on intelligence tests were not worth bragging about. Back then, I never really understood Gardener's theory but seized on the idea that being smart didn't necessarily mean being smart in one way. More recently, in response to his own bad experiences being labeled dumb in school, intelligence expert Robert Sternberg offered a "Triachic Theory of Successful Intelligence." Being smart, he said, isn't just being analytical but being creative and practical, too. Strength in one can compensate for weakness in the other two ("Robert J. Sternberg"). Yet I always sensed that, no matter what Gardener or Sternberg said, there was a kind of intelligence that really counted and that I didn't possess. It was school smarts—the ability to pick apart an argument, to recognize the logical fallacy, and to make an arresting point—all of the things, I see now, that my father could do so well. As an academic, I see these qualities in some of my colleagues, whom I admire and envy. A very few of them, however, use their intelligence to bully people like my father bullied me.

Before I entered the profession, I imagined that many professors were like these intellectual bullies, people who bludgeon others with reason, looking to wound rather than to enlighten. The literary critic Jane Tompkins once wrote that college teachers are often driven by fear, "fear of being shown up for what you are: a fraud, stupid, ignorant, a clod, a dolt, a sap, a weakling, someone who can't cut the mustard" (654), and this is what drives us to do everything we can to prove to our students and others that we're intellectually superior. In rare cases, this fear of being found out turns teachers into intellectual bullies. More often, their anxiety in the classroom leads to what Tompkins calls the "performance model" of instruction: teachers talking at their students, teachers trying desperately to demonstrate how smart they are. It probably is no surprise that this tendency moves easily from the classroom to the department faculty meeting where the stakes feel higher.

I can't recall exactly how things began to change for me, when I started to see that I might revise the script that had governed my life for so long, but I started to notice it in those department meetings. Whether I spoke or not ceased to matter. I didn't decide one day that I was just as smart as my colleagues. I didn't suddenly start believing the strong evidence that I must have some intellectual ability because I enjoyed a successful career as a college professor. There was no sudden epiphany or dramatic moment. I think I just stopped being afraid.

It has helped to know, too, that my own ideas about intelligence don't travel well. In a famous study, developmental psychologist Joseph Glick asked a Liberian Kpelle tribesman to sort 20 items—food, tools, and cooking utensils—in a way that made "sense" to him. He did this quickly enough, pairing a knife with an orange, a potato with a hoe, and other matches that reflected the practical, functional relationships between the items. "This is what a wise man would do," said the tribesman. The researchers then asked, "What would a fool do?" The Liberian then sorted the items in what we would consider "logical" categories, putting food in one pile, cooking utensils in another, tools in another, and so on (Cole, Gay, Glick, and Sharp 84–87). I live a world away, of course, where as I write this my wife, Karen, is putting away the groceries using a logic that a Kpelle tribesman might find curious. The definition of a fool, obviously, depends on who and where you are.

My self-doubts will never go away completely, but I think they have made me a better teacher. I have empathy for my own students in whom I see the same struggle. Just the other night in a graduate seminar, Greg, a particularly bright student, derailed himself in midsentence while interpreting a passage from a Montaigne essay we were reading. "My head just isn't working tonight," he said. "I don't know what's wrong with me." I reassured him that he was making perfect sense, but for the rest of the class Greg was solemn, his hand fixed on his forehead, concealing a brow darkened by frustration. Ironically, Montaigne, a sixteenth-century philosopher and father of the personal essay, constantly questioned his own intelligence, and in the piece we were reading that night, Montaigne writes that his "mind is lazy and not keen; it can not pierce the least cloud" (213). And yet, Montaigne's work celebrated his shortcomings as well as his strengths, the very things that make us human. Learning's highest calling, he thought, was to know oneself, and the essay seemed the best vessel into which this self-reflection might be poured, as I have done here.

On the advice of a friend, I recently took up meditation, a practice that often involves visualization. Sometimes as I listen to the slow rhythm of my breathing, there are moments when I meet myself on a beach on Nantucket Island, a place I spent a spring nearly 30 years ago. There are just the two of us there—one young version of myself, with a navy blue beret and his hands thrust in the pockets of his khaki pants, and the other the grayer, bearded man I see in the mirror these days. I am walking with that younger self on the empty beach at sunset, and I have my arm around his shoulders. I am whispering something to him meant to be comforting. I might be saying many things, but lately I imagine it is this: "You're going to be okay." I think that learning to fully believe this will be the smartest thing I'll ever do.

Works Cited

Aronson, Joshua, Carrie B. Fried, and Catherine Good. "Reducing the Effects of Stereotype Threat on African American College Students by Shaping Theories of Intelligence." *Journal of Experimental Psychology*, vol. 38, no. 2, 2002, pp. 113–25.

Blanchflower, David G., and Andrew J. Oswald. "Is Well-Being U-Shaped over the Life Cycle?" National Bureau of Economic Research Working Paper No. 12935, 2007.

Cole, Michael, et al. *The Cultural Context of Learning and Thinking.* Basic Books, 1971.

Kinlaw, Ryan C., and Beth Kutz-Costes. "Children's Theories of Intelligence: Beliefs, Goals, and Motivation in the Elementary Years." *Journal of General Psychology,* vol. 34, no. 3, 2007, pp. 295–311.

Montaigne, Michel de. *Essays.* Translated by J. M. Cohen, Penguin, 1958.

"Robert J. Sternberg." *Human Intelligence: Historical Influences, Current Controversies, and Teaching Resources,* Indiana U., 7 Oct. 2010, www.intelltheory.com/sternberg.shtml

Tompkins, Jane. "Pedagogy of the Distressed." *College English,* vol. 52, no. 6, 1990, pp. 653–60.

Creative Research Papers?

Question: How often will I get to write a research paper like "Theories of Intelligence"?

Answer: Not often.

Question: So why should I write one now?

Answer: Because writing a research *essay,* one that also uses some of the conventions of academic writing like citation, is a great introduction to the essentials of academic inquiry. These essentials include the following:

1. **Powered by questions.** In the beginning, at least, the motive behind nearly any kind of research is to answer questions or solve a problem. The research rests on a simple hope: discovery. You write about the doubts about intelligence or the habits of a housefly or the motives of a terrorist because you want to find out something. Formal academic writing shares this motive, too, but it's less apparent in the product, which focuses mostly on the persuasiveness of its conclusions. In the research essay, the process of discovery is often a visible part of the product.

2. **Extend an ongoing conversation.** The purpose of research writing is not simply to show readers what you know. It is an effort to *extend a conversation about a topic* that is ongoing, a conversation that includes voices of people who have already spoken, often in different contexts and perhaps never together. Research writers begin with their own questions and then find the voices that speak to them. They then write about what others have helped them to understand. This experience of entering into a conversation with sources is much more likely when you are visibly part of it, even if this means using the first person.

3. **Write across, not up.** Normally, when we write conventional research papers, we have a narrow conception of audience: the teacher. In a sense, we tend to write *up* to the instructor because he or she knows more about the subject than we do. That's actually quite different from most academic writing, which is written to an audience of peers. You should write your research

essay to an audience like that; you're trying to make your topic relevant and interesting to people who share in your own "discourse" community. As you advance in college, that community will become more specialized, and so will your writing.

No matter what form your paper takes for this class—whether it's an exploratory research essay or an argumentative one—what happens behind the scenes is similar: If the goal is to engage in genuine inquiry, the kind your professors do, then you begin with this simple question: "What can I learn from this?" From there you begin to listen in to what has already been said by others about your topic; when you know enough, you join the conversation. The process must begin, of course, with figuring out what you want to know. That's the subject of the next chapter.

Chapter 1
The First Week

Learning Objectives

In this chapter, you'll learn to . . .

- Use invention strategies to discover a topic for your project.
- Identify the characteristics of a strong research question, and apply a working knowledge of your topic to propose your initial research question.
- Apply genre knowledge to understand an academic article.
- Understand the elements of a research proposal, and apply them to your topic.

The Importance of Getting Curious

Despite what they say, curiosity is not dead. You know the obituary: At some point around the age of (fill in the blank), we stop wondering about things. We lose that childlike sense that the world is something to explore. Actually, we never stop being curious, especially if we feel like there's a good reason for it. More than ever, we live in an information-rich environment, and the Internet makes information more accessible than ever before. Say you're having a conversation with a friend about deodorant. "I wonder what the first deodorant was?" asks she. "That's the kind of question that the Internet was made for," says you. And within a minute, you report that the first commercial deodorant was a product called "Mum," invented in the 1880s, though noncommercial deodorants were in use 5,000 years ago. This kind of short-term curiosity—sometimes called "situational curiosity"—is incredibly common in this Internet age.

On the other hand, genuine research relies on a sustained interest in something. It can begin with situational curiosity. For example, I once wrote an entire book on lobsters, an interest that was initially triggered by childhood memories of eating them during the holidays with my family and, many years later, reading a newspaper article that reported the lobster catch was down 30 percent and some believed the lobster fishery was on the verge of collapse. I wondered, will lobster go the way of caviar and become too expensive for people like me?

That was the question that triggered my research, and it soon led to more questions. What kept me going was my own curiosity. If your research assignment is going to be successful, you need to get curious, too. If you're bored by your research topic, your paper will almost certainly be boring as well. By chapter's end, you'll make a proposal about what you want to investigate. But begin by simply wondering a little.

Seeing the World with Wonder

Your curiosity must be the driving force behind your research paper. It's the most essential ingredient. The important thing, then, is this: *Choose your research topic carefully. If you lose interest in it, change your topic to one that does interest you, or find a different angle.*

In most cases, instructors give students great latitude in choosing their research topics. (Some instructors narrow the field, asking students to find a focus within some broad, assigned subject. When the subject has been assigned, it may be harder for you to discover what you are curious about, but it won't be impossible, as you'll see.) Some of the best research topics grow out of your own experience (though they certainly don't have to), as mine did when writing about lobster overfishing. Scholars tell us that a good way to sustain your curiosity in a topic is to find something to research that has some personal relevance. Begin searching for a topic by asking yourself this question: *What have I seen or experienced that raises questions that research can help answer?*

Getting the Pot Boiling

A subject might bubble up immediately. For example, I had a student who was having a terrible time adjusting to her parents' divorce. Janabeth started out wanting to know about the impact of divorce on children and later focused her paper on how divorce affects father–daughter relationships.

Tim bikes to school nearly every day, and he started to notice that it was changing him. His interaction with impatient automobile drivers made him testy. "I started to realize that when I was on my bike, I turned into a guy I didn't know, a guy I didn't want to be." He became interested in cities that have tried to reduce bicycle/car conflicts and wrote an essay on best practices.

Manuel was a divorced father of two, and both of his sons had recently been diagnosed with attention deficit disorder (ADD). The boys' teachers strongly urged Manuel and his ex-wife to arrange drug therapy for their sons, but they wondered whether there might be any alternatives. Manuel wrote a moving and informative research essay about his gradual acceptance of drug treatment as the best solution for his sons.

If you're still drawing a blank, try the following exercise in your notebook.

Exercise 1.1

BUILDING AN INTEREST INVENTORY

STEP 1: From time to time I'll hear a student say, "I'm just not interested in *anything* enough to write a paper about it." I don't believe it. The real problem is that the student simply hasn't taken the time to think about everything he knows and everything he might want to know. Try coaxing those things out of your head and onto paper by creating an "interest inventory."

Start with a blank journal page or word-processing document. Create three columns per page with these words:

> PLACES, TRENDS, THINGS, TECHNOLOGIES, PEOPLE, CONTROVERSIES, HISTORY, JOBS, HABITS, HOBBIES

Under each title, brainstorm a list of words (or phrases) that come to mind when you think about *what you know and what you might want to know* about the category. For example, for TRENDS, you might be aware of the use of magnets for healing sore muscles, or you might know a lot about extreme sports. Put both down on the list. Don't censor yourself. Just write down whatever comes to mind, even if it makes sense only to you. This list is for your use only. You'll probably find that ideas come to you in waves—you'll jot down a few things and then draw a blank. Wait for the next wave to come and ride it. But if you're seriously becalmed, start a new column with a new word from the preceding list and brainstorm ideas in that category. Do this at least four times with different words. Feel free to return to any column to add new ideas as they come to you, and don't worry about repeated items. Some things simply straddle more than one category. For an idea of what this might look like, here's what one student did with the exercise (Figure 1.1).

Figure 1.1
Interest Inventory:
A Student Example

PLACES
Freedom Tower (WTC)
Syria
Subway tunnels
Mines and caves
South Africa
Rural Western America (Wyoming, Idaho, Montana)
Galapagos
Venice (sinking?)
Guantanamo Bay

CONTROVERSIES
Westboro Baptist Church
LDS and FLDS
Scientology
Racism—Trayvon Martin
Marriage equality
Paparazzi and celebrities (Kanye assault charge)
Teen suicide
The Millennial generation
Sugar addiction
Diversity in the fashion industry
Rights issues and copyright
NSA and security

JOBS
Police officer
Public office (mayor, comptroller, governor, borough president)
Wedding planner
Stylist
Nutritionist/personal trainer
Animal trainer
Computer hacker
Postal worker
Publisher
Schoolteacher
Marine biologist
Weapons manufacturer
Drug dealer
Soldier

TRENDS
3-D printing
Stupid baby names (North West, Blue Ivy)
Hip diets (paleo, gluten-free, intermittent fasting)
TV on the Internet vs. live TV
Cats on the Internet (Grumpy Cat, Lil' Bub)
Internet memes
Vampires/zombies
Mustaches
Micro-apartments

Allot a total of 20 minutes to do this step: 10 minutes to generate lists in four or more categories, a few minutes to walk away from it and think about something else, and the remaining time to return and add items to any column as they occur to you. (The exercise will also work well if you work on it over several days. You'll be amazed at how much information you can generate.)

STEP 2: Review your lists. Look for a single item in any column that seems promising. Ask yourself these questions: Is this something that raises questions that research can help answer? Are they potentially interesting questions? Does this item get at something I've always wondered about? Might it open doors to knowledge I think is important, fascinating, or relevant to my life?

Circle the item.

STEP 3: For the item you circled, generate a list of questions—as many as you can—that you'd love to explore about the subject. This student's interest inventory turned up a topic she didn't expect: teeth whitening. Here are some of her opening questions:

Are tooth whiteners safe?

What makes teeth turn browner over time?

How has society's definition of a perfect smile changed over time?

Are whiter teeth necessarily healthier than darker teeth?

Is it true that drinking coffee stains your teeth?

How much money is spent on advertising tooth-whitening products each year?

What percentage of Americans feel bad about the shade of their teeth?

Do dentists ever recommend that people whiten their teeth?

Is there any way to keep your teeth from getting darker over time?

Can teeth get too white?

Why do I feel bad that my teeth aren't perfect?

Do other cultures have the same emphasis on perfectly white teeth as Americans do?

Are there the same standards for men's teeth and women's teeth?

What judgments do we make about people based simply on the color of their teeth?

How does America's dental hygiene compare with that of other countries? Is the "Austin Powers" myth really true?

The kinds of questions she came up with on her tentative topic seem encouraging. Several already seem "researchable." What about you? Do any of your questions give you a hunger to learn more?

Browse for a Topic

If you're still stumped about a tentative topic for your paper, consider the following:

- **Surf the Net.** The Internet is like a crowded fair on the medieval village commons. It's filled with a range of characters—from the carnivalesque to the scholarly—all participating in a democratic exchange of ideas and information. There are promising research topics everywhere. For instance, you might even scour Tweets that you've received from a person or organization you're following. Follow the Tweets from news organizations and major magazines, which often provide summaries of their major articles.

- **Search a research database.** Visit your library's Web site and check a database in a subject area that interests you. For example, suppose you're a psychology major and would like to find a topic in the field. Try searching PsycINFO, a popular database of psychology articles. Most databases can be searched by author, subject, keyword, and so on. Think of a general area you're interested in—say, bipolar disorder—and do a subject or keyword search. That will produce a long list of articles, some of which may have abstracts or summaries that will pique your interest. Notice the "related subjects" button? Click that and see a long list of other areas in which you might branch off and find a great topic.

- **Browse Wikipedia.** Although the online "free content" encyclopedia isn't a great source for an academic paper, Wikipedia is a warehouse of potential research topic ideas. Start with the main page, and take a look at the featured or newest articles. You can also browse articles by subject or category.

- **Consider essays you've already written.** Could the topics of any of these essays be further developed as research topics? For example, Diane wrote a personal essay about how she found the funeral of a classmate alienating—especially the wake. Her essay asked what purpose such a ritual could serve—a question, she decided, that would best be answered by research. Other students wrote essays on topics like the difficulty of living with a depressed brother and an alcoholic parent, which yielded wonderful research papers. A class assignment to read Ken Kesey's *One Flew Over the Cuckoo's Nest* inspired Li to research the author.

- **Pay attention to what you've read recently.** What articles or Web sites have sparked your curiosity and raised interesting questions? Rob, a hunter, encountered an article that reported the number of hunters was steadily declining in the United States. He wondered why. Karen read an account of a particularly violent professional hockey game. She decided to research the Boston Bruins, a team with a history of violent play, and examine how violence has affected the sport. Don't limit yourself to articles or Web sites. What else have you read recently—perhaps magazines or books—or seen on TV that has made you wonder?

- **Consider practical topics.** Perhaps some questions about your career choice might lead to a promising topic. Maybe you're thinking about teaching but wonder about current trends in teachers' salaries. One student, Anthony, was being recruited by a college to play basketball and researched the tactics coaches use to lure players. What he learned helped prepare him to make a good choice.

- **Think about issues, ideas, or materials you've encountered in other classes.** Have you come across anything that intrigued you, anything that you'd like to learn more about?

- **Look close to home.** An interesting research topic may be right under your nose. Does your hometown (or your campus community) suffer from a particular problem or have an intriguing history that would be worth exploring? Jackson, tired of dragging himself from his dorm room at 3:00 A.M. for fire alarms that always proved false, researched the readiness of the local fire department to respond to such calls. Ellen, whose grandfather worked in the aging woolen mills in her hometown, researched a crippling strike that took place there 60 years ago. Her grandfather was an obvious source for an interview.

- **Collaborate.** Work together in groups to come up with interesting topics. Try this idea with your instructor's help: Organize the class into small groups of five. Give each group 10 minutes to come up with specific questions about one general subject—for example, American families, recreation, media, race or gender, health, food, history of the local area, environment of the local area, education, and so forth. Post these questions on newsprint as each group comes up with them. Then rotate the groups so that each has a shot at generating questions for every subject. At the end of 40 minutes, the class will have generated perhaps 100 questions, some uninspired and some really interesting. You can also try this exercise on the class Web site using the discussion board or group features.

Making the Most of an Assigned Topic

Frequently, you'll be encouraged to choose your own topic for a research essay. But if your instructor either assigns a topic or asks you to choose one within a limited subject, you don't have to forfeit your curiosity. You just have to find the question that makes you genuinely wonder. Alternatively, examine your assigned topic through the following "lenses." One might give you a view of your topic that seems interesting.

- **People.** Who has been influential in shaping the ideas in your topic area? Is there anyone who has views that are particularly intriguing to you? Could you profile that person and his or her contributions?

- **Trends.** What are the recent developments in this topic? Are any significant? Why?

- **Controversies.** What do experts in the field argue about? What aspect of the topic seems to generate the most heat? Which is most interesting to you? Why?

- **Places.** Can you ground a larger topic in the particulars of a specific location that is impacted by the issue? For example, controversies over wolf management in the West can find a focus in how the debate plays out in Challis, Idaho, where some of the stakeholders live.

- **Impact.** What about your topic currently has the most effect on the most people? What may have the most effect in the future? How? Why?

- **Relationships.** Can you put one thing in relationship to another? If the required subject is Renaissance art, might you ask, "What is the relationship between Renaissance art and the plague?"

From Topic to Question

Taylor, a sports medicine major, wanted to write a research essay on concussions. "That's great," I said. "But it's a pretty big topic. Who, exactly, are we talking about? Athletes, toddlers, the elderly?"

"Well, I think I want to write about women athletes."

"Which female athletes?" I said.

"Um, I'm not sure. Probably soccer players."

"Okay, why are you interested in concussions among female soccer players?"

"Because most people assume that it's only football players who get concussions. But they're surprisingly common among women soccer players."

"Why is that?" I said.

"You know, I'm not really sure," she said.

In less than a minute conversation, Taylor opened the door on a research topic and walked through it. Like most students, she started with a big idea—concussions—but quickly narrowed the focus: *why are concussions common among women soccer players*? Taylor's still not there. This is a question of fact and factual questions aren't great inquiry questions because they don't often involve evaluation and judgment. But factual questions are exactly the kind we often begin with at the beginning of investigating a topic: *What is known about this*?

You need to turn your tentative topic into an opening question. Taylor found her question when I started to ask her "W" questions, which include who, what, where, when, and why. But there are other ways to find your question, and in Exercise 1.2 I'll show you an approach that works for my students. But first, why is transforming a research topic into a research question so important?

Where's Waldo? and the Organizing Power of Questions

Want to know what it's like to be in a small dinghy in the middle of an ocean of information? Propose a research topic on something big, something like, say, whales. To be interested in whales is a good thing, but to be a researcher who wants to learn more about the topic "whales" is an invitation to information overload. Narrowing the topic is the obvious solution—blue whales!—but you'll still be at sea. Narrowing the topic further will surely help, and transforming it into a research question will help even more. Why? Because a good question is a navigation aid, not only pointing you in a particular direction but also helping you to manage what you find. The visual puzzles in the *Where's Waldo?* series of children's books illustrate the power of focused questions to manage information. As you know, Waldo, with his red-and-white-striped stocking cap and jersey, is hidden in a picture among hundreds of other people, many of whom look a lot like him. The challenge, quite simply, is to find Waldo in all of this data. Imagine, though, if the game didn't ask, "Where's Waldo?" but "Where are the men?" or

"Where are the women?" in the picture. Suddenly, much more information is relevant and the search isn't nearly as focused. A better question might be, "Where are the people wearing yellow?" That eliminates some of the data but still leaves a lot to work with. Obviously, "Where's Waldo?" is the best question because you know what you're looking for and what you can ignore.

Similarly, a good preliminary question will focus your investigation of any topic. Starting with an answer—a thesis or main point—before you do any research is also efficient; it sets you on a steady march to a destination you already know. But beginning with questions, although sometimes a messier process, is a much more powerful method of discovery, which is, after all, the purpose of academic inquiry. But there's more. The right questions can transform a familiar, even commonplace topic into something unexpectedly interesting, as the following exercise demonstrates.

Exercise 1.2

THE MYTH OF THE BORING TOPIC

This exercise requires in-class collaboration. Your instructor will organize you into four or five small groups and give each group a commonplace object; it might be something as simple as a nail, an orange, a pencil, a can of dog food, or a water bottle. Whatever the object, it will not strike you as particularly interesting—at least not at first.

STEP 1: Each group's first task is to brainstorm a list of potentially interesting questions about its commonplace object. What questions do you have about this thing, or, even more importantly, this *category* of thing (i.e., not just this particular water bottle but water *bottles*)? Choose a recorder who will post the questions as you think of them on a large piece of newsprint taped to the wall. Inevitably, some of these questions will be pretty goofy ("Is it true that no word rhymes with orange?"), but work toward questions that might address the *history* of the object, its *uses,* its possible *impact on people,* or *the processes* that led to its creation in the form in which you now see it.

STEP 2: After 20 minutes, each group will shift to the adjacent group's newsprint and study the object that inspired that group's questions. Spend 5 minutes thinking up additional interesting questions about the object that didn't occur to the group before yours. Add these to the list on the wall.

STEP 3: Stay where you are or return to your group's original object and questions. Review the list of questions, and choose *one* you find interesting. More specifically,

imagine that you are an editorial team assigned to propose a researched article that focuses on this object for a general interest magazine, what might be a good opening question for the investigation? Once your group has settled on a possible question, evaluate how "researchable" it might be. A researchable question is one that might sustain the research over time, and it should be a question that meets the following criteria:

- People have a stake in the answer to the question. It's potentially significant.
- There is no simple answer to the question. (It might even raise more questions).
- The question isn't too broad.
- It's a question that other researchers may have asked, and as result there should be some answers.

STEP 4: Before you share your question with the rest of the class, go to Table 1.2 on page 37 and identify what type of question you are asking. Be prepared to discuss not only why you settled on a particular question from the many possibilities, but what it might imply about how to find the answer. Where will you look? What information can you ignore? What does the question *type* imply about the kind of article that might result from the investigation (e.g., a proposal, argumentative essay, narrative, report, etc.)?

In the absence of much knowledge about a topic, we typically ask questions of fact or definition. In the next section, you'll see how these provide the working knowledge that help you to craft better inquiry questions, questions that will force you to go beyond simply reporting information but evaluating and analyzing it. But the more important idea is the "myth of the boring topic": the remarkable power of questions to make even the most commonplace things interesting.

In Idaho where I live, there are stones called *geodes*. These are remarkably plain-looking rocks on the outside, but with the rap of a hammer they easily break open to reveal glittering crystals in white and purple hues. The most familiar subjects and objects are easy to ignore because we suspect there is nothing new to see or know about them. Sometimes it takes the sharp rap of a really good question to crack open even the most familiar subjects, and then suddenly we see that subject in a new light. What I'm saying is this: A good question is the tool that makes the world yield to wonder, and knowing this is the key to being a curious researcher.

Developing a Working Knowledge

In inquiry-based research, you often begin a project not knowing much about the topic. But to find the questions that will sustain your investigation, you have to quickly listen in to what other people have said about it. For example, take Jacky's interest in reality TV (see Figure 1.2). She certainly knows *something* about reality TV because she is addicted to the show *Hoarders*. She knows enough to ask a preliminary question: Why do people watch programs like this? But Jacky needs to have working knowledge of her topic before she will be

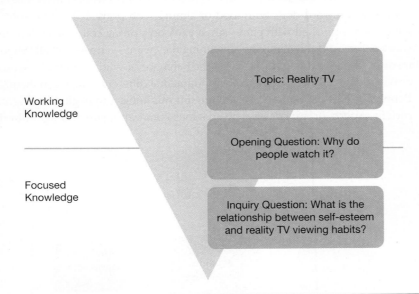

Working Knowledge

Focused Knowledge

Topic: Reality TV

Opening Question: Why do people watch it?

Inquiry Question: What is the relationship between self-esteem and reality TV viewing habits?

Figure 1.2 Steps for Developing an Inquiry Question

You need some background (or working) knowledge on your topic before you can settle on a researchable inquiry question. In this example, Jacky begins with a general factual question, and after learning enough about her topic (focused knowledge), is able to craft the inquiry question that will guide her research for the next few weeks.

ready to pose an inquiry question that might work. But what kinds of things do you need to know to ask a good question?

Here's another example of how to find an inquiry question, this time from my life. It began with this question, *Which theory of dog training works best?*

CASE STUDY ON DEVELOPING WORKING KNOWLEDGE: THEORIES OF DOG TRAINING   A few years ago, we took our Lab puppy, Stella, to eight weeks of dog training. We thought things went well: She learned a "down stay," she would come when we called, and she wouldn't pull on her leash. Then we took our new golden retriever, Ada, to a different trainer, and the first thing he said was that the method we used with Stella "simply wouldn't work" with Ada. He disapproved of our first trainer's approach. "I don't know how she stays in business," he said. The experience confirmed the feeling I already had: that despite advances in the study of animal behavior, there is little agreement on the best way to make Fido sit on command.

If I develop a working knowledge (see Figure 1.3) on theories of dog training, what might I discover?

1. **Definitions.** I quickly discover that there are competing definitions about things I thought were settled. What, for example, is a "well-behaved" dog? What do trainers mean when they use the term *correction*? What's the difference between operant and classical conditioning?
2. **Conversations.** After just 10 minutes of searching online, it's obvious that there are fundamental disagreements among dog trainers on a whole range of issues. Should you reward dogs with food or simply with praise? Should disobedient dogs be punished with pain—say, a yank on a prong collar or a jolt from a shock collar—or with removing something they want—a treat or a ball? Should theories of dog training be based on the behavior of wild canines like wolves or based on the belief that there are fundamental differences between them?
3. **People.** It doesn't take much searching on this subject to begin to recognize certain experts or advocates whose names come up again and again in the

Figure 1.3

To have a working knowledge, a researcher discovers who are key people who are interested in an inquiry topic, the questions that are often debated, what key terms and concepts mean, and what kinds of experts are involved in the conversation.

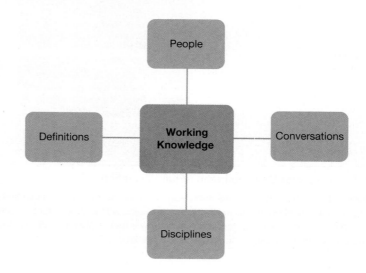

debates. There is, for example, the "Dog Whisperer" on cable TV, Cesar Milan, who applies some of the principles of the wolf pack to dog training. Then there are behaviorists like Patricia McConnell and Victoria Stilwell, who advocate positive reinforcement.

4. **Disciplines.** Before long, I realize that I can understand dog training in more than just the context of debates among trainers. This is a topic that leashes together a whole range of disciplines: animal behavior, social psychology, wildlife biology, and anthropology.

Research Strategies for Developing Working Knowledge

Academic research demands that you develop new research routines (see "What Are Your Research Routines" on page 43), and that starts here. So much of the casual research we do online—say looking for wireless router reviews or following debates about immigration—involves finding and reading sources written by people who aren't necessarily credentialed experts on the topic. There's nothing wrong with this. On the contrary, reading sources like that is how we start building our knowledge on a topic. But for most academic projects, your research routines for developing working knowledge must go beyond popular and general sources, even at this early stage. In other words, you might certainly begin, as you often do, with a Google search, but then you'll need to at least dip into the conversations that experts are having on your research question. Google Scholar is a stride in that direction. Later, you'll learn how to use the databases in your university library, which are more powerful in many ways that Google Scholar, but it will allow you to listen in to the many ways that experts are talking about your topic. Encyclopedias are helpful, too. In general, your research strategy here is to work from more general information to more specialized information. But there are also some targeted research strategies (see discussion that follows) you might try, approaches that will help find key conversations, definitions, people, and disciplines.

Researching the conversation What are the main questions or themes in the conversation about your topic?	• Google search with keywords • Google Scholar search with keywords • Add the word *research* to a topic query on Google News
Researching the definitions What common terms or concepts are part of the public and scholarly conversation?	• Check Wikipedia • Search topic in a general or subject encyclopedia (see page 32 for examples)
Researching the people Who are the leading experts? What work gets cited or mentioned most?	• Search topic in news sources (*New York Times*, NPR.org, TED.org, etc.) to discover who is interviewed or featured • In Google Scholar, check "cited by" link in results to see what articles and authors are cited most
Researching the disciplines What fields or areas of expertise participate in the conversation on your topic?	• Search topic in *several* subject encyclopedias • Search topic in Google Scholar adding a disciplinary keyword (e.g., ethics, psychology, legal, etc.). List the field first in the query (e.g., **ethics** concussions women's sports).

**WIKIPEDIA AND BEYOND: ENCYCLOPEDIAS AND WORKING KNOWL-
EDGE** With a heavy heart, I recently gave away my bound volumes of the
Encyclopedia Britannica, a work that has sentimental meaning only for people of a
certain age. But the encyclopedia is no less relevant today (if widely underused
by student researchers), especially in developing working knowledge of a topic.
When you think of encyclopedias, it's likely that Wikipedia is the first thing that
comes to mind, and it can be useful in combination with other works. You'll
often find online versions of the *Encyclopedia Britannica* in your library or you
can go to *Encyclopedia.com*. Both are examples of **general encyclopedias**. These
are texts that cover lots of territory, so the treatment of a topic is necessarily
cursory. But there are also **subject encyclopedias** (see list that follows), and
these can be amazingly helpful in the early stages of research. There are subject encyclopedias on hundreds of subjects: art history, war, African American
literature, nutrition—you name it. (My favorite is the *Encyclopedia of Hell*.) You
can frequently find these online at your university library. Though it may take a
little effort to find them, you should strongly consider searching for your topic
in the appropriate subject encyclopedia; in a short time, you'll get an invaluable
snapshot of what is known about the topic.

Subject Encyclopedias

Humanities	Social Sciences
Dictionary of Art	*African-American Encyclopedia*
International Dictionary of Films and Filmmakers	*Dictionary of Psychology*
Encyclopedia of World Art	*Encyclopedia of Marriage and the Family*
Encyclopedia of Religion	*Encyclopedia of Psychology*
Encyclopedia of Philosophy	*The Blackwell Encyclopedia of Social Psychology*
Encyclopedia of African American Culture and History	*Encyclopedia of Educational Research*
Encyclopedia of America	*Encyclopedia of Social Work*
Encyclopedia of Sociology	*Encyclopedia of World Cultures*
Social History	*Encyclopedia of the Third World*
	Encyclopedia of Democracy
	Guide to American Law: Everyone's Legal Encyclopedia

Science	Other
Dictionary of the History of Science	*Encyclopedia of the Modern Islamic World*
Dictionary of the History of Medicine	*The Baseball Encyclopedia*
Encyclopedia of the Environment	*Encyclopedia of Women and Sports*
Concise Encyclopedia of Biology	*Encyclopedia of World Sport*
Encyclopedia of Bioethics	*The World Encyclopedia of Soccer*
Encyclopedia of Science and Technology	*Worldmark Encyclopedia of the Nations*
Macmillan Encyclopedias of Chemistry and Physics	
Food and Nutrition Encyclopedia	

USING APPS TO MANAGE YOUR RESEARCH There are a growing number
of free applications you can use to keep track of your research. These programs
will not only help you organize online sources but will also help you build a bibliography. See Table 1.1 for some of the current options.

Exercise 1.3

BUILDING A BIBLIOGRAPHY

Conclude your working knowledge search by collecting the basic bibliographic information on the most useful sources you found. You'll learn later how to format these citations so they'll conform to the system required by your instructor. In the meantime, though, you can use a free online "citation generator." There are quite a few of these, including "EasyBib," "RefMe,"

and "Citation Machine." (Make sure that whatever citation builder you choose uses the latest MLA conventions, which were updated in the eighth edition of the *MLA Handbook).* Your instructor may ask you to submit your bibliography or annotate it. For more on how to annotate, see Exercise 3.4 "Building an Annotated Bibliography" on page 000.

Table 1.1 Software for Managing Research

	Zotero	Mendeley	RefWorks	EndNote
Web-based or desktop?	Web-based	Web-based, but has desktop program that syncs with Web program	Web-based	Desktop only, but Web option, EndNote Web, is available after purchase
Available offline?	Yes	Yes	No	Yes
Available in app?	Third-party apps	iPhone and iPad apps	No	No, but has mobile capability
Cost	Free	Free	$100. May be available free through your university's library	$249.99. May be available free through your university's library
Import capabilities	Can import from databases and Web pages	Can import from databases and Web pages, with Mendeley browser plug-in	Can import from databases and Web pages	Can import from databases and Web pages
Citation capture from Web pages	Yes. Can archive page and annotate	Yes, from certain sites. Can archive page and annotate	Yes	Yes, with Ref-Grabit plug-in
Citation styles	Many available, difficult to modify	Many available, difficult to modify	Many available and can modify and add styles	Many available. Can modify but cannot add new styles
Storage size	Unlimited local storage. 100 MB available online (more for purchase)	Unlimited local storage. 1 GB available online (more for purchase)	Limited to 10,000 citations in Web program, but unlimited in desktop program	100 MB per user but can be increased to 5 GB
Sharing options	Create groups, share references	Share references, create one three-member group free (more available for purchase)	Create groups, share references	Create groups, share references

THE REFERENCE LIBRARIAN: A LIVING SOURCE There are compelling reasons to visit the library, even at this early stage in your research. First and foremost is that the reference desk is where reference librarians hang out, and these are people you should get to know. They can save you time by guiding you to the best sources on your topic, and they often give great advice on how to narrow your research question. Reference specialists are invaluable to college researchers; without a doubt, they're the most important resource in the library.

Narrowing the Subject

Consider these two photographs. The first is a long shot of a school in my neighborhood. It's not particularly interesting. The shot is straight-on—the most obvious way of seeing—and although it's clear what the subject is in the photograph, there's isn't much that catches the eye.

The second image is a much closer shot of *a part of* the school—the same subject but much more narrowly focused. Although it's hardly a great picture, the photo is far more visually interesting than the long shot, with the geometric shadows of the stair railings clashing with the orderly horizontal lines of the cement steps. This is what often happens in photography when you begin to look more closely at a larger subject that interests you, varying distance, angle, and light.

In writing, when we talk about narrowing your focus, this is what we mean: Maybe start with a long shot but then find some aspect of the topic to look at

more closely. This is especially important with projects that involve research because they involve so much information. An investigation with too broad a focus is a hindrance to writers because it's hard to know what information *not* to include, and the result is usually a paper that is general and uninteresting. On the other hand, if you can move in for a closer shot, you'll see an *aspect* of your topic that's less obvious, more interesting, and more efficient to research. With a camera, narrowing a focus is easy: Get closer to your subject. In writing, it's a little more difficult. You have to find the right inquiry question to direct your gaze. You've already made some progress doing this when you turned your topic into a preliminary question, probably a question of fact or definition. But let's push this along further in the exercise that follows.

Other Ways to Narrow Your Subject

1. **Time.** Limit the time frame of your project. Instead of researching the entire Civil War, limit your search to the month or year when the most decisive battles occurred.

2. **Place.** Anchor a larger subject to a particular location. Instead of exploring "senioritis" at American high schools, research the phenomenon at the local high school.

3. **Person.** Use the particulars of a person to reveal generalities about the group. Instead of writing about the homeless problem, write about a homeless man.

4. **Story.** Ground a larger story in the specifics of a "smaller" one. Don't write about dream interpretation, write about a dream *you* had and use the theories to analyze it.

Exercise 1.4

FINDING THE QUESTIONS

With some working knowledge of your topic, you're ready to further refine the focus of your inquiry by using what you know to generate even more questions. Your goal here is to find one or more questions that will be the focus of your investigation, at least initially. Although you can do this exercise on your own, your instructor will likely ask that you do it in class this week. That way, students can help one another. (If you do try this on your own, only do Steps 3 and 4 in your research notebook.)

STEP 1: Post a large piece of paper or newsprint on the wall. (In a computer classroom, you can do this exercise in an open Word document.) At the top of the paper, write the title of your tentative topic (e.g., "Plastics in the Ocean").

STEP 2: Take a few minutes to briefly describe why you chose the topic.

STEP 3: Spend 5 minutes or so briefly listing what you know about your topic already. This is information you harvested this week from your effort to develop working knowledge on your proposed topic. You might list any surprising facts or statistics, the extent of the problem, important people or institutions involved, key schools of thought, common misconceptions, observations you've made, important trends, major controversies, and so on.

STEP 4: Now spend 15 or 20 minutes brainstorming a list of questions *about your topic* that you'd like to answer through your research. Make this list as long as you can; try to see your topic in as many ways as possible. Push yourself on this; it's the most important step.

STEP 5: As you look around the room, you'll see a gallery of topics and questions on the walls. At this point in the research process, almost everyone will be struggling to find a focus. You can help one another. Move around the room, reviewing the topics and questions other students have generated. For each topic posted on the wall, do two things: Add a question *you* would like answered about that topic that's not on the list, and check the *one* question on the list you find most interesting. (It may or may not be the one you added.)

If you do this exercise in class, note the question about your topic that garnered the most interest. This may not be the one that interests you the most, and you may choose to ignore it altogether. But it is helpful to get some idea of what typical readers might want most to know about your topic.

You also might be surprised by the rich variety of topics other students have tentatively chosen for their research projects. The last time I did this exercise, I had students propose papers on controversial issues such as the use of dolphins in warfare, homelessness, the controversy over abolishment of fraternities, legalization of marijuana, and censorship of music. Other students proposed somewhat more personal issues, such as growing up with an alcoholic father, date rape, women in abusive relationships, and the effects of divorce on children. Still other students wanted to learn about historical subjects, including the role of Emperor Hirohito in World War II, the student movement in the 1960s, and the Lizzie Borden murder case. A few students chose topics that were local. For example, one student recently researched the plight of nineteenth-century Chinese miners digging for gold in the mountains just outside of Boise. Another did an investigation of skateboard culture in town, a project that involved field observation, interviews, and library research.

Crafting Your Opening Inquiry Question

What do you do with the gazillion questions you've generated on your research topic? Throw most of them away. But not yet! If you look carefully at the list of questions you (and your peers) generated in Exercise 1.3, you will likely see

Table 1.2 Types of Inquiry Questions

Type	Question	Example
Fact	What is known about _____?	How many people watch reality TV in the United States? What are the demographics of that viewing audience?
Definition	What is _____ called, and what do key people think that means?	What is "reality" TV?
Policy	What should be done about _____?	What might be ethical guidelines for how participants are treated in reality TV shows?
Hypothesis	What is the best explanation for _____?	Is the popularity of reality TV shows another manifestation of the breakdown of community in the United States?
Relationship	What is the relationship between _____ and _____? What might be the cause of _____?	Does watching reality crime shows affect viewers' attitudes toward the police?
Interpretation	What might _____ mean?	How might we interpret the politics of race relations on *Survivor*?
Value	How good is _____?	Which reality crime show provides the most realistic picture of police work?
Claim	What does the evidence about _____ suggest is true?	Is there evidence that shows like *Intervention* help viewers develop more sympathetic attitudes toward addiction?

patterns. Some of your questions will clump together in more general categories. We've already talked about two: questions of fact and definition. These are often the engines behind developing a working knowledge about a topic, but unless you're writing a report, they don't typically work well as inquiry questions. Do any of the other questions on your list fall into any of the categories listed in Table 1.2? Might they be revised or combined to create an inquiry question you're interested in, one that will challenge you to make a judgment or evaluation?

Your work this week will culminate in the crafting of a tentative inquiry question and research proposal that will guide your research and writing next week. This question will constantly evolve as you learn more; but for now, create the one question around which you will launch your project.

Alternative Methods for Focusing Your Paper: An Example

A clear, narrow research question is the one thing that will give you the most traction when trying to get your research project moving. It's also one of the hardest steps in the process. Like gulping air after a dive into the deep end of a pool, our natural instinct at the beginning of a research project is to inhale too much of our subject. We go after the big question—why is poverty a problem?—and quickly wonder why we are submerged in information, struggling to find a direction. That's why I've spent so much time on giving you a range of methods to craft a workable research question.

In Table 1.2, I offered one approach to finding a strong inquiry question using policy, interpretation, hypothesis, claim, value, and relationship questions. Here's another approach based on time, person, place, and story, which is described in the "Other Ways to Narrow Your Subject" on page 35. Any one of these questions would be a good starting place for an inquiry into fad diets.

Topic: Fad diets

Opening question: What is the basis for our culture's current obsession with fad diets?

1. Time: How does human gastronomic history play a role in the popularity of the "Paleo" diet?
2. Person: How did Dr. Atkins' low-carb diet launch the dieting industry, which is now so powerful today?
3. Place: Where is each diet the most popular? What do cost and accessibility have to do with popularity?
4. Story: What were the effects of the 1944–1945 Minnesota Starvation Experiment? How have these findings influenced dieting strategy and healthfulness today?

 Presenting Research in Alternative Genres

Four Genres

You're probably used to considering how to approach a research topic in a conventional paper format. But if your assignment also involves alternative genres, then you also might start to imagine how other formats might help you to dramatize, inform, or persuade on the problem or issue. Though it's way too early to choose an alternative genre—that decision will be based on the purpose of an essay you haven't yet written or researched—it might be helpful to consider the possibilities. With your limited time and expertise, I think the most suitable alternative genres might be one of the following:

- **Slide presentation.** This is a format you know. Undoubtedly you've developed PowerPoint or Keynote presentations in other classes. They can be really boring, of course, but done well a slide presentation can present key information in a targeted—and even dramatic way—to an audience who is already interested in your topic.
- **Infographic.** Facts, if selected thoughtfully, can tell powerful visual stories, and the infographic is a popular way to do that. It's a genre that is especially useful for comparing data. New online software, some of it free, makes it easier than ever to create an infographic.
- **Poster.** The conference poster has long been a staple of research presentations in the sciences, but they're also a popular genre for showcasing undergraduate research in any discipline. A poster combines minimal text and images to present key findings in a visually appealing way. It's designed to stand alone *and* be presented.
- **Photo essay.** The photographic essay is one of the most accessible forms of visual storytelling. It's challenging, too, because you have to reimagine your topic in a sequence of images that has a narrative logic. A photo essay can make an argument or dramatize an issue. They can rely on pictures you take or archival photographs.

In later chapters I'll give you some basic planning and design tips for each of these, but you'll have to do more research on your own. You might begin by a Google search on "best practices" for the multimedia genre that interests you and follow the links. Also exploit the resources of the university library, including "how-to" books.

Possible Purposes for a Research Assignment

As you're considering your inquiry question, think a bit about the motive behind your project. Are you primarily interested in exploring what you think or making an argument? Although any essay can have more than one purpose, which would you say is your *main* motive in writing your paper—at least at this moment?

1. **To explore.** You pose the question *because* you're unsure of the answer. This is what draws you to the topic. You're most interested in writing an essay, not a paper; that is, you want to write about what you found out in your research and what you've come to believe is the best or truest answer to the question you pose. Your essay will have a thesis, but it will probably surface toward the end of the paper rather than at the beginning. This is what I would call a *research essay* rather than a research paper, and it's the most open-ended form for academic inquiry. Exploratory essays often begin with sense-making or relationship-analyzing questions.

2. **To argue.** You know you have a lot to learn about your topic, but you have a strong hunch about what the answer to your research question might be. In other words, you have a hypothesis you want to test by looking at the evidence. Inspired by a hypothesis question ("Is it true that…?"), you report on your investigation. However, you may quickly move from a hunch to a conviction; and then you move immediately into arguing your claim, trying to influence what your readers think and even how they behave. For example, you might already have a tentative thesis like this: *Buying grade schoolers things like bullet-proof backpacks to protect them from random gun violence gives parents a profoundly false sense of security.* It may well change as you learn more, but when you write your paper, your purpose is to state a central claim and make it convincing. Frequently, that claim is stated near the beginning of the paper.

Reading for Research

When you read for research you drop into on-going conversations about your topic. Scholar Kenneth Burke uses the metaphor of a parlor conversation to describe how knowledge is made—a bunch of people in a room with interest and expertise on a subject engage in a "never-ending conversation" (see page 000). Imagine that these conversations are taking place in different rooms in a large hotel. The largest ballroom is reserved for more public

Exercise 1.5

RESEARCH PROPOSAL

Try to capture what you've learned so far in a research proposal, one that includes the following four elements.

1. Draft Inquiry Question	The opening question that will drive your initial research. Typically, this isn't a question of fact or definition but one that will lead to evaluation or judgment.
2. Purpose	Will your project be exploratory or argumentative? • If exploratory, what draws you to the topic? What do you hope to discover? How might what you discover matter to you and others? • If argumentative, what is your tentative claim or thesis? What are the main counterarguments?
3. Thought narrative	Tell the story of your thinking about the topic so far. What were your assumptions when you started? Did they change? Specifically, what did you encounter in your initial research that most influenced those assumptions?
4. Working bibliography	List the sources that helped you to identify the focus of your inquiry.

discussions led by non-experts who happen to have a keen interest in the topic. The smaller ballrooms are for relevant disciplines, scholars who have done research on the topic or who have something to say about it because of their expertise. Once you have a research topic, you can go from room to room, listening in (reading). If your research topic was, say, how hoarding is handled on reality TV, in the biggest hotel ballroom you would read "Hoarding Reality Shows Might Do More Harm than Good" on the *Huffington Post.* A few doors down, you might pop into a smaller room and read "Hoarding Memories: The Work of Nostalgia in Two Reality TV Shows" in the *Journal of Popular Culture.* The conversation in each room is different. The smaller they get, the more different you feel from everyone else there, and the more difficult the conversation is to follow.

For some research, you never have to leave the biggest ballroom, and it's often the best place to begin if you don't know much about the topic. But the real action, especially for the academic writer, is often in the smaller venues, where the latest ideas and discoveries are being discussed. There you'll encounter journal articles and books that will, at first, seem alien because they weren't written for you. But even non-experts can glean fascinating information and ideas from academic scholarship. They just have to learn where to look.

How to Read an Academic Article

Recent studies on the research routines of college students are mostly unsurprising: Students rely heavily on Google and largely skim off the top of the search results. They also tend to avoid using library databases. Naturally, one explanation for this is that students simply don't know how to use them (see the next chapter for help with that). Another is that they simply don't want to deal with scholarly articles. Because these are genres that are often crucial to academic research, let's explore how they might be read by a non-expert.

An article in the biological sciences is different from an article in political science, which is different from one in criminology. But there are some basic similarities. This describes the structure of a lot of academic articles:

1. This is the problem or question I propose to explore.
2. This is what people have already said about it.
3. This is my claim or hypothesis.
4. This is how I propose to test the hypothesis or argue the claim.
5. Here are my results or here are the reasons and evidence that support the claim.
6. This is what is significant about what I found.
7. Here are a few things that merit further study.

Knowing that this is roughly the structure of most academic articles, you know where to look for the things you want to know. For example, you know to look about a third of the way in an article to find the hypothesis or claim and just before that you can often find a review of the literature. Unless the article is directly relevant to your research question, you probably won't actually read the whole article in most cases but will "skim and scan."

Rhetorical Reading Strategies

The table that follows offers suggestions about how to put your genre knowledge of academic articles to work.

First Look	Second Look
To determine relevance	Mining material in a relevant article
• Read the abstract, if there is one. • Skim the introductory material. Do the literature review and discussion of the research question seem to point in your chosen direction? • Check titles and subtitles. Do they include terms or concepts you've seen before?	• Subtitles, if present, are often signposts for content. • The "discussion" section in some articles provides a rich analysis of the findings. • Scan the first few sentences of every paragraph in relevant sections.
To glean the basic argument or hypothesis	Harvest key phrases and terms
• The abstract, if present, will often state this. • Toward the end of the introductory material, you'll often find the phrase "this paper will argue" or "we predicted" or "we hypothesize."	• The introductory material, particularly the literature review, will provide you with the terms and phrases experts typically use to discuss the topic. Collect these to use as keywords in subsequent searches.
Peruse the bibliography	To find quotable material
• The review of literature in the introduction will summarize other studies, books, or articles that address the topic. Harvest relevant citations for follow-up. • Scan the bibliography. Do any titles seem promising?	• Avoid the tendency to quote a statistical discussion (paraphrase instead). • Look for well-put explanations or summaries of the findings or argument. These can be found anywhere but are often in the final sections.

Reading Strategies for Research Writers

- First develop a working knowledge.
- Let your own purposes guide you: example, context, challenge.
- Anticipate your own resistance.
- Learn the organizing principles of articles.
- Read with a pen in your hand.

Chapter 2
The Second Week

 ## Learning Objectives

In this chapter, you'll learn to . . .

- Identify your typical research routines and adapt them to college-level research.

- Apply keyword and subject search techniques to find sufficient information.

- Use the concept of "focused knowledge" of a topic to guide research goals.

- Apply a rhetorical understanding of sources to evaluate what sources are best for a research project.

- Evaluate the usefulness of surveys, interviews, and field observations for research.

What Are Your Research Routines?

Most of us have a research strategy, and it's simple: Google it. One scholar describes this as a kind of affliction. "Google dependence," she writes, has the following symptoms: The afflicted one "always returns to Google when confused; repeatedly asserts that 'Google is my friend'; demonstrates the belief that Google has everything; uses Google as an all-inclusive tool." I'm as addicted as anyone to Google's powerful search engine, and one of my purposes in this chapter is to help you use it better (see "Google Tips and Tricks" on page 49).

But even if you use it well, Google alone won't cut it for academic research. We'll explore other options. However, what databases you search is only part of the story; *what you do* with what you find is even more important. Let's begin by thinking about your current habits as an academic researcher. Look at the following table. Which of the terms—*fast surfer, broad scanner*, or *deep diver*—applies to your typical school research routines?[1]

---

[1]See Heinstrom, Jannica. "Fast Surfing, Broad Scanning, and Deep Diving: The Influence of Personality and Study Approach on Students' Information-seeking Behavior." *Journal of Documentation* 60.2 (2005): 228–47.

Fast surfer	• I'd prefer to read only the sources that are written so that I can understand them. • If I don't find much on my topic when I search, I usually assume that there isn't much written about it. • I always feel under a lot of time pressure when I do research. • I pretty much limit myself to searching for the kinds of sources that I'm familiar with. • I just look for what I need and little more.
Broad scanner	• I search for a range of sources on my topic, a process that I don't necessarily plan but that develops slowly as I work. • I often find my best sources accidentally. • I'm pretty careful about evaluating the reliability of the relevant sources I do find.
Deep diver	• I'm more interested in getting the highest-quality sources than in finding a lot of sources. • I'm open to changing my mind about what I think on my topic. • I spend some time planning my research because I want to be thorough.

Depending on what and why we're researching—and for whom—any one of these profiles might apply. That doesn't make you a lousy researcher. But because academic research needs to be *authoritative*—presenting the strongest evidence and solid reasoning—and because, as a student, you need to be *efficient* with your time, it pays to be a deep diver.

Deep divers possess a quality we've already talked about: *the willingness to suspend judgment*. I can't overstate how important this is to academic inquiry—and to maximizing your learning. But you also need to plan your research rather than proceed haphazardly, hoping for happy accidents.

Planning for the Dive

A research strategy is built from a good inquiry question. We spent considerable time on that last week. With a tentative question in place, a working knowledge of your topic, and perhaps a research proposal, you're ready to plunge more deeply into relevant sources. There's you and an ocean of information. You need a research strategy, and it's one that has to solve three problems:

1. Finding the appropriate amount of information—not too much and not too little.
2. Locating the relevant conversations, the sources that address your research question.
3. Selecting the best sources, those that will make the work interesting and convincing.

In the sections that follow, we'll look at approaches that will help you to solve these problems. We'll begin with the power of words, then plumb the deep wells of databases, and finally look at the Web. We'll also consider what makes "good" sources by looking at them rhetorically.

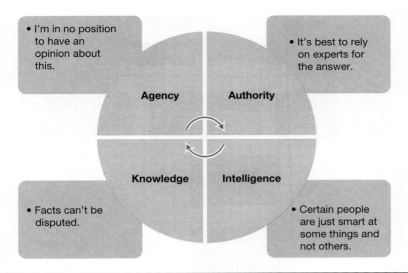

Figure 2.1 Our knowledge beliefs include how we feel about our agency, or ability to contribute, our attitude toward authority, our view about intelligence and learning, and most importantly, our ideas about the nature of knowledge. Is it certain or uncertain? When we do research, these beliefs figure into how we react to challenges and feel about our performance. For example, the person who agrees with the statements above would likely be comfortable writing a research report and frustrated by the kind of academic research we're discussing here.

The Power of Words to Find and Filter Information

Yesterday my daughter Julia got evicted from her San Francisco apartment, along with all the other tenants. The landlord apparently wanted to break the lease so he could raise the rent, something that is happening a lot in that city. This is the kind of moment when many of us start urgently typing words into Google: *San Francisco tenant rights eviction*. It's hard to find anyone who doesn't have experience with keyword searches for information, so you're already aware of how it works. But to solve the problem of getting the right amount of information on your research topic, and finding sources that address your research question, you should become more sophisticated at manipulating search language.

KEYWORD SEARCHES   Seizing on the first words that came to mind that seemed relevant to Julia's housing crisis—*San Francisco tenant rights eviction*—I didn't do too badly. Google helped me along, too, by suggesting some alternative wording in a drop-down list below the search window. But let's analyze why this keyword search works so we can get better at doing it. From a research question, a good keyword search mines key concepts, proper names, and vocabulary to narrow and filter the results (see Figure 2.2). From there, you might refine concepts into synonyms or more specific terms. For example, a subcategory of the

Figure 2.2

Build keyword searches from the language of your research question. The more specific the question, the easier it is to craft keywords that will yield relevant results.

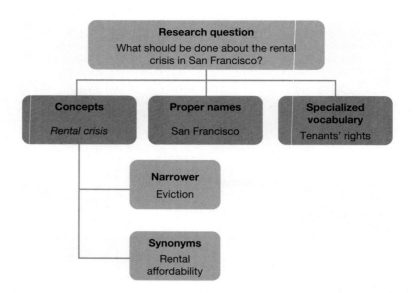

concept *rental crisis* is *eviction,* which is relevant here because the problem is Julia is being forced to leave her apartment. A synonym for *rental crisis* is *rental afford-ability.* It helps, too, that we're focused on a particular place (*San Francisco*) rather than, say, all American cities. Specialized vocabulary is the language—terms or phrases—that experts use in the discourse of their field to talk about the topic. *Tenants' rights* is a term that frequently comes up in discussions of the rental crisis among legal advocates for renters. This specialized language is the kind of thing you may have discovered when you developed working knowledge of your topic, and you should continue to look for it as you dig more deeply.

SUBJECT OR INDEX SEARCHES   We're accustomed to doing keyword searches on the Web, so naturally we repeat the routine when we search library databases. That's fine, but if you don't learn how to do a subject search—sometimes called an "index" search—you'll fail to exploit one of the great advantages of library data-bases: their organization. Unlike the Web, libraries not only index information but have a special language for searching it. It's not an alien language—the words are familiar—but it is a language that requires that certain words be used to reflect the way librarians organize information. These subject (or index) searches may there-fore initially seem less straightforward than the more familiar *keyword searches.*

More specifically, reference librarians use something called the *Library of Congress Subject Headings* (*LCSH*), which divides all knowledge into areas. These divisions are the *index terms* that you can use for subject searches, which will almost always help you to find more relevant books on your topic. How do you find out these index terms? A couple ways: There is a four-volume book in your library's reference room—sometimes called the "Red Book." These volumes are the standard reference to index terms. You can also go online to search the *LCSH* (http://authorities.loc.gov/) (see Figure 2.3). There you can search by subject, name, or title, and the software will tell you what subject headings to use when searching for books in the library. But the easiest method to know what Library of Congress (LOC) terms to use is to go to your library's online book database and do an initial search with terms you *think* might work. When you find relevant books, you'll likely see the relevant LOC terms in your results. For example, I did a keyword search using the term *cyberterrorism* in my library's book database and found a great book: *Cyberterrorism: The Use of the Internet for Terrorist Purposes.* The results page also suggested the following index terms as active links that would help me narrow my search:

Cyberterrorism—Prevention
Computer networks—Security measures
Computer security—Law and legislation

Knowing these index terms is a huge help, particularly in the early stages of a research project. Just enter the suggested terms in your library online book index, and you'll be surprised by the quality of the results.

REFINING KEYWORD SEARCHES USING BOOLEAN CONNECTORS If you're still not getting the results you're looking for—there are too many, too few, or they don't address your research question—then there's another technique you can use. Many libraries and Internet search engines use something called *Boolean* connectors to help you when you search databases. (These connectors were invented by George Boole, a British logician, more than 100 years ago.)

The system essentially requires the use of the words AND, OR, and NOT between the search terms or keywords. The word AND, say, between "animal" and "rights" will search a database for documents that include *both* of those terms. Just keying in *animal rights* without the AND connector will often get the same results because the AND is implied. If you want to search for *animal rights* as an exact phrase, library databases ask you to put the phrase in parentheses or quotation marks.

The use of the connector OR between search terms, obviously, will produce a list of documents that contain either of the terms. That can be a lot of results.

The Library of Congress   >> Go to Library of Congress Online Catalog

LIBRARY OF CONGRESS AUTHORITIES

Help ❶ | Search | Search History | Headings List | Start Over

SOURCE OF HEADINGS: Library of Congress Online Catalog
Authority Headings Search

Search Text:	rental crisis affordability United States tenant rights
Search Type:	Subject Authority Headings
Scroll down for Search Hints	Name Authority Headings
	Title Authority Headings
	Name/Title Authority Headings
	Keyword Authorities (All)

100 records per page ▾   Begin Search | Clear Search

Figure 2.3 To effectively search library databases, especially for books, it's extremely helpful to know the index terms that librarians use to organize information on your topic. The online "Library of Congress Authorities" will help you find the best terms. Enter your keywords, and in "search type" choose "Subject Authority Headings."

Exercise 2.1

WORKSHEET FOR POWER SEARCHING

Let's combine the two methods—keyword and subject searches—and generate some scripts that are most likely to help you find what you're looking for.

STEP 1: We'll begin with generating some keywords. Write your inquiry question at the top of a page, and then circle concepts, proper names, specialized terms, and possible keywords.

STEP 2: List each concept and for each, build a list of narrower ideas or synonyms (see Figure 2.2).

STEP 3: If your initial research last week failed to yield any specialized vocabulary, try to find some now. One way to do this is to use the keywords you developed in the last two steps and search on Google Scholar (scholar.google.com). Browse the titles and abstracts of the articles to see what alternative terms experts and practitioners who write about your topic use to talk about it.

STEP 4: Drawing from what you've gathered so far, propose an initial search string of keywords. Put what you think might be the most important words first and least important last

STEP 5: Now let's work on language for subject searches. Go to your library's Web site. Open the database for books, and in the search window type in the keywords that you generated in step four. Search for promising titles—books that seem like they address your research question. You may have to add or subtract keywords to get relevant results. Open one or more of these and look for a list of "related subjects," or index words you can use to search for similar books. These are often hyphenated (e.g. Housing policy—United States). Write the most promising of these on your worksheet.

STEP 6: We'll use one more approach for finding index words. Open authorities.loc.gov in your browser and type in your keywords. The order of the terms makes a big difference here since the results are keyed to the first words you use. For "search type," click on "Subject Authority Headings" (see below) and then "begin search."

Look for promising subject headings and write them down on your worksheet. If you combine these with your list of possible keywords you generated in previous steps, you've got a rich script you can use to find relevant sources. These search terms will likely change as you go along. For one thing, your research question will continue to evolve, but so will your understanding of your topic. You'll discover fresh vocabulary to try in search, the names of key experts, and synonyms you may not have thought of. But the time you spent in the front-end of the project planning possible search terms will pay off immediately to stronger results.

However, there are a few more advanced search techniques you should consider, and in the next section will look at two of these: manipulating keywords using Boolean connectors and exploiting some of Google's advanced features.

In the early stages of your project, you might want to browse a heap of results; that way you can explore different angles on your topic, see the more common treatments, and discover some alternative search terms. The NOT connector is less frequently used but really can be quite helpful if you want to *exclude* certain documents. Suppose, for example, you were interested in researching the problem of homelessness in Washington State, where you live. To avoid getting information on Washington D.C., where it's also a problem, use the connector NOT.

Homeless AND Washington NOT D.C.

As you can see from the example, it's possible to use the connectors between a number of terms—not just two. In fact, the art of creating keyword searches is both using the right words (those used by librarians) and using them in the right combinations (those that in combination sufficiently narrow your search and give you the best results).

One final search technique that can be useful, especially in library database searches, is something called *nesting*. This involves the use of parentheses around two or more terms in a phrase. This prompts the computer to look for those terms first. For example, suppose you were searching for articles on the ethics of animal rights, but you were particularly interested in information in two states, Idaho and Montana. You might construct a search phrase like this one:

(Montana OR Idaho) AND animal AND rights AND ethics

Putting the two states in parentheses tells the software to prioritize Montana or Idaho in the results, generating a much more focused list of sources related to animal rights and ethics.

Google Tips and Tricks

If You Want To...	Use...	For Example...
Find related pages	**related:** followed by Web site address	**related:** www.epicurious.com
Automatically search within a specific site or type of site	**site:** followed by Web site or Web site type	microbiology **site: edu** or crime **site:** www.nytimes.com
Search for words or phrases in an open Web document	**Control-F (Windows)** or **Command-F (Mac)** and a search window opens	Search for the term *revision* in an article about writing
Search by file type	**file type:** followed by 3-letter abbreviation	Obamacare file type: **PDF**
Ignore words in your search	**minus sign** (–) followed by word to ignore	pet training – **cats**
Include words in your search	**quotation marks (" ")** around word to include	**"the" borrowers**
Include results with synonyms	**tilde sign** ~ before word	eggplant ~ **roasting**
Retain stop words in phrases without quotes	**plus sign** + in front of stop word to retain	fish +**and** chips
Search for two options	capitalized **OR** between two options	yellow **OR** black Labradors
Match any single word in a search	**asterisk (*)** to find matching word or words	"four score and * years ago" or "undergrad program pre*"
Search number range	**two dots (..)** between values	used laptops **$50..$1000**
Log and search your own search history	**Web history:** www.google.com/history	

Figure 2.4
How Multiple
Search Terms
Narrow Results

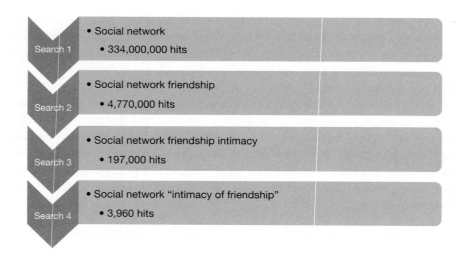

- Search 1
  - Social network
    - 334,000,000 hits
- Search 2
  - Social network friendship
    - 4,770,000 hits
- Search 3
  - Social network friendship intimacy
    - 197,000 hits
- Search 4
  - Social network "intimacy of friendship"
    - 3,960 hits

What's a Good Source?

An ad in a recent *Smithsonian Magazine* made a pitch for fragrance that promised to "increase your attractiveness and the affection you receive from others." This wasn't any old perfume but a human pheromone, one endorsed by Winnifred Cutler, Ph.D., who claimed that three "double-blind studies" had confirmed its effectiveness. A personal testimonial from a satisfied customer followed: "I had come out of a mall wearing (the product) and it was very windy. And there was a middle-aged man about 20 meters away. The wind caught me, my scarf was blowing in his direction. He stopped dead in his tracks, turned to me and said: 'I just wanted to tell you, you are so beautiful.'"

Like all ads, this was making an argument: Buy this fragrance and people will think you're, well, beautiful. And the evidence behind the claim? A Ph.D. with expertise in human pheromones says it will work, and so does a woman coming out of a mall. But are these "good" sources? It depends, right? But on what?

A RHETORICAL PERSPECTIVE ON SOURCES   To say a source is "good" is to say that it is *authoritative.* It is information a particular audience values because they believe it's convincing, which brings me back to the woman in the mall with the flowing scarf and the admiring middle-aged man. Does the *Smithsonian* ad use convincing sources? As writers of college essays, we would surely say no. It's not enough to simply claim that three double-blind studies suggest that standing downwind of someone with a human attraction pheromone can expect a compliment. What were those studies? What did they exactly say? Are there any conflicting findings from other research? And although Dr. Cutler appears to have expertise, her commercial ambitions cast that in a different light.

But for this genre—an ad—and this rhetorical situation—a pitch in a popular magazine aimed at middle-aged (and older) readers—these might be perfectly convincing sources. **We can only evaluate the authority of a source in**

Other Ways to Look at Sources

1. **Type.** Is it "primary" or "secondary?" A primary source presents the original words of a writer—his speech, poem, eyewitness account, letter, interview, or autobiography. A secondary source analyzes somebody else's work.
2. **Objective or Subjective.** Is the information gathered systematically to minimize author bias? Is the information organized around the author's perspective?
3. **Stable or Unstable.** The distinction between online and published sources is blurring. But exclusively online sources can disappear or be rarely updated.
4. **Currency.** Depending on the topic, genre, and audience, it matters whether a source was published recently.

context. This was one of the major themes of the 2015 *Framework for Information Literacy for Higher Education,* a statement by the professional organization of college librarians about what twenty-first century consumers and creators of information need to know. The librarians note that the authority of sources is determined by discourse communities—disciplines, professional fields, social groups—all of which may have different expectations about what is a good source of information. Some of these expectations are baked into the genres of communication these communities rely on to share information and arguments. For example, advertisers use ads, and these don't tend to include citations.

As college writers, you're learning what those genres and expectations are; for instance, in an academic context, typically the best sources of information are "peer reviewed," or research that other experts have found methodologically sound and well-reasoned. Figure 2.5 neatly summarizes the hierarchy of sources like this that readers of many academic genres of writing value most. But the table doesn't tell the whole story. For one thing, sources aren't simply published texts like books and articles but can include observations, data from experiments, anecdotes, images, narratives, interviews, and so on. In addition, some writing you'll do in other classes is informal or intended for audiences who aren't experts on a topic, and this might not require that you use scholarly sources.

To ask, then, what is a good source for a research project is to see the question rhetorically. Ask yourself,

- **What is your purpose?** This begins with your research question, of course, and whether a source is relevant to it. But on a less grand scale, you might choose to use a source for a whole range of reasons: To demonstrate what it *doesn't* say; to expose its bias; to use as a counterargument; to show a popular perspective, and many other purposes.

- **Who is the audience,** and how much do they already know about the topic? (Less knowledgeable readers probably don't expect the rigorous evidence that knowledgeable readers do).

Figure 2.5
Pyramid of Library
Sources for
Academic Writing

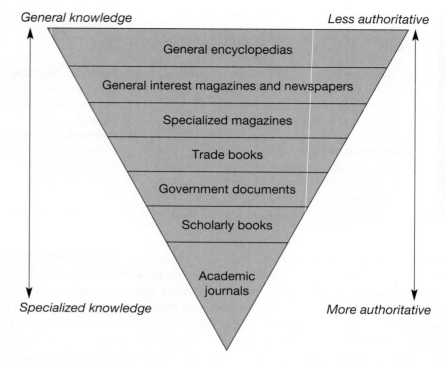

General knowledge   *Less authoritative*

- General encyclopedias
- General interest magazines and newspapers
- Specialized magazines
- Trade books
- Government documents
- Scholarly books
- Academic journals

Specialized knowledge   *More authoritative*

- **What's the genre?** What kinds of sources and evidence do users of that genre typically expect? (A 500-word reading response to a textbook chapter will lean mostly on passages and ideas from the book. A marketing plan for a start-up business will include the demographic profiles of target customers, information you might glean from the U.S Census Bureau. A podcast on campus sustainability might rely solely on interviews.)

SEEING SOURCES FOR WHAT THEY DO AND NOT WHAT THEY ARE   You get a research paper assignment, and it says, "you are required to use five journal articles and at least one book." It's easy to infer from this that the most important thing to consider when finding a source is what *kind* it is. The composition scholar Joseph Bizzup turns this idea notion on its head. "If we want students to adopt a rhetorical perspective towards research-based writing then we should use language that focuses their attention on their sources and other materials are…but on what they as writers might do with them."[2] Bizzup uses the acronym BEAM (background, exhibit, argument, and method) to describe writers' motives for using a source. Here's how I might apply his ideas to a current research project of my own.

- **Background.** I am writing a research essay recently on the history of the manual typewriter, and there is pretty wide agreement about who invented the first commercial machine—and when. I would consider sources that tell

[2]Bizzup, Joseph. "BEAM: A Rhetorical Vocabulary for Teaching Research-Based Writing." *Rhetoric Review,* 27, no 1, p. 75.

this story as providing *background,* or relatively uncontested, authoritative facts. These are sometimes uncited.

- **Exhibit.** Was the typewriter's introduction into the workplace good or bad for women? Early historians of the machine said "good"—it created an almost exclusively female profession at first—but other analysts wonder being a "type-writer girl" was really a form of emancipation. Sources that make these claims are *exhibits,* information that can be analyzed, interpreted, or explained. They're complicated in interesting ways, so it's worth taking a closer look at them.

- **Argument.** If after exploring these competing ideas about the impact of the early typewriters on women workers, I conclude that the machine was hardly emancipatory because the "typewriter girls" were grossly under-paid, then I might turn around and use a source that was initially an exhibit (along with other sources I find) into information that services an argument: to support, counter, complicate, or extend a claim I want to make.

- **Methods.** I own something like 16 manual typewriters. This seems odd (especially to my wife). In writing about the machines, I am interested in the psychology of collecting—what prompts people to collect salt shakers, porce-lain dolls, Pez dispensers, or typewriters? This question led me to the work of the philosopher William James, who opines about how bound we are to see ourselves through things. This source is an example of a *method:* a theory, idea, approach, or methodology for looking at or answering a question.

If you begin to see sources like this—as information that does certain kinds of work in your writing rather than containers—you're more likely to actively look for the information you need.

THINKING CRITICALLY ABOUT SOURCES IN ACADEMIC WRITING   Seeing sources for what they do in your writing is key to seeing them rhetorically. So is thinking critically about them. What you need to develop for much of the aca-demic writing you do, including this project, is a disposition toward sources—a kind of mental program that you run in the background—that helps you to filter what you find. When you encounter any source, consider who's speaking and what their motives are. Evaluate their level of expertise on the subject. Look for evidence (e.g., a bibliography) that the author is familiar with the conversation on the topic, including, in some cases, recent findings. Finally, look at the nature of the evidence (see "Other Ways to Look at Sources" on p. 51) that the author chooses. Is it appropriate given the author's purpose and genre?

The reference scholar Sara Robertson suggests that one way of thinking about what kinds of sources are best for academic writing is to ask a simple question: Is it professionally reviewed, and if so, by how many people and for how long? A reviewer might be a fact-checker who spends a few hours to a panel of experts who take 6 months evaluating an article draft. In general, academic writing fa-vors sources that undergo some kind of review. This ranges from a magazine like *Atlantic* or *Psychology Today* that employs fact-checkers, to journals like the *Journal*

What Does "Peer Reviewed" Mean?

Broadly speaking, periodicals, books, Web sites, and magazines are one of two types: scholarly or popular. Popular publications include magazines like *Newsweek* or online sites like *Slate*, which are staff written, usually by non-experts for a more general audience. Scholarly publications are written and edited by experts for others in their fields, and the best of these are "peer reviewed." This means that before an article is published online or in print, a group of fellow experts read and comment on its validity, argument, factual accuracy, and so on. The article doesn't appear in print until this review is completed and the journal editor is satisfied that the other scholars think the work is respectable.

What does this mean for you? It means that you can count on the authoritative muscle of a peer-reviewed source to help you make a strong point in your paper.

of Experimental Psychology that doesn't publish anything unless it passes muster from peer reviewers (see "What Does Peer Reviewed Mean?" on p. 000).

What does all of this mean as you proceed with your own project? *The Curious Researcher* emphasizes a genre of the academic research paper—the research *essay*—that is a bit less formal than conventional scholarship, and written for a less specialized audience. But because it *is* an academic research essay, the best sources are often the kinds that most scholars prefer: peer-reviewed books and articles, stable online sources, and work by authors who are recognized by others as experts on the topic or as thoughtful commentators

EVALUATING ONLINE SOURCES FOR ACADEMIC ESSAYS You want to buy a new wireless router, so you Google *wireless router reviews*. You get about 9.5 million results and skim the first few pages, clicking on router reviews from *PC Magazine*, a magazine you once subscribed to. Maybe you check a few other Web pages as well, focusing on review sites that you're vaguely familiar with: CNET, Consumer Reports. As a method of evaluating sources to buy a new router—choosing online publications that cover technology with which you're somewhat familiar—this works pretty well. But for much academic writing, with its emphasis on authoritative sources that reflect current thinking, sound methods, scholarly evidence, good reasoning, and an informed perspective, the router scenario is way too loose and haphazard as a method for evaluating online sources. This is especially critical because the sources *are* online.

In the last few years, the distinction between online sources and published ones blurred. Now lots of sources are *both* online and off. You can find that same article published in *Journal of Psychopathology* on alien abduction delusions in print and on the Web. But for those sources that are exclusively online—things like blogs, Web pages, and e-magazines—you should supplement your rhetorical perspective (see p. 56) on what's a good source with some general guidelines when you're doing academic work.

- **Always keep your purpose in mind.** For example, if you're exploring the lobbying methods of the National Rifle Association, then you will want to hear, and see, what this organization has to say on its Web site. In looking at the NRA Web pages, you'll know full well that they are not unbiased; however, for your purpose, they are both relevant and authoritative. After all, who knows more about the NRA than the NRA?

- **Favor governmental and educational sources over commercial ones.** There are plenty of exceptions to this, but in general you're wise to rely more heavily on material sponsored by groups without a commercial stake in your topic. How can you tell the institutional affiliation of sources? Sometimes it's obvious: They tell you. But when it's not obvious, the *domain name* provides a clue. The .com that follows a server name signifies a commercial site, whereas .edu, .org, or .gov usually signals an educational, nonprofit, or governmental entity. The absence of ads also implies that a site is noncommercial.

- **Favor authored documents over those without authors.** There's a simple reason for this: You can check the credentials of an author. You can do this by sending an e-mail message to him or her, a convenience often available as a link on a Web page, or you can do a quick search to see if that author has published other books or articles on your topic. If writers are willing to put their names on a document, they might be more careful about the accuracy and fairness of what they say.

- **Favor Web pages that have been recently updated over those that haven't been changed in a year or more.** Frequently, at the bottom of a Web page there is a line indicating when the information was posted to the Internet or when it was last updated. Look for it.

- **Favor Web sources that document their claims over those that don't.** Most Web documents won't feature a bibliography. That doesn't mean that they're useless to you, but be suspicious of a Web author who makes factual assertions without supporting evidence.

A Key to Evaluating Internet Sources. As an undergraduate, I was a botany major. Among other things, I was drawn to plant taxonomy because the step-by-step taxonomic keys for discovering the names of unfamiliar plants gave the vegetative chaos of a Wisconsin meadow or upland forest a beautiful kind of logic and order. The key that follows is modeled after the ones I used in field taxonomy. This one is a modest attempt to make some sense of the chaos on the Web for the academic researcher, particularly when the usual approaches for establishing the authority of traditional scholarship and publications fail—for example, when documents are anonymous, their dates of publication aren't clear, or their authors' affiliations or credentials are not apparent.

If you're not sure whether a particular Web document will give your essay credibility, see Figure 2.6 and work through the following steps:

1. Does the document have an author or authors? If *yes*, go to Step 2. If *no*, go to Step 7.

Figure 2.6

Follow the flowchart for a rigorous review of a Web document or page, beginning with whether the author is obvious or not. Sites that earn stars are generally more trustworthy. Those with question marks still may be useful, depending on the situation. Be particularly wary of information on commercial or special interest sites.

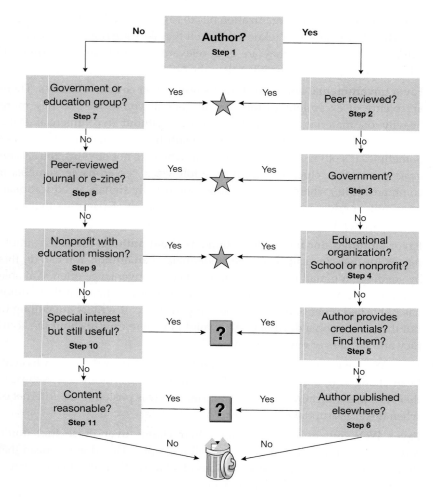

Authored Documents

2. Does the document appear in an online journal or magazine that is "refereed"? In other words, is there any indication that every article submitted must be reviewed by other scholars in the field before it is accepted for publication? If *yes*, you've found a good source. If *no* (or you're unsure), go to Step 3.

3. Is the document from a government source? (Online, look for the .gov domain.) If *yes*, then it is likely a good source. If *no*, go to Step 4.

4. Does the document appear in an online publication affiliated with a reputable educational institution (e.g., a university) or nonprofit educational organization (e.g., the American Cancer Society)? (Online, look for the .edu or .org domain.) If *yes*, it's likely to be trustworthy. If *no*, go to Step 5.

5. If the author isn't clearly affiliated with a reputable institution, does he or she offer any credentials that help establish expertise on the topic? (For example, an advanced degree in the relevant discipline is encouraging.) If credentials

are missing, can you find an author's credentials by Googling the author's name? Is there an e-mail link to the author so you can inquire about affiliations or credentials? If *no,* go to Step 6.

6. Has the author published elsewhere on the topic in reputable journals or other publications? Check this at the library by searching under the author's name in the catalog or appropriate databases. If *no,* reconsider the value of the source. You could be dealing with a lone ranger who has no expertise on your topic and no relevant affiliations.

Unauthored Documents

7. If the online document has no author, is it from an institutional source like a university (.edu) or the state or federal government (.gov)? If *yes,* then chances are the document is useful. If *no,* go to Step 8.

8. Is the anonymous document published in an online journal or magazine? Is it refereed? (See Step 2.) If *yes,* it's likely a good source. If *no,* go to Step 9.

9. Is the document part of a publication or Web page from a nongovernment source whose mission is described in the document, and does it suggest that the organization's goals include research and education? Is there a board of directors, and does it include professionals and academics who are respected in the field? If *no,* go to Step 10.

10. Even if the organization offering the information represents a special interest group or business with an axe to grind, the information may be useful as a means of presenting its point of view. Make sure, if you use it, that the information is qualified to make the source's bias obvious.

11. Does the site seem reasonable? Try to apply the usual criteria for evaluating a source to this anonymous document. Does it have a citations page, and do the citations check out? Was it published on the Internet recently? Does the argument the writer is making seem sound? Do the facts check out? If the answer is *no* to all of the above, then don't trust the document. If you can answer *yes* to more than one of these questions, the material might have some marginal value in a college paper.

Developing Focused Knowledge

If working knowledge equips you to sustain a 1-minute dinner conversation on your topic, then focused knowledge is enough for you to make a 15- or 20-minute presentation to the rest of the class (see Exercise 2.1). You'll hardly be an expert, but you'll probably know a lot more about your topic than any of your peers.

You have arrived at this level of knowing about your topic when you notice the following things happen as you're doing your research:

1. You have settled on some good search terms, consistently turning up good sources.

2. The names of certain experts start to become familiar to you.

3. You more or less get what the debate is about: what the key issues are, the general areas of agreement and disagreement, and some of the key terms and concepts that pop up regularly in the ongoing conversation about your topic.

4. You can read a pretty technical academic article on the topic with some interest and understanding.

5. You know enough to revise your research question. It might be more focused, or it might incorporate some of the relevant terms or concepts you've discovered in your research.

SEEING PATTERNS   In general, whenever we dig past the superficial layers of knowing about a research topic, we start looking for patterns in what we find. Scholars who study the differences between how experts and novices do research often notice this: Experienced researchers see patterns in data that novices don't notice. Experts *expect* patterns, and you should look for them, too. Does the information you find seem to tell a story? Does the most persuasive information suggest a particular answer to your research question? Are there relationships among facts, theories, or claims that surprise you? Are there any unexpected contradictions, causes, or connections? For example, in Figure 2.7, I've created a "word cloud" of the last 320 words you just read. A "word cloud" takes some text and creates an image that represents word frequency in the text. The visually bigger words are repeated more than the smaller ones. Note the pattern of emphasis on certain subjects and relationships—questions and information, relevance and research, change and focus. In a sense, when you develop focused knowledge on your topic, you gather a cloud of information much like

Figure 2.7
Looking for
Patterns

this one, except richer and more complicated. Constantly analyze the relationships in what you're finding—what are the most frequent arguments, which ideas seem connected, what facts stick out?

What about a Thesis?

Ultimately, you must have a thesis, something you are saying about your research question. But when should you know what that is?

ARE YOU SUSPENDING JUDGMENT?   Should you have a thesis at this point? That depends on the purpose of your project. If it's exploratory, if your motive is to discover what you think, then it's too early to make any bold statements that answer the question you're researching. It might even be counterproductive. Inquiry-based investigations depend on your willingness to *suspend judgment* long enough to discover what you think.

ARE YOU TESTING ASSUMPTIONS?   If, however, you feel that you have developed some ideas about what you want to say, now might be an excellent time to make a list of your theories, assumptions, or beliefs about your topic. They will be invaluable guides for your research this week because you can examine these beliefs against the evidence and potentially break through to new understandings about your research question.

WHAT ARE YOU ARGUING?   In some cases, you know that what you think is the best answer to your research question even before you've done much investigation of the topic, and your motive is to build a convincing argument around that claim. For example, consider this claim: *Lawnmowers make a significant contribution to CO_2 emissions in the United States.* Maybe this is something you heard or read somewhere from a reputable source, and it's something you strongly suspect is true. Maybe your instructor asked you to make that argument, or you're writing an opinion piece for an assignment. Conventional research papers are frequently organized from the beginning around a thesis or claim. If that's the kind of project you're working on, now would be a good time to craft a sentence that states your most important assertion or main idea. This may well be refined or even discarded later on as you learn more, but it will help with your research this week.

To generate a *tentative* thesis statement at this point, try finishing one of the following sentences:

1. Although most people think _____ about _____, I think _____.
2. The most convincing answer to my research question is _____.
3. The main reason that _____ is a problem is _____, and the best solution is _____.
4. Among the causes of _____, the least understood is _____.
5. Though much has been said about _____, little attention has been paid to _____.
6. All of the evidence so far about _____ points to _____ as a significant cause/solution/effect/problem/interpretation/factor.

Presenting Research in Alternative Genres

Genre Power

Typically, we think of genres as categories. There are genres of music, books, and film. Although helpful as a means of sorting out "family resemblances"—things that certain groups of things share—it's a limited way of looking at genre. Genre is also a perceptual frame, something through which we look at the world that directs or gaze at this rather than that, and in one way or rather than another. Taylor was working on a research essay on the dangers of concussions in women's soccer, and her draft went into some detail about definitions of concussions, statistics on its occurrence in amateur and professional sports, and the particular vulnerability of some women athletes to the condition. When asked to present some of this research as an infographic, Taylor said it forced her to look at the same information in a different way. How could she tell a *visual* story, especially one that exploits comparisons, about the dangers of concussions in women's soccer? In other words, she had to turn 2000 words of text into a series of graphics with 200 words. What did she see? A brain, of course, and a ball, and the story—in pictures with very little text—of what a brain looks like when it violently collides with a soccer ball. To present your research in an alternative genre, then, is to choose a particular way of seeing your topic. Of course, genres don't live in a vacuum. They are social creatures, things that are created by certain communities to serve particular purposes. The peer-reviewed science article is a genre designed to advance scientific understanding, written for an audience of fellow experts with a shared interest in the topic. Those readers expect to see certain conventions followed, including a reliance on sound methodology and empirical evidence. An infographic, on the other hand, is intended for a general audience—non-experts who may have a passing interest in the topic—and it often relies on data from secondary sources. The best evidence is often presented graphically. Therefore, when you choose an alternative genre for presenting your research, you need to recognize its *rhetorical situation*. How will it influence your gaze, what purposes can it serve, for whom, and in what situations? In later "Presenting Research in Alternative Genre" features, we'll look more closely at how slides, infographics, posters, and photo essays each have their own rhetorical purposes and affects.

You'll be implementing your research strategy this week and next, looking at sources in the library and on the Web. The exercises that follow will help guide these searches, making sure that you don't overlook some key source or reference. Your instructor may ask you to hand in a photocopy of the exercise as a record of your journey.

Keeping Track of What You Find: Building a Bibliography

For the next two weeks, you're going to collect a lot of material on your research question: PDF copies of articles, books, bookmarked Web pages, images, and perhaps even audio and video files. You will make your life easier if you don't just collect but *record* what you find. Your options include the following:

- **Basic bibliography.** This is the minimalist approach. You simply keep a running list, using the appropriate citation method, of information on each source you think you'll use in your essay. If you're using MLA, for example, this will become your Works Cited page. An online citation machine, like bibme (http://www.bibme.org), can help you build it. You can, of course, wait until the last minute to do this but, trust me, you will regret it.

- **Working bibliography.** This is one step up from the basic bibliography (see Figure 2.8) and is the simplest form of what's called an "annotated bibliography." A working bibliography provides a brief *summary* of what the source says: what topics it covers and what the basic argument or main ideas are. If you're using a double-entry journal, then you can find the material you need for your summary there. Your annotation may be a brief paragraph or more, depending on the source.

- **Evaluative bibliography.** In some ways, this is the most useful annotated bibliography of all because it challenges you not only to "say back" what

---

Topic: Theories of Dog Training

Inquiry Question: Should dogs be trained using positive reinforcement exclusively?

1. Katz, Jon. "Why Dog Training Fails." *Slate Magazine.* 14 Jan. 2005. www.slate
.com/articles/news_and_politics/heavy_petting/2005/01/train_in_vain.html
   Katz argues that most theories of dog training fail to take into account the realities of raising an animal in a "split-level," not a training compound. He calls his own method the "Rational Theory," which he describes as an "amalgam" of techniques that takes into account the actual situation of both dog and owner.

2. Schilder, Matthijs B. H., and Joanne A. M. van der Borg. "Training Dogs with the Help of the Shock Collar: Short and Long Term Behavioural Effects." *Applied Animal Behaviour Science,* vol. 85, 2004, pp. 319–34. www
.appliedanimalbehaviour.com/article/S0168-1591(03)00248-X/abstract
   Researchers had two groups of German shepherds, one training with shock collars and the other training without them. They then studied both "direct reactions" of dogs to the shock and their later behavior. Study found that dogs trained with shock collars consistently showed more signs of stress during and after training, including "lower ear positions." Finding "suggests that the welfare of these shocked dogs is at stake, at least in the presence of their owner."

3. Shore, Elise, Charles Burdsal, and Deanna Douglas. "Pet Owners' Views of Pet Behavior Problems and Willingness to Consult Experts for Assistance." *Journal of Applied Animal Welfare Science,* vol. 11, no. 1, 2008, pp. 63–73.
   Study notes that 30 percent of dogs that are given to shelters are there because owners complained of behavior problems; yet only 24 percent of owners surveyed enrolled in obedience classes. Researchers surveyed 170 dog and cat owners and determined that the highest concern was about animals who threatened people, and those owners were most likely to ask for assistance and they mostly turned to the Web unless there was a charge.

Figure 2.8
Working
Bibliography:
An Example

you understand sources to be saying but also to offer some judgments about whether you find them persuasive or relevant. You might comment on what you consider the strengths of the source or its weaknesses. Is writing an evaluative bibliography more work? You bet. But ultimately you are writing your paper as you go because much of the material you generate for the bibliography can be exported right into your essay. Your double-entry journal provides the raw material for these annotations.

Your instructor will tell you what kind of bibliography you should build for this project, but at the least you should consider maintaining a basic bibliography as you go. Put it on a "cloud," like Google Docs or Evernote, that will store your draft bibliography on the Web and always be available wherever you find a new source—in the library, at home, or in the campus computer lab.

Searching Library Databases for Books and Articles

Despite the appeal of the Web, the campus library remains your most important source of information for academic research, and it's vital for developing focused knowledge on your topic. Sure, it can be aggravating. There's that missing book or that article that isn't available in full text. You needed that article! Most of all, there's the sense of helplessness you might feel as a relative novice using a large, complicated, and unfamiliar reference system.

In this chapter and the last one, you were introduced to basic library search strategies, knowledge that will help give you some mastery over the university library. Now you'll expand on that knowledge, and at the same time you'll move from a working knowledge of your topic to a deeper understanding, one that will crystallize by reading and writing about what you find.

It's hard for newcomers to the university to fully appreciate the revolution the last decade brought to how we do college research. All you need to know, really, is that finding sources is infinitely easier. And with the growing availability of full-text PDFs of articles and e-books, you can end a session of searching with not just a citation but also the printout of the article.

Because there are still relatively few digital versions of books, you should use the library the old-fashioned way: Journey into the "stacks," which at big schools can be cavernous, floor-to-ceiling aisles of books. The trip is well worth it because even if you discover that the book you want isn't right for your project, that book is surrounded by 100 others on your topic or related ones. Browse like you do on Amazon.

You will save time if you know *where* to look for the book you want, and so you must be familiar with how librarians organize books.

Finding Books

There are two systems for classifying books: the Dewey Decimal and the Library of Congress systems.

The Library of Congress system, which uses both letters and numbers, is much more common in college libraries. This is the system with which you should become most familiar. Each call number begins with one or two letters, signifying a category of knowledge, which is followed by a whole number between 1 and 9,999. A decimal and one or more Cutter numbers sometimes follow. The Library of Congress system is pretty complex, but it's not hard to use. As you get deeper in your research, you'll begin to recognize call numbers that consistently yield useful books. It is sometimes helpful to simply browse those shelves for other possibilities.

UNDERSTANDING CALL NUMBERS   The call number, that strange code on the spine of a library book, is something most of us want to understand just well enough to find that book on the shelf. How much do you need to know? First, you should know that there is more than just the alphabet at work in arranging books by their call numbers, and that the call numbers tell you more than merely where books are shelved. Take for example the call number for *The Curious Researcher*.

The call number shown in Figure 2.9 tells you the subject area of the book, a little something about its author, and when the book was published. This is useful to know not only because it will help you find the book, but it also might prompt you to find other, possibly more recent, books on the same subject on a nearby shelf. In Figure 2.10, you can see how Library of Congress call numbers determine the arrangement of books on the shelf.

COMING UP EMPTY HANDED?   In the unlikely event that you can't find any books by searching directly using the online catalog, there's another reference you can check that will help locate relevant articles and essays that are *a part* of a book whose title may otherwise seem unpromising. Check to see if your library has a database called the Essay and General Literature Index. Search that database with your keywords or subject and see if it produces something useful. List the relevant results as instructed previously. In addition, Google Book Search (http://books.google.com) allows users to do full-text searches of many titles.

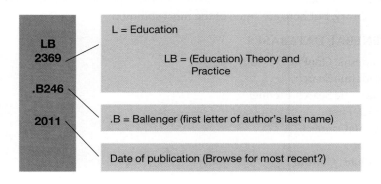

Figure 2.9
Deciphering the Call Number Code

Figure 2.10

How Books Are
Arranged on the
Library Shelf

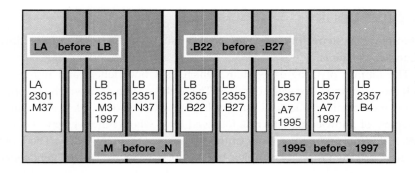

Those books in the public domain (i.e., the rights have lapsed) are available to any user in digital versions. This is a particularly rich resource for older texts, including some dating back hundreds of years.

CHECKING BIBLIOGRAPHIES   One tactic that might lead to a mother lode of sources for your essay is to look at the bibliographies at the back of (mostly) scholarly books (and articles). Don't ever set aside a promising book until you've checked the bibliography! Jot down complete bibliographic information from citations you want to check out later. Keep a running list of these in your research notebook.

INTERLIBRARY LOAN   If your library doesn't have the book (or article) you really want, don't despair. Most college libraries have a wonderful low- or no-cost service to students called interlibrary loan. The library will search the collections of other libraries to find what you're looking for and have it sent, sometimes within a week or less. Use the service by checking with the reference desk or your library's Web site.

Article Databases

There are two kinds of article databases at your library: general databases that cover multiple disciplines and specialized databases that are discipline specific. The general databases cover multiple subjects, so their coverage is wide but shallow. The specialized databases are subject specific, so their coverage is deep but narrow. Of course, I don't know which of these general databases you have at your library, but here are some of the most common:

> **GENERAL DATABASES**
>
> Academic OneFile
> Academic Search
> Academic Search Premier
> ArticleFirst
> IngentaConnect
> JSTOR
> ProQuest Central
> Web of Science

Many of these multidisciplinary databases index popular magazines and some newspapers, and even some scholarly journals, which makes them useful. For example, Academic Search Premier indexes nearly 14,000 magazines and journals. Increasingly, these databases include full-text articles, an extraordinary convenience for students working from home.

Common Specialized Databases

Humanities	Science and Technology	Social Sciences
America, History and Life	AGRICOLA (Agriculture)	Anthropological Index
Arts and Humanities Citation Index	Applied Science & Technology Index	ComAbstracts (Communication)
Historical Abstracts	Biological Abstracts	Contemporary Women's Issues
Humanities Index	CINAHL (Nursing)	Criminal Justice Abstracts
Literature Resource Center	Computer Literature Index	PAIS (Public Affairs)
MLA International Bibliography (Literature and composition)	GeoRef Abstracts (Geology)	PsycINFO
Music Index	Health Reference Center	Social Sciences Index
Project Muse	MathSciNet	Social Work
Religion and Philosophical Collection	Medline Web of Science (Medicine)	Sociological Abstracts
		Worldwide Political Science Abstracts

Business	Education
ABI/Inform	Education Full Text
Business Source Elite	Education Index
FreeEDGAR	ERIC

Specialized databases are subject specific. These are usually listed by discipline on your library's Web pages. The advantage of using these databases is that they will produce many scholarly articles that might be relevant to your research question, though they may not all be full text. For a list of some of these, see the table on page 000.

Finally, certain article databases are focused on certain *types* of publications. The most important of these are indexes to newspapers (see following list, "Newspaper Databases"). They don't index the small-town papers, but they do provide citations to the so-called national newspapers such as the *New York Times*, the *Washington Post*, the *Los Angeles Times*, the *Wall Street Journal*, and the *Christian Science Monitor*. What's good about the national newspapers is that they're among the most authoritative journalistic sources; in other words, because of their large and experienced staffs, the information they provide is more trustworthy than that of smaller newspapers and online news outlets.

If you're looking for state or local newspapers, you have a couple of options. The larger papers (and many magazines, for that matter) also have their own Web sites, where you may be able to search their archives and retrieve full-text articles. Some sites charge for this service, though you can usually request them from your campus library for free. A convenient method for searching some of these sites is to use a news search engine, which will consult thousands of papers in a few seconds. Two of the best of these search engines are Google News (http://news.google.com) and Yahoo News (http://news.yahoo.com).

Occasionally, the local papers are also indexed online by the university library, and copies are available on microfilm. More and more frequently, however, local papers, like their larger counterparts in major cities, have their own Web sites, where you can use keyword searches to scour their archives.

NEWSPAPER DATABASES

Alternative Press Index
Ethnic Newswatch
LexisNexis Academic
National Newspaper Index
National Newspapers
Newspaper Source
ProQuest Central

Saving Search Results

Most online book indexes and article databases allow you to save your search results. Some of these databases allow you to mark the relevant results and then print them out. Some databases and most university libraries also allow you to create an account and a file for your search results. Through the Web page at my library, I can save searches, build a list of books I want to check out, and even publish my bibliographies so others can see them (and I can see theirs). Finally, you can always e-mail your search results page to yourself and organize a bibliography on your own computer.

Exercise 2.2

SEARCH BOOK AND ARTICLE DATABASES

Develop your focused knowledge by doing a thorough search using your library's book index and article databases. Unlike in Web and database searches, in book searches it often pays off to begin with broad subject terms. I got better results, for example, when I searched for books on theories of dog training with *animal behavior-canine* than I did with *dog training theories*. Searches that begin broadly might lead you to a relevant chapter in an otherwise irrelevant book.

Choose one of the bibliographies (see pages 60–62) as a way of collecting relevant results. Your instructor may ask you to hand these in to gauge your progress. Remember that online citation machines like bibme.org can help you compile these results in the appropriate format (MLA or APA).

Advanced Internet Research Using Google Scholar

You worked with Google Scholar last week. In some ways, your library's databases make the search engine superfluous. For one thing, databases allow you to search by subject as well as keyword, and you can filter the results by type of publication. Library databases are also more comprehensive than Google Scholar, allowing you to a wider range of journals, magazines, and books.

On the other hand, sometimes you're trying to find a specific article and it's not turning up in a database search. And Google Scholar is often simply more convenient to use. To make the most of your searches, refine your Google Scholar search skills with some of the following techniques.

LINK TO YOUR LIBRARY   One of the downsides to Google Scholar when compared to your college library's database is that sometimes you may be asked to pay for a full-text article on Google. Therefore, the first thing you should do is set up the preferences in Google Scholar to link to your library where access to articles is free.

1. Click settings on the Scholar homepage.
2. Click on library links. A page will open like the one shown. Enter the name of your school, then search. Your university library should appear on a list. Check and save it. Now if your library's database has an article that appears in your search results, you'll see a link to retrieve it for free.

EXPLOIT RELATED RESULTS   One of the nifty but largely ignored features of Google Scholar are the links at the bottom of each result. Lets' take a closer look at a few of these.

[HTML] Genesis of suicide **terrorism**
S Atran - Science, 2003 - sciencemag.org
... significant causal relations between our society's policies and actions and those of **terrorist** organizations and ... As with the somewhat tendentious and self-serving use of "**terror**" as a policy concept ... to ignore these relations as legitimate topics for inquiry into what **terrorism** is all ...
Cited by 693   Related articles   All 42 versions   Web of Science: 206   Cite   Save

1. **Cited by.** To start with, this is a useful metric for evaluating the authority of an article. Typically, articles that are cited in other works is scholarship that other experts value. Here "Genesis of Suicide Terrorism" is cited by 693 other sources. If you click on this link, you can see some of these other articles, some of which might be helpful to you.
2. **Related articles.** Click on this and you'll find related works to the article you've chosen. In this case, I found 101 articles relevant to "Genesis of Suicide Terrorism," including books like *Dying to Kill: The Allure of Suicide Terror.*
3. **Versions.** This cool feature allows you to see the formats and publication venues for each Scholar result. This is particularly helpful when you want to find a version with a link to your library or a full-text copy that you can download.
4. **Cite.** The "cite" button can help you in two ways. First, it will give you a formatted citation of an article in MLA, APA, Chicago, and several other formats that you can simply cut and paste into your working bibliography. It also provides links to some of the more popular citation software like Endnote in case you use one of those programs.

FILTER USING ADVANCED SEARCH   Click on the downward pointing arrow on the right of the Google Scholar search window and a box will open (see image that follows) that can help you do Boolean-like searching without the need to use the connectors (see pages 47–49). For example, you can launch a search for results that contain all or at least one of your keywords. Perhaps more useful are options that allow you to control *where* in the results you want those words to appear, something that's particularly useful if you're looking for a particular article and you don't know the author. Finally, some disciplines, especially those in the sciences, value more recent publications. Using the advanced search you can specify results limited to certain dates.

Living Sources: Interviews and Surveys

Arranging Interviews

A few years ago, I researched a local turn-of-the-century writer named Sarah Orne Jewett for a magazine article. I dutifully read much of her work, studied critical articles and books on her writing, and visited her childhood home, which is open to the public in South Berwick, Maine. My research was going fairly well, but when I sat down to begin writing the draft, the material seemed flat and lifeless. A few days later, the curator of the Jewett house mentioned that there was an 88-year-old local woman, Elizabeth Goodwin, who had known the writer when she was alive. "As far as I know, she's the last living person who knew Sarah Orne Jewett," the curator told me. "And she lives just down the street."

The next week, I spent 3 hours with Elizabeth Goodwin, who told me of breakfasting with the famous author and eating strawberry jam and muffins. Elizabeth told me that many years after Jewett's death, the house seemed haunted by her friendly presence. One time, when Elizabeth lived in the Jewett house as a curator, some unseen hands pulled her back as she teetered at the top of the steep staircase in the back of the house. She likes to believe it was the author's ghost.

This interview transformed the piece by bringing the subject to life—first for me as the writer, and later for my readers. Ultimately, what makes almost any topic compelling is discovering why it matters to *people*—how it affects their lives. Doing interviews with people close to the subject, both experts and non-experts, is often the best way to find that out.

If you'd like to do some interviews, now is the time to begin arranging them.

TYPES OF INTERVIEWS   You should be realistic about the kind of interviews that you have time for in this project. The most involved are those like my interview with the wife of the lobster fisher, which involved going into the field, holding an interview on site, and then doing some follow-up with the subject. These are often the most rewarding interviews to do. But you simply may not have time for that. What are other options? The table that follows lists some types of interviews you might incorporate in your project, from the most time-consuming to the least.

Interview Type	What's Involved	Time Required
Field interviews	Arranging to meeting your subject where they work or in a location relevant to the research topic. May involve follow-up. Preparation, including some subject knowledge, is often helpful	These are often the most fruitful but also the most labor intensive interviews. May require travel to a remote location, and significant preparation.
On-campus interviews	Meet with university experts on your topic or with other students affected by the problem. Interviews could be in offices or informal settings on campus.	An appealing approach because of the accessibility of experts on your own campus as well as students who might have experience with your topic.
Online interviews	These could be live—through programs like FaceTime or instant messaging software—with subjects in remote locations. Or they might involve submitting questions by e-mail.	With messaging software, it's possible to interview someone nearby or on the other side of the world. E-mail interviews are even easier to arrange but may involve a wait for responses.
Informal interviews with friends and family	Depending on what you're writing about, the people you know might have interesting things to say. These subjects are often accessible and willing.	The least time-consuming of all, for obvious reasons. But are friends and family really the best people to interview on your topic?

FINDING PEOPLE TO TALK TO   No matter what type of interview you plan you have to find the right people to talk to. These will include people with expertise on your research topic and people who are affected directly or indirectly by the problem. Say you're writing about the rental crisis for low-income residents in San Francisco. Your first instinct, and it's a good one, is to ask yourself "Who do I know that is affected by the problem?" Maybe you're good friends with your landlord. Does she have any views on the rental crisis? What about your friend who just got evicted and is desperately looking for an affordable place to rent? Is there someone in your campus' Student Affair's office who might tell you what they say to prospective students about finding off-campus rentals? You certainly could take a trip down the Mission District, where gentrification is pushing out lower-income residents. Maybe you could talk to someone on the staff of the nonprofit tenant's rights group?

Now cast a wider net. Imagine how to reach people affected by the problem who you might find online. You Google your topic and find the name of a reporter for the *San Francisco Chronicle* who writes on the rental housing crisis in the city. Maybe e-mail him? What about the leader of the organization that opposed the 2015 referendum intended to confront the rental crisis?

What about experts on rental affordability? Is there a faculty member at your own university who has written or spoken about it? Does your English instructor have any suggestions about colleagues you might talk to? In your research did you find a great article by a scholar at another school? You go to that university's Web site and find his e-mail address to query her about an interview.

As you imagine people to talk to move outward from people you know to people you don't, and people who are close by to people who are remote. Think imaginatively, brainstorming ideas. Then consider who might have the most relevant, useful things to say, who is accessible, and how much time it might take to set up the interview and get a response. Finally, make some realistic choices about how to proceed given your time constraints, including the deadline for submitting your draft.

MAKING CONTACT   You'll be asking for an interview face-to-face, by phone, or e-mail. When contacting an expert for an interview, first state your name and then briefly explain your research project. If you were referred to the subject by someone she may know, mention that. A comment like "I think you could be extremely helpful to me" or "I'm familiar with your work, and I'm anxious to talk to you about it" works well. When thinking about when to propose the interview with an expert on your topic, consider arranging it *after* you've done some research. You will not only be more informed, but you will also have a clearer sense of what you want to know and what questions to ask.

E-mail interview queries are often less effective than actually speaking to a potential interview subject, but e-mail is an especially appealing approach for reaching out to strangers. Once you find the e-mail address of someone who seems a likely interview subject, proceed courteously and cautiously. One of the Internet's haunting issues is its potential to violate privacy. Be especially careful if you've gone to great lengths in hunting down the e-mail address of someone involved with your research topic; she may not be keen on receiving unsolicited e-mail messages from strangers. It would be courteous to approach any potential interview subject with a short message that asks permission for an online interview. To do so, briefly describe your project and why you think this individual might be a good source for you. As always, you will be much more likely to get an enthusiastic response from someone if you can demonstrate your knowledge of her work on or experience with your topic.

Let's assume your initial contact has been successful and your subject has agreed to answer your questions. Your follow-up message should ask a *limited* number of questions—say, four or five—that are thoughtful and, if possible, specific. Keep in mind that although the e-mail interview is conducted in writing rather than through talking, many of the methods for handling conventional interviews still apply.

CONDUCTING INTERVIEWS   You've already thought about whether interviews might contribute to your paper. If there's a chance that they will, build a list of possible interview subjects and contact several of them. By the end of this week, you should begin interviewing.

I know. You wouldn't mind putting it off. But once you start, it will get easier and easier. I used to dread interviewing strangers, but after making the first phone call, I got some momentum going, and I began to enjoy it. It's decidedly easier to interview friends, family, and acquaintances, but that's the wrong reason to limit yourself to people you know.

What Questions to Ask? The first step in preparing for an interview is to ask yourself, What's the purpose of this interview? In your research notebook, make a list of *specific questions* for each person you're going to interview. Often, these questions are raised by your reading or other interviews. What theories or ideas encountered in your reading would you like to ask your subject about? What specific facts have you been unable to uncover that your interview subject may provide? What don't you understand that he could explain? Would you like to test one of your own impressions or ideas on your subject? What about the subject's work or experience would you like to learn? Interviews are wonderful tools for clearing up your own confusion and getting specific information that is unavailable anywhere else.

Now make a list of more *open-ended questions* you might ask some or all of the people you're going to talk to. Frankly, these questions are a lot more fun to ask because you're likely to be surprised by some of the answers. For example:

- In all your experience with _____, what has most surprised you?
- What has been the most difficult aspect of your work?
- If you had the chance to change something about how you approached _____, what would it be?
- Can you remember a significant moment in your work on _____? Is there an experience with _____ that stands out in your mind?
- What do you think is the most common misconception about _____? Why?
- What are significant current trends in _____?
- Who or what has most influenced you? Who are your heroes?
- If you had to summarize the most important thing you've learned about _____, what would it be?
- What is the most important thing other people should know or understand?

As you develop both specific and open-ended questions, keep in mind what you know about each person—his work in the field and personal experience with your topic. You may end up asking a lot of the same questions of everybody you interview, but try to familiarize yourself with any special qualifications a subject may have or experiences he may have had. That knowledge might come from your reading, from what other people tell you about your subject, or from your initial telephone call to set up the interview.

Also keep in mind the *kinds* of information an interview can provide better than other sources: anecdotes, strong quotes, and sometimes descriptive material. If you ask the right questions, a live subject can paint a picture of his experience with your topic, and you can capture that picture in your paper.

During the Interview. Once you've built a list of questions, be prepared to ignore it. Interviews are conversations, not surveys. They are about human interaction between two people who are both interested in the same thing.

I remember interviewing a lobsterman, Edward Heaphy, on his boat. I had a long list of questions in my notebook, which I dutifully asked, one after the other. My questions were mechanical and so were his answers. I finally stopped, put my notebook down, and talked informally with Edward for a few minutes. Offhandedly, I asked, "Would you want your sons or daughter to get in the business?" It was a totally unplanned question. Edward was silent for a moment, staring at his hands. I knew he was about to say something important because, for the first time, I was attentive to him, not my notepad. "Too much work for what they get out of it," he said quietly. It was a surprising remark after hearing for the last hour how much Edward loved lobstering. What's more, I felt I had broken through. The rest of the interview went much better.

Much of how to conduct an interview is common sense. At the outset, clarify the nature of your project—what your paper is on and where you're at with it. Briefly explain again why you thought this individual would be the perfect person to talk to about it. I find it often helps to begin with a specific question that I'm pretty sure my subject can help with. But there's no formula. Simply be a good conversationalist: Listen attentively, ask questions that your subject seems to find interesting, and enjoy sharing an interest with your subject. Also, don't be afraid to ask what you fear are obvious questions. Demonstrate to the subject that you *really* want to understand.

Always end interviews by making sure you have accurate background information on your subjects: name (spelled correctly), position, affiliation, age (if applicable), phone number. Ask if you can call them with follow-up questions, should you have any. And always ask your subjects if they can recommend any additional reading or other people you should talk to. Of course, mention that you're appreciative of the time they have spent with you.

Notetaking. There are basically three ways to take notes during an interview: Use a digital recorder or smartphone, a notepad, or both. I adhere to the third method, but it's an individual choice. I like recording with a smartphone because I don't panic during an interview that I'm losing information or quoting inaccurately. I don't want to spend hours transcribing interviews, so I also take notes on the information I think I want to use. If I miss anything, I consult the recording later. Sometimes, I find that there is no recording—the machine decided not to participate in the interview—but at least I have my notes.

Get some practice developing your own notetaking technique by interviewing your roommate or taking notes on the television news. Devise ways to shorten often-used words (e.g., *t* for *the, imp* for *important,* and *w/o* for *without*).

Let's assume your initial contact has been successful and your subject has agreed to answer your questions. Your follow-up message should ask a *limited* number of questions—say, four or five—that are thoughtful and, if possible, specific. Keep in mind that while the e-mail interview is conducted in writing rather than through talking, many of the methods for handling conventional interviews still apply.

Planning Informal Surveys

Christine was interested in dream interpretation, especially exploring the significance of symbols or images that recur in many people's dreams. She could have simply examined her own dreams, but she thought it might be more interesting to survey a group of fellow students, asking how often they dream and what they remember. An informal survey, in which she would ask each person several standard questions, seemed worth trying.

You might consider it, too, if the responses of a group of people to some aspect of your topic could reveal a pattern of behavior, attitudes, or experiences worth analyzing. Informal surveys are decidedly unscientific. You probably won't get a large enough sample size, nor do you likely have the skills to design a poll that would produce statistically reliable results. But you probably won't actually base your paper on the survey results, anyway. Rather, you'll present specific, concrete information about some patterns in your survey group or, perhaps, use some of your findings to help support your assertions.

DEFINING GOALS AND AUDIENCE   Begin planning your informal survey by defining what you want to know and whom you want to know it from. Christine suspected that many students have dreams related to stress. She wondered if there were any similarities among students' dreams. She was also curious about how many people remember their dreams and how often and whether this might be related to gender. Finally, Christine wanted to find out whether people have recurring dreams and, if so, what those were about. There were other things she wanted to know, but she knew she had to keep the survey short.

If you're considering a survey, make a list in your research notebook of things you might want to find out and specify the group of people you plan to talk to. College students? Female college students? Attorneys? Guidance counselors? Be as specific as you can about your target group.

PAPER OR ELECTRONIC?   After you mull over the purpose of your survey, you need to decide whether you'll distribute it electronically or on paper. These days, free online software like the popular SurveyMonkey (see Figure 2.11) allows users to easily create basic digital surveys. You can distribute the survey to a targeted list of recipients by e-mail or post it on a blog, Web site, or even on social media like Facebook and Twitter. In addition, a program like SurveyMonkey helps you analyze the results and filter, compare, and summarize the data with charts and graphs. Web-based surveys are also cheaper than paper surveys.

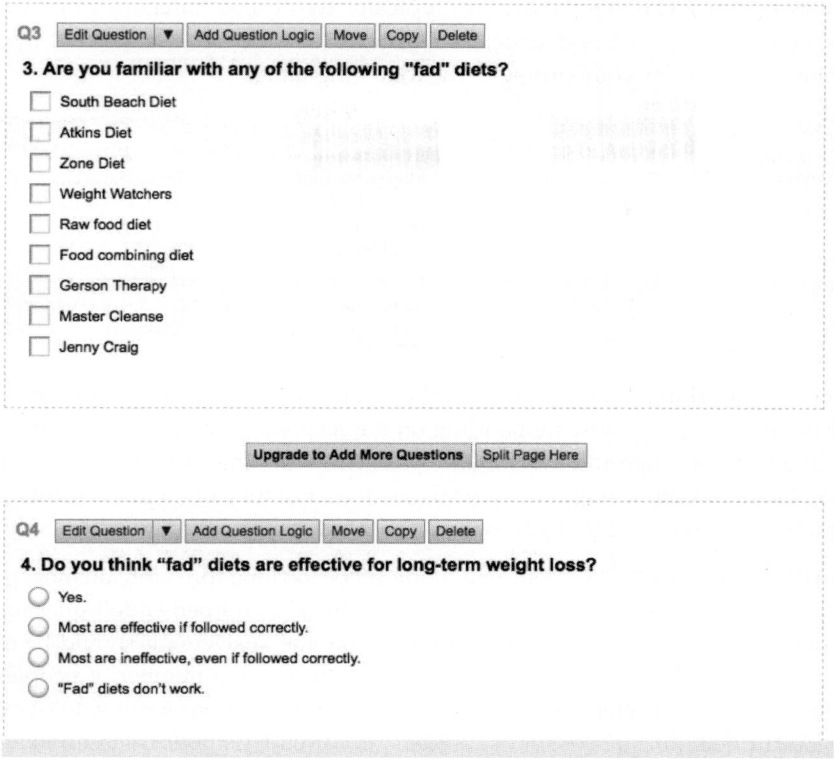

Figure 2.11
A Sample Online Survey

A student researching fad diets used SurveyMonkey to design and distribute her survey. This screen shot shows several of her questions, which are structured rather than open ended. The key with structured questions like these is that you have to know enough about your subject to know the appropriate answers.

Why *wouldn't* you want to go digital instead of using old-fashioned paper surveys? A couple of reasons:

- With paper, you can target an audience much more easily, particularly if you can actually *locate* those potential respondents in a specific time or place. For example, if you want to survey your school's football fans, distributing your survey on game day at the tailgate party will give you direct access to your survey audience.

- Not everyone has easy Internet access.

- The free versions of the online software may limit the number of responses you can gather.

- Response rates to electronic surveys can be lower than response rates to paper surveys.

Despite these drawbacks, a Web-based survey is often the best choice for an undergraduate research project, particularly if you can find ways to target your audience, make a personal appeal for a response, and send out a reminder or two.

TYPES OF QUESTIONS   There are typically two broad categories of survey questions: open ended and structured. You can see the advantages and disadvantages of each for your survey in the following table.

Question Type	Examples	Advantage	Disadvantage
Open ended	Brief response, essay question	May get surprising answers. More insight into respondents' thoughts and ideas.	Takes more time. Can't easily be measured.
Structured	Multiple choice, true/false, Likert, ranking	Easier to analyze responses. Doesn't take much time.	Must know enough to provide appropriate choices.

Generally speaking, you should limit the number of open-ended questions you use because they are more demanding on the respondents. But don't hesitate to use them if you hope to open a window on the thinking of your survey audience. These responses might not reveal a pattern, but they often provide interesting anecdotal evidence that you can use in your essay.

CRAFTING QUESTIONS   A survey shouldn't be too long (probably no more than six or seven questions, and fewer if you rely mostly on open-ended questions), it shouldn't be biased (questions shouldn't skew the answers), it should be easy to score (especially if you hope to survey a relatively large number of people), it should ask clear questions, and it should give clear instructions for how to answer.

As a rule, informal surveys should begin (or end) as polls often do: by getting vital information about the respondent. Depending on the purpose of your survey, you might also want to know whether respondents are registered to vote, whether they have political affiliations, what year of school they're in, or any number of other factors. Ask for information that provides different ways of breaking down your target group.

Avoid Loaded Questions.   Question design is tricky business. Biased questions should be avoided by altering language that is charged and presumptuous. Take, for example, the question *Do you think it's morally wrong to kill unborn babies through abortion?* This wording is charged and is also presumptuous (it is unlikely that all respondents believe that abortion is killing). One revision might be *Do you support or oppose providing women the option to abort a pregnancy during the first 20 weeks?* This is a direct and specific question, neutrally stated, that calls for a yes or no answer.

Controversial topics, like abortion, are most vulnerable to biased survey questions. If your topic is controversial, take great care to eliminate bias by avoiding charged language, especially if you have strong feelings yourself.

Avoid Vague Questions.   Another trap is asking vague questions. One such question is *Do you support or oppose the university's alcohol policy?* This wording assumes that respondents know what the policy is, and it ignores the fact that the policy has many elements. A revised question might ask about one part of the policy: *The university recently established a policy that states that underage students caught drinking* *in campus dormitories are subject to eviction. Do you support or oppose this policy?* Other equally specific questions might ask about other parts of the policy.

Drawbacks of Open-Ended Questions. Open-ended questions often produce fascinating answers, but they can be difficult to tabulate. Christine's survey on dream interpretation asked, *Please briefly describe the dream you best remember or one that sticks out in your mind.* She got a wide range of answers—or sometimes no answer at all—but it was hard to quantify the results. Almost everyone had different dreams, which made it difficult to discern much of a pattern. However, she was still able to use some of the material as anecdotes in her paper, so it turned out to be a question worth asking.

Designing Your Multiple-Choice Questions. As you've seen, the multiple-choice question is an alternative to the open-ended question, leaving room for a number of *limited* responses, which are easier to quantify.

The challenge in designing multiple-choice questions is to provide choices that will likely produce results. For example, from her reading and talking to friends, a student studying fad diets came up with a comprehensive list of the most popular diets (see Figure 2.11). Design choices you think your audience will respond to, but consider giving them room to say your choices weren't theirs by including a "none of the above" option or an open-ended "other" selection that allows respondents to insert their own answers.

Using Scaled Responses. The best-known of these types of questions is the Likert scale, which provides respondents with the chance to express their levels of agreement or disagreement with a statement. Typically, you'd provide a related group of statements. For example, suppose you wanted to collect some data on how students feel about rider traffic on campus. Using a Likert's scale, you might develop a series of questions like those that follow.

	Strongly Agree	Agree	Undecided	Disagree	Strongly Disagree
1. Speeding bicyclists are a problem on the quad.	1	2	3	4	5
2. Speeding skateboarders are a problem on the quad.	1	2	3	4	5
3. The university should consider a policy that requires bicyclists to dismount when on the quad.	1	2	3	4	5
4.	1	2	3	4	5

CONDUCTING SURVEYS Once you have finalized your questions, you can make plans to distribute the survey to the target group you defined previously. Though surveys can be distributed by phone and mail (remember that?), it's far more likely that you'll distribute your survey online or in person. We'll concentrate on those two methods.

In-Person Surveys. The university community, where large numbers of people are available in a confined area, lends itself to administering surveys this way. A survey can be distributed in dormitories, dining halls, classes, or anywhere else the people you want to talk to gather. You can stand outside the student union and stop people as they come and go, or you can hand out your survey to groups of people and collect them when the participants have finished. Your instructor may be able to help distribute your survey to classes.

Although an exclusively university audience won't always be relevant, for some research questions it is exactly what's needed. Anna, writing a paper on date rape, surveyed exclusively women on campus, many of whom she found in women's dormitories. For his paper on the future of the fraternity system, David surveyed local "Greeks" at their annual awards banquet.

How large a sample should you shoot for? Because yours won't be a scientific survey, don't bother worrying about statistical reliability; just try to survey as many people as you can. Certainly, a large (say, more than 100) and representative sample will lend more credence to your claims about any patterns observed in the results.

Internet Surveys. You can reach respondents online in the following ways:

1. E-mail
2. Social media like Facebook
3. Listservs, discussion groups
4. Posting survey link on a blog or Web page

Of these, targeted e-mail and online discussion groups of relevant people are likely to be the most productive. Marketing specialists often buy e-mail lists, an unlikely option for the undergraduate. That's why posting a link to your survey on a relevant online forum or listserv can be so effective because you can match the subject of your survey to people who discuss that subject online. You must, of course, first subscribe to one or more of these lists, and it always helps to listen in on the conversation before you make an appeal for survey respondents. Make sure this group is the appropriate one to answer your questions. Try searching Google Groups to find potential respondents.

Posting a link to your survey on Facebook or Twitter will get it out to potentially many more people, but you should expect a very low response rate.

Fieldwork: Research on What You See and Hear

My daughter Julia, as a senior in high school, belonged to the school's theater group, performing in plays and taking theater classes. She enjoyed it. But she also claimed that certain qualities distinguished "theater kids" from other students. How did she come to these conclusions? By hanging out with the theater

crowd. To use a more academic phrasing, Julia was a "participant-observer," though there was certainly no method involved. We all make judgments about social groups, inferences that come from experience. Usually there's nothing systematic about this process, and sometimes these judgments are unfair.

Yet the data that comes from observation, particularly if we take care to collect and document it, can be a rich vein to mine. This kind of data is also relevant to research in the social sciences and humanities and even to research essays in composition courses. Suppose, for instance, that your research question focuses on comparing crowd behavior at college and high school football games. How can you research that essay *without* observing a few games? If your topic has anything do to with subcultures or social groups—say, international students on your campus or the snowboarding community—fieldwork can be invaluable.

Preparing for Fieldwork

The kind of fieldwork you're able to do for your essay simply won't be the more rigorous and methodologically sophisticated work that academic ethnographers, anthropologists, or sociologists do. For one thing, you don't have the time it requires. But you can collect some useful observations for your paper. There are three tools for this you might find useful:

1. **Notebook.** You can't do without this. For convenience, you might choose a pocket notebook rather than a full-size one.
2. **Digital camera.** Use your camera or smartphone to take pictures of the site you're observing and the people participating in an activity for later study. Also photograph objects (ethnographers call these *artifacts*) that have symbolic or practical significance to the people you're observing.
3. **Digital recorder.** Use it for interviews and other recording in the field. (Remember to ask permission to record interviewees.) Smartphones these days can fulfill both your recording and your video needs.

Where you go to conduct field observations of course depends on your topic. Typically you choose a physical space in which people in particular social or cultural groups meet to participate in meaningful (to them) activities. If your research is on the high school theater group as a subculture, you might go to rehearsals, auditions, or perhaps a cast party. A researcher interested in adult video gaming addiction might spend a few evenings watching gamers do their thing at someone's home. A writer of an essay on Kwanazaa, an African American holiday tradition, might observe some families participating in its rituals.

Notetaking Strategies

What do you look for and how do you document it? Well, that depends on your project. Generally, of course, the task is to watch what people do and listen to what they say. More specifically, though, consider the following:

- **Look for evidence that confirms, contradicts, or qualifies the theories or assertions you've read about in your research.** Is it true that when they're not playing, adult video gamers can appear irritable and depressed? Do dogs that are punitively corrected during a training class demonstrate submissive behavior?

- **Look and listen to what people say during moments with particular significance for participants.** How do fans behave when the referee doesn't call the foul? What does one gamer say to another when she beats him?

- **Describe** *artifacts*—**things that people in the situation typically use.** A skater's skateboard. The objects in an actor's dressing room. The clothing traditionally worn by women celebrating Kwanzaa.

When you take notes, consider using the double-entry journal system that is discussed in detail in the next chapter. Use the left-facing page of your notebook to scribble your observations and the right-facing page to later freewrite about what strikes you about these observations. Make sure that you clearly indicate when you are quoting someone and when you are describing something.

Using What You See and Hear

Unless your research topic is an ethnography—an investigation that describes and interprets the activities of a cultural group in the field—it's likely that you will use your own fieldwork in your essay in a relatively limited way. Still, it can really be worth the effort. For example, fieldwork can be especially useful to:

- **Give your topic a face.** Nothing makes a problem or idea more meaningful than *showing* how it affects people. Can you use your descriptions of individuals (perhaps along with your interviews) to show rather than simply explain why your topic is significant?

- **Make a scene.** Observations in the field give you the ingredients of a scene: In a particular time and place, people are *doing something*. If what they are doing is significant and relevant to your research question, you can describe the place, the people, the action, and even the dialogue. Few techniques give writing more life.

- **Incorporate images.** Depending on the nature of your project, the digital pictures you take in the field can be powerful illustrations of what you're writing about.

- **Develop a multimodal research essay.** Using the digital recordings you made in the field and free editing software like Audacity, you can create a podcast of your research essay, even incorporating music. You can use free software like Microsoft Photo Story to use images, text, and voice narration to present your findings.

Chapter 3
The Third Week

 ## Learning Objectives

In this chapter, you'll learn to . . .

- Practice notetaking as a conversation with a source.
- Use writing *as you read* to clarify what a source is saying and think through what it means for your research question.
- Identify different types of borrowing from a source, which of these risk plagiarism, and what to do about it.
- Understand the triad of notetaking strategies—paraphrase, summary, and quotation—and use them in your own notes.
- Consider several techniques for notetaking that encourage written conversations with sources, and choose one that works for you as a research writer.
- Draft an annotated bibliography that explains and evaluates key sources on your topic.

Writing in the Middle: Conversing with Sources

Tim's inquiry question explores the impact that an adult's addiction to video games has on family and friends. He spends a week collecting research—mostly printing out articles from library databases and Web sites. Tim skims things, underlining a line or a passage from time to time, but for the most part he's like a bear in a blueberry patch, voraciously collecting as much information as he can. This is all in preparation for the writing, which he'll postpone until right before the paper is due.

Sound familiar? This is certainly similar to the way I always did research.

Here's how I would rewrite this scene for Tim: Tim is still hungrily collecting information about video gaming addiction, *but as he collects it, he's writing about what he's found.* Tim's notebook is open next to his laptop, and he's jotting down quotations and summaries and maybe an interesting fact or two. He's also marking up the electronic copy, highlighting passages of an article he might want to return to, or cutting and pasting relevant passages into an open Word document. Then, when he's done reading the article, Tim writes furiously in his notebook for 10 minutes or so, exploring his reaction to what he's read.

I now believe that the writing that takes place in the *middle* of the research process—the notetaking stage—may be as important as, if not more important than, the writing that takes place at the end—composing the draft. Writing in the middle helps you take possession of your sources and establish your presence in the draft. It sharpens your thinking about your topic, and it is the best cure for unintentional plagiarism.

I realize I have a sales job to do on this. Writing in the middle, particularly if you've been weaned on notecards, feels like busywork. "It gets in the way of doing the research," one student told me. "I just want to collect as much stuff as I can, as quickly as I can. Notetaking slows me down." Though it may seem inefficient, writing as you read may actually make your research *more* efficient. Skeptical? Read on.

Notetaking as a Scene of Writing

In class the other night, my students enlightened me about the digital dating scene. One was a veteran of OkCupid, the largest of the online sites, and she regaled me and the rest of the class with tales of weird online encounters, a few of which turned into face-to-meetings with likely prospects. In the end, she met a man she liked, and they're now in a relationship. But my student mentioned how difficult it was to deal with the sometimes aggressive and even insulting messages she received. As a long married guy, I knew nothing about the online dating scene, and so naturally I did a little online research. Here's an excerpt from "Why Online Dating is Good for Women" by Jo Piazza:

> Digital dating and the vast amount of information that accompanies it—with a market estimated at 27 million Americans—arm women with the knowledge needed to make a better choice before the date even begins. The Pill allowed women to metaphorically road-test the car. Online dating allows a woman to get an inspection before she bothers heading to the lot.

Imagine for a moment that my casual search was instead a research project that was investigating this preliminary inquiry question: "What role does gender play in how people represent themselves on digital dating sites?" This passage from "Why Online Dating Is Good for Women" would be a great find. Here's why:

- It's not only relevant to my question, but it also includes some useful data about how many Americans are involved in the online dating phenomenon.

- It makes an interesting claim: Finding dates online is actually *good* for women.

- It is distinctively written: Online dating is like inspecting a car before you drive it out of the lot.

I like the passage for my hypothetical research project, but now what do I do with it? Faced with this situation, a lot of my students don't do anything at all. Or at best, they save the file somewhere on their hard drive where they can find it when they begin the draft. What students rarely do when the encounter a good source is write.

When we do research we are following the story of our thinking. The drama of doing research is found in moments like the one I described here—having a question and then finding another voice that speaks to it in ways that lead to a new episode of understanding. Really, online dating can *empower* women? Every interesting encounter with a surprising fact or a fresh perspective moves that narrative of thought along, and before long, if we're paying attention, we realize how much we understand now that we didn't when we started. It's a story we build from small scenes like this one—an encounter with a reading from your research. Making this a scene for writing helps you to both remember the encounter and understand how it is moving the story of your thinking along.

What I'm talking about here is a kind of notetaking that isn't the usual triad—paraphrase, quotation, or summary—but writing that is *exploratory*, an examination of first and second thoughts about the things you read. It's a kind of writing that is conversation with yourself and a source that might begin questions like this:

- Does my experience and previous understandings lead me to believe this is true?
- What do I find surprising about this?
- How does it change the story of my thinking so far?

In the following exercise, I'll show you how this can work.

Exercise 3.1

GETTING INTO A CONVERSATION WITH A FACT

Through writing, facts can ignite thought, if we let them. They can help us discover what we think and refine our point of view. But for this to happen, you have to interact with information. Rather than a monologue—simply jotting down what an author is saying—you engage in a conversation—talking *with* an author: questioning, agreeing, speculating, wondering, connecting, arguing. You can do this in your head, but it's far more productive to have this dialogue through writing.

Let's try it.

I'm going to share with you two facts—one at a time—that together start to tell an interesting story about gender, beauty, and culture. Each fact will be a prompt for about 5 minutes of fastwriting in which you explore your thinking about the fact.

STEP 1: How do women see men's "attractiveness"? Apparently, not favorably. *Harper's Magazine* recently reported that U.S. women said that they judge the "attractiveness" of 80 percent of men to be "worse than average." Methodological questions aside for the moment (how exactly *did* the study come up with this finding), a lot of us might find the apparent harshness of this judgment surprising. Do you? Assuming the finding is true, how might you explain it? Write fast for 4 minutes, exploring your own reaction to the "fact." Think through writing, trying to sort out your first and second thoughts.

STEP 2: Naturally, we want to know how U.S. men judge women's "attractiveness." *Harper's* reported that men were apparently much less judgmental. Men judged 20 percent of women as having "worse than average" attractiveness. In a culture where women often feel judged by men over physical beauty, does it surprise you that men might be less critical of attractiveness than women? If true, how might you explain this? Together, what does this information about both men and women's views say to you about gender and "attractiveness"? Again, fastwrite for 4 minutes, following your narrative of thought.

Reflect on what you just did. Did your thinking about gender and "attractiveness" evolve with each episode of writing? Can you follow the story of your thinking? Did any ideas and insights emerge from the writing that you didn't expect? What you accomplished in this exercise (if anything) might have occurred in a conversation with others about the finding. But in the absence of others, writing can spark a conversation, too, and one that provides you with a record of what happened. Later in the chapter, we'll look at several ways to structure your notetaking so it encourages conversing with information.

What I Hear You Saying

Most *good* conversations make demands on both speakers. The most important of these is simply to listen carefully—and *to understand*—what the other person is saying. In couples' therapy there's a method to help this along called "say back"—each partner has to listen first and then repeat what he or she heard the other say. Response or reaction comes later. Researchers entering into a conversation with their sources need to engage in the same practice: You need to listen or read carefully, first making an effort to understand a subject or an author's arguments or ideas and then exploring your response to them, as you did previously in this exercise.

Taking the time to summarize your understanding of a source and what it says is especially important when you're reading difficult texts, something you'll do pretty often in academic research projects. It's also important when you're reading something that is making an argument that you don't agree with.

The academic equivalent of say back is paraphrasing or summarizing, something we'll look at in more detail later in this chapter. It takes practice to do well. In Exercise 3.2, you will try combining say back or summary with exploratory writing. Then you'll work up a synthesis of the two to draft a thoughtful response to a question.

Exercise 3.2

EXPLORE, "SAY BACK," AND SYNTHESIZE

In 20 minutes or so, you can test your skills in this exercise by using exploratory writing to summarize some data and to come up with a synthesis that reflects your thinking on a question.

STEP 1: Begin with a little exploratory writing on the topic of digital dating. Maybe you've tried it. Maybe you've never tried it. Maybe you never will. But consider how dating has changed since the emergence and popularity of sites like Match.com, Tinder, or OkCupid. Is this a good thing? A bad thing? A complicated thing? What does it say about the challenges of developing relationships in the twenty-first century? Fastwrite for 4 minutes. As always, follow your writing to see where it goes.

STEP 2: The Pew Research Center does lots of research on online behavior, including trends in how users and non-users view digital dating. Take a look at some of Pew's recent data on online dating, information I've culled from the organization's annual surveys from 2014 to 2016.

Who Dates Online?

Survey of Americans who have used online dating Web sites or apps, (2013):

Age Group	Percentage
18–24	10
25–34	22
35–44	17
45–54	8
55–64	6
Older than 65	3

Have American Attitudes Toward Online Dating Changed?

Percentage who agree with the statement:

	2005	2013	2015
Online dating is a good way to meet people.	44	59	59
People who use online dating are desperate.	29	21	23

How Do Online Daters Feel About the Experience?

Percentage of users and non-users of online dating services who agree with the statement (2015):

	Users	Non-users
Online dating is a good way to meet people	80	55
Online dating allows people to find a better match for themselves	62	50
Online dating is easier and more efficient than other ways	61	44
Online dating is more dangerous than other ways	45	60
Online dating keeps people from settling down	31	32
People who use online dating are desperate	16	24

Will Online Dating Result in a Lasting Relationship?

Percentage in each category who "know someone who has entered a long-term relationship via online dating" (2015):

All adults	29
High school or college grad	18
Some college	30
College graduate	46
Less than $30,000	20
More than $75,000	43

Look over these tables carefully, and then say back what you believe are the key ideas about trends in online dating implied by the data. Summarize your analysis in a short paragraph.

STEP 3: Imagine that you're in a conversation with a friend who says, "Digital dating sites are for losers." Drawing on your understanding of the information from the tables, how would you respond? Draft a response to her that incorporates some of the Pew findings.

STEP 4: Finally, make it personal. Let's pose the question rather than the claim: Is online dating for losers? What do you think? Drawing on your fastwrite in Step 1 of the exercise, the data from Pew, your experience and observations, and other relevant information or ideas, write a paragraph that addresses your thoughts about the question.

In this exercise, you've combined exploratory writing with say back and summary to address a question. This is the kind of thinking and writing you'll be doing through-out your research project. But you've also practiced incorporating information from a source in your writing, and you might analyze how that went. For instance, did you have any difficulty smoothly integrating the Pew findings? Did you clearly signal to the reader when you were citing the Pew data? Does the exercise raise any questions for you about how to properly use a source?

Your Voice and Theirs: Using Sources Responsibly

I've been arguing up until now that the way to make the most of the sources you encounter in your research is to use writing to *think through* them. That's quite different from an approach that treats others' voices, data, findings, claims, and evidence as untouchable exhibits, things presented for show to impress the guests. Instead, try to blend your ideas with the ideas of others; you assert your own purposes and analyses on the sources and the sources influence what you think and say.

The tricky part of this blending, however, is to preserve the integrity of what a source says—making sure you don't distort its findings or arguments—and also clearly give credit to a source for information that sparked your thinking. We've already discussed a technique that helps guard against mischaracterizing what a source says: say back or summary and paraphrases that explain, in your own words, what you understand is the argument, point, or analyses sources put forward. Making sure that you flag where the information came from is important, too. As you know, we do this in several ways:

- **Attribution tags:** *According to …, _____ argues that …, _____ reported that …,* and so on.

- **Quotation marks.** We clearly signal when we are borrowing the words of others.

- **Citation.** In academic writing, references to the source are integrated into our texts so readers can see where the information came from.

Of course, one of the reasons you want to signal what's yours and what's not in your writing is to avoid plagiarism, something that many of us do—if we do it at all—unintentionally. So let's be clear about how to borrow information responsibly. Here's a passage from a controversial 2013 *Time* article on Millennials, "The Me Me Me Generation," by Joel Stein.

> Though they're cocky about their place in the world, millennials are also stunted, having prolonged a life stage between teenager and adult that this magazine once called twixters and will now use once again in an attempt to get that term to catch on. The idea of the teenager started

in the 1920s; in 1910, only a tiny percentage of kids went to high school, so most people's social interactions were with adults in their family or in the workplace. Now that cell phones allow kids to socialize at every hour—they send and receive an average of 88 texts a day, according to Pew—they're living under the constant influence of their friends.

Every generation has to bear the burden of where critics place it in the constellation of generations that came before it, and my 20-something students are often hit hard on their narcissism. Stein echoes this claim. As an exercise, it would be great practice for you to say back the basic argument he's making in the passage. But let's look a little more closely at how the passage might be used well—and badly—in a summary.

A Taxonomy of Copying

My colleague Casey Keck, a linguist, studied how students paraphrase sources and ways to describe students' brushes with plagiarism. Casey notes that there are four kinds of borrowing: near copy, minimal revision, moderate revision, and substantial revision. Let's see what each category might look like in summaries of the Stein excerpt on Millennials and narcissism. The bolded passages in each example are words or phrases lifted directly from the excerpt.

- **Near copy:** About half of the borrowed material is copied from the source, usually in a string of phrases.

  *Example: Stein argues that **Millennials are stunted** because instead of having **social interactions** with adults they're **under the constant influence of their friends**.*

- **Minimal revision:** Less than half but more than 20 percent is copied from the original. Notice that the quotation marks appropriately signal at least two borrowed words from the original. But there are still three phrases that are lifted from the source verbatim.

  *Example: Millennials are both "cocky" and "stunted," according to Stein, stuck in a **life stage** that critics **once called twixters**, which is that time **between teenager and adult** when they're mostly influenced by peers, not adults.*

- **Moderate revision:** Less than 20 percent is copied from the original, and mostly individual words are mentioned only once in the source.

  *Example: Stein's argument rests on the idea that Millennials are **stunted** because their **social interactions** are mostly with peers rather than adults.*

- **Substantial revision:** Though the summary might include a few general words that are used a few times in the original text, there are no copies of phrases or unique words that appear in the source unless they are directly quoted.

  Example: The term "teenager" is a relatively recent invention, according to Stein, used to describe a period in young peoples' lives during which relationships with peers were far more common than relationships with adults.

Plagiarism Q & A

1. **So I can't take *any* words from the original source?** Yes, of course you can, but try to steer clear of unique words, and especially avoid using the same string of words unless you put them in quotation marks.

2. **If I add an attribution tag (e.g., "According to _____ ...," or _____ argues that...") or include a citation, does that mean I can copy things from a source?** Attribution tags and citations are really useful for your readers and are a good way to credit authors for their ideas, but they aren't licenses to use source material without the usual signals—like quotation marks—that you've copied something.

3. **Is it a problem if I paraphrase a source and follow pretty much the same structure of the original in terms of the order of ideas?** Technically, that is a form of plagiarism, and practically speaking, it's far better to restate a source in the order that reflects what *you* think are the important ideas.

4. **How do I credit the same information that I found in, say, four different books?** You may not have to. Check out the "common knowledge" exception on page 89.

5. **I've got a lot of my own ideas about my topic. Do I risk plagiarizing if someone else has the same ideas but I don't know about it?** No, you can't know what you don't know. But the point of research is that it helps *expand* your ideas about a topic. If you encounter a source that repeats an idea you already hold, look more closely to see what you didn't already know: a fresh context, a slightly different angle, a new bit of supporting evidence. Then think again. Can you revise your own ideas, discovering new insights that do reflect your own thinking?

Why Plagiarism Matters

It may seem that concern over plagiarism is just a lot of fuss that reflects English teachers' obsession with enforcing rules. In reality, the saddest days I've ever had as a writing teacher have always been when I've talked with a student about a paper she downloaded from the Internet or borrowed from her roommate. Most instructors hate dealing with plagiarism.

Deliberate cheating is, of course, an ethical issue, but the motive for carefully distinguishing between what is yours and what you've borrowed isn't just to "be good." It's really about making a gesture of gratitude. Research is always built on the work that came before it. As you read and write about your topic, I hope that you come to appreciate the thoughtful writing and thinking of people before you who may have given you a new way of seeing or thinking.

Knowledge is a living thing (see Figure 3.1), growing like a great tree in multiple directions, adding (and losing) branches that keep reaching higher

Figure 3.1 As researchers, we're tree climbers, standing on branches that other researchers before us have grown. Citation identifies the wood we're standing on that has helped us to see further into our topic.

toward new understandings. As researchers we are tree climbers, ascending the branches in an effort to see better. It's only natural that as we make this climb, we feel grateful for the strength of the limbs supporting us. Citing and acknowledging sources is a way of expressing this gratitude.

What Is Plagiarism?

Each college or university has a statement in the student handbook that offers a local definition. But that statement probably includes most or all of the following forms of plagiarism:

1. Handing in someone else's work—a downloaded paper from the Internet or one borrowed from a friend—and claiming that it's your own.
2. Handing in the same paper for two different classes.
3. Using information or ideas from any source that are not common knowledge and failing to acknowledge that source.
4. Using the exact language or expressions of a source and not indicating through quotation marks and citation that the language is borrowed.
5. Rewriting a passage from a source, making minor word substitutions, but retaining the syntax and structure of the original.

The Common Knowledge Exception

Although you always have to tell readers what information you have borrowed and where it came from, things that are common knowledge are excluded from this. But what is *common knowledge*? The answer, in part, is considering what is common knowledge to *whom*. Each field makes different judgments about that.

In addition, knowledge is constantly changing, so what may be accepted fact today could be contested tomorrow. What's the undergraduate researcher to do? Scholar Amy England suggests that you consider something common knowledge if you find the exact same information in four or more different sources.

The Notetaker's Triad: Quotation, Paraphrase, and Summary

Because so much research has moved online, including work with digital documents rather than printed ones, student researchers typically do one of two things when they find a relevant source

1. Save it to look at later, usually when they're writing the draft.
2. Cut-and-paste relevant passages, and save them in a separate document.

These two approaches have one thing in common: There's no writing. Since the beginning of this chapter, I've made the argument that encounters with relevant sources can be powerful scenes of writing, beginning with exploratory notes in which you try to explain to yourself what a sources says, and what about it you find interesting or significant. This exploratory writing tells the writer the story of his thinking, which is an essential part of taking control of the project. It is how you find the ideas and questions that you'll build the draft around.

Understanding what a source says—something we've called "say back" in this chapter—is an essential part of this exploratory work. Summary, paraphrase, and quotation are at the heart of this. This triad also produces prose that you can later import into your draft, so by taking the time now to create these kinds of notes, you save time. Let's look at each more closely.

Paraphrasing

In Exercise 3.2, you practiced say back, a technique that helps many married couples who may be headed for divorce. As I mentioned, *paraphrase* is the academic equivalent of this therapeutic method for getting people to listen to each other. Try to say in your own words—and with about the same length as the author said it—what you understand the author to mean. This is hard, at first, because instead of just mindlessly quoting—a favorite alternative for many students—you have to *think*. Paraphrasing demands that you make your own sense of something. The time is well worth it. Why? Because not only are you lowering the risk of unintentional plagiarism and being fair to the source's ideas, *you are also essentially writing a fragment of your draft.*

To put it most simply, at the heart of paraphrasing is this simple idea: *Good writers find their own ways of saying things.*

Summarizing

To sell a movie to Hollywood, a screenwriter should be able to summarize what it's about in a sentence. "*Juno* is a film about a smart, single, pregnant teenager who finds unexpected humor in her situation but finally finds that her wit is not enough to help her navigate the emotional tsunami her pregnancy triggers in the lives of those around her." That statement hardly does justice to the film—which is about so much more than that—but I think it basically captures the story and its central theme.

Presenting Research in Alternative Genres

Three Rhetorical Goals

Though it's enormously tempting to arbitrarily choose an alternative genre to present your research, postpone that decision until you've clarified what you hope to accomplish and *then* choose the best genre for accomplishing those purposes. Let's consider three goals: **to dramatize** the problem you're writing about, **to persuade** certain audiences to do something about it, or **to inform** a particular audience about your topic in a timely way. Here's a way to look at this rhetorically:

Keep in mind that the four alternative genres I'm suggesting—the slide presentation, photo essay, infographic, and poster—all incorporate less text than a research paper. Typically, written text is working in conjunction with other "modes," like images, tables, graphics, and even animation. In other words, some genres are better vehicles for transmitting information, others are more effective at dramatizing, and still others might combine formats in ways that make them persuasive. For example, the table that follows is one way of thinking about how to match your rhetorical goals with the right genre.

Goal	What?	Who?
Dramatize	What question, dilemma, idea, or problem?	Audiences who might be receptive to the story?
Persuade	To do what? What action or behavior?	Audiences whose action on the problem is needed?
Inform	About what? What information will be most relevant and useful?	Audiences who can *use* the information?

Genre	Primary Purpose	Amount of information
Photo essay (See page 000)	Dramatize	Relatively low content
Infographic (See page 000)	Dramatize, inform, persuade	Moderate content
Poster (See page 000)	Inform or persuade	Relatively moderate to high content
Slide presentation (See page 000)	Dramatize, inform, persuade	Moderate content (more with handouts)

Obviously, that's what a *summary* is: a reduction of longer material into a brief statement that captures a basic idea, argument, or theme from the original. Like paraphrasing, summarizing often requires careful thought. This is especially the case when you're trying to capture the essence of a whole movie, article, or chapter that's fairly complex. Many times, however, summarizing involves simply boiling down a passage—not the entire work—to its basic idea.

Although a summary can never be purely objective, it needs to be fair. After all, each of us will understand a text differently, but at the same time we have to do our best to represent what a source is actually saying without prejudice. That's particularly a challenge when you have strong feelings about a topic.

Quoting

I'll never forget the scene from the documentary *Shoah,* an 11-hour film about the Holocaust, that presents an interview with the Polish engineer of one of the trains that took thousands of Jews to their deaths. As an old man still operating the same train, he was asked how he felt about his role in World War II. He said quietly, "If you could lick my heart, it would poison you."

It would be difficult to restate the Polish engineer's comment in your own words. But more important, it would be stupid even to try. Some of the pain and regret and horror of that time in history are embedded in that one man's words. You may not come across such a distinctive quote as you read your sources this week, but be alert to *how* authors (and those quoted by authors) say things. Is the prose unusual, surprising, or memorable? Does the writer make a point in an interesting way? If so, jot it down in your journal or cut and paste it into a digital file, making sure to signal the borrowed material with quotation marks.

There are several other reasons to quote a source as you're taking notes.

- To bring in the voice, not just the ideas, of a notable expert on your topic.
- To quote someone who says something effectively that supports a key point you're trying to make.
- When you're writing an essay that uses primary sources—a literary text, a transcript, and so on—quoted material is essential.

As a general rule, however, the college research paper should contain no more than 10 or 20 percent quoted material. This principle sometimes gets ignored because it's so easy to just copy a passage from a source and paste it into an essay. But keep in mind that a writer who quotes does not really need to think much about and take possession of the information, shaping it and allowing herself to be shaped by it. Still, you can retain a strong presence in your work even when using the words of others if you remember to do the following:

1. **Quote selectively.** You need not use all of the passage. Mine phrases or sentences that are particularly distinctive, and embed them in your own prose.
2. **Provide a context.** The worst way to use a quote is to just drop it into a paragraph without attribution or comment. If you're going to bring someone else's voice into your work, you should, at the very least, say who the source is and perhaps indicate why what this person says is particularly relevant to what you're saying.
3. **Follow up.** In addition to establishing a context for a quotation, seize the chance to analyze, argue with, amplify, explain, or highlight what is in the quotation.

As an example of effective use of quotation, consider the following excerpt from Bill Bryson's book *At Home: A Short History of Private Life*. Bryson is especially talented at telling compelling nonfiction stories using research, and here he explains the fears of people in the nineteenth century about being buried alive. In this case, Bryson incorporates a "block quotation"—that is, the passage he quotes is set off and indented, as is required in MLA style for passages of more than four lines.

> According to one report, of twelve hundred bodies exhumed in New York City for one reason or another between 1860 and 1880, six showed

signs of thrashing or other postinternment distress. In London, when the naturalist Frank Buckland went looking for the coffin of the anatomist John Hunter at St. Martin-in-the-Fields Church, he reported coming upon three coffins that showed clear evidence of internal agitation (or so he was convinced)....A correspondent to the British journal *Notes and Queries* offered this contribution in 1858:

> A rich manufacturer named Oppelt died about fifteen years since at Reichenberg, in Austria, and a vault was built in the cemetery for the reception of the body by his widow and children. The widow died about a month ago and was taken to the same tomb; but, when it was opened for the purpose, the coffin of her husband was found open and empty, and the skeleton discovered in the corner of the vault in a sitting posture.

> For at least a generation such stories became routine in even serious periodicals. So many people became morbidly obsessed with the fear of being interred before their time that a word was coined for it: *taphephobia*.

Notice that Bryson provides a context for his quotation—the name of the source—and then follows up the quoted passage by noting that the story it tells is typical of nineteenth-century fears of being buried alive. He also notes that the anecdote is an illustration of what was then called taphephobia. Bryson's book is not an academic work, so you don't see citations, something that you will incorporate into your own essay, but you can see how a powerful quotation can bring the work to life, especially when it's sandwiched within the commentary of a writer who chooses to allow another voice to speak.

Notetaking Methods

There's the skills part of notetaking—knowing how to cite, summarize, paraphrase, and quote correctly—and then there's the more interesting, harder part—making *use* of what you're reading to discover what you think. So far, we've talked about this latter process using the metaphor of conversation. In Exercise 3.1, you tried out this idea, responding in writing to facts about gender and notions of "attractiveness." This conversation metaphor doesn't originate with me. Lots of people use it to describe how all knowledge is made. One theorist, Kenneth Burke, famously explained that we might imagine that all scholarship on nearly any subject is much like a parlor conversation between people in the know (see the box "The Unending Conversation" on the following page). These are the experts who, over time, have contributed to the discussions about what might be true and who constantly ask questions to keep the conversation going.

As newcomers to this conversation, we don't really have much to contribute. It's important that we listen so that we begin to understand what has already been said and who has said it. But at some point, even novices like us are expected to speak up. We're not there to simply record what we hear. We're writers. We're supposed to discover something to say.

The Unending Conversation

Imagine that you enter a parlor. You come late. When you arrive, others have long preceded you, and they are engaged in a heated discussion, a discussion too heated for them to pause and tell you exactly what it is about. In fact, the discussion had already begun long before any of them got there, so that no one present is qualified to retrace for you all the steps that had gone before. You listen for a while, until you decide that you have caught the tenor of the argument; then you put in your oar. Someone answers; you answer him; another comes to your defense; another aligns himself against you, to either the embarrassment or gratification of your opponent, depending upon the quality of your ally's assistance. However, the discussion is interminable. The hour grows late, you must depart. And you do depart, with the discussion still vigorously in progress.

Kenneth Burke

Fortunately, we rarely enter the parlor empty handed. We have experiences and other prior knowledge that are relevant to the conversation we're listening in on. For example, you certainly know something about the subject of Thomas Lord's essay, "What? I Failed? But I Paid for Those Credits! Problems of Students Evaluating Faculty." After all, you've probably filled out an evaluation or two for a course you've taken. But clearly, Lord, as a science educator, has spent considerably more time than you considering whether these evaluations are useful for judging the quality of teaching. Yet college writers, even if they have limited expertise, are expected to speak up on a topic they're writing about, entering the conversation by raising questions, analyzing arguments, speculating, and emphasizing what they think is important.

Exercise 3.3

DIALOGIC NOTETAKING: LISTENING IN, SPEAKING UP

Drop into the conversation that Thomas Lord has going in his essay, and, drawing on what you've learned so far, use your journal writing to listen in and speak up.

STEP 1:

1. Begin by listening in. Read Thomas Lord's essay once straight through. Underline and mark passages that you think are:
   a. important to your understanding of the article,
   b. puzzling in some way,
   c. surprising, or
   d. connected with your own initial ideas and experiences.

2. Reread the opening paragraph, the last few paragraphs, and all of your marked passages; then, without looking at the article, compose a three- or four-sentence summary of what you understand to be the most important thing the article is saying. Write this down on the left-hand page of your notebook.

3. Find two passages in the article that you think are good examples of what you state in your summary. Copy these on to the left-hand page of your notebook, too. Or if you're doing this on your computer, use the Table function to create two columns, and use the left one.

STEP 2: Now speak up. Use the right-hand side of your notebook to explore your thinking about what Lord is saying. Look on the left-hand pages to remind yourself of some of his ideas and assertions. This is an open-ended fastwrite, but here are some prompts to get you writing and thinking:

- Tell the story of your thinking:
    - *Before I read about this topic, I thought _____, and then I thought _____, and then _____, and then...but now I think _____.*
- Consider ways you've begun to think differently:
    - *I used to think _____, but now I'm starting to think _____.*
- Try both believing and doubting:
    - *The most convincing points Lord makes in his essay are _____. or Though I don't*

necessarily agree with Lord, I can understand why he would think that _____.
- And then: *The thing that Lord ignores or fails to understand is _____. or The least convincing claim he makes is _____ because _____.*
- Consider questions:
    - *The most important question Lord raises is _____.*
    - *The question that he fails to ask is _____.*

Discuss in class how this notetaking exercise worked. What went well? What was difficult? How did your initial thoughts influence your reading of the article? Did your thinking change? Which of these techniques will you continue to use in your notetaking?

What? I Failed? But I Paid for Those Credits! Problems of Students Evaluating Faculty*

by Thomas Lord

Late one afternoon several days ago, I was startled by a loud rap on my office door. When I opened it, I immediately recognized a student from the previous semester clutching the grade slip he had just received in the mail. Sensing his anger and frustration, I invited him in to discuss his scores. I was surprised that he had not anticipated the failing grade because his exam scores were abysmal, his class work was marginal, and his attendance was sporadic. When I scooted my chair over to my computer to open the course's spreadsheet to review his grade, he told me he didn't have an argument with the test, class, and attendance records. His reason for coming to see me was to ask how he could get his refund. He had, after all, paid for the credits, right? I was astonished. In all my years in higher education, this was the first time I had been asked for a refund.

A day later over lunch, a colleague remarked that with the nation's troublesome economy, many universities have turned to the business model of running the institution. "The business model," he acknowledged, "focuses on financial efficiency while maintaining a quality product."

"Perhaps so," another colleague responded, "but the principal foundation of the business model is the notion of satisfying the customer. Because the products of a college are its graduates, it requires the college to meet their expectations for both a quality education and a gratifying experience. This is nearly impossible if the college wants to retain its integrity and high standards."

*"What? I Failed? But I Paid for Those Credits! Problems of Students Evaluating Faculty" by Thomas Lord from *Journal of College Science Teaching*, November/December 2008. Used by permission of the National Science Teachers Association.

Furthermore, what students expect from their college experience varies greatly. A quality, highly respected education is, of course, always desirable, but that's about as common as the expectations get. Some college students relish the liberal challenges universities can provide, some look for a cultural experience, and others simply want to be trained for a career. A large number of undergraduates seek strong intercollegiate athletic or theater programs, and some students are most interested in an exciting social life. This diversity is where the difficulty lies. With such an assortment of demands and expectations, it's simply not possible for any institution to provide it all and maintain a student-as-consumer philosophy. Many universities have tried, and in so doing, have undercut their reputation. Several decades ago, education theorist David Reisman (1981) wrote, "This shift from academic merit to student consumerism is one of the two greatest reversals of direction in all the history of American Higher Education; the other being the replacement of the classical college by the modern university a century ago."

Despite Reisman's statement, the student-as-consumer philosophy has become more widely spread in academic institutions over the last two decades, and with it has come a tendency for students to have a stronger voice in higher education (d'Apollonia and Abrami 1997). It is common nowadays for student representatives to serve on university committees. Students are often consulted on ventures that include curriculum, discipline, regulation, and campus construction. In many schools, segments of the institution's governance are shared with students. My institution, for example, retains two students on the University Executive Board.

But by far the greatest number of student voices impacting the institution is in the evaluation of the instructors. The practice was first implemented at Purdue University in 1927, when surveys were distributed to students in a sociology class to solicit their opinions of the course (Remmers 1927). The surveys were not shared with the administration, but were retained by the professors as feedback for self-improvement. Two years later, Remmers revised the surveys to include "student ratings of their instructor's teaching and what they have learned in the course." The researcher reported his finding at a national professional meeting, and soon other universities began soliciting instructor ratings on their campuses. Course and instructor evaluations remained benign until the 1960s, when students discovered the power their united voices could make in higher education. During this time, students began vocalizing their resistance to the war in Vietnam, the ills of the environment, and the materialism of society. It was a time of student free speech about ethical, cultural, and racial issues. Suddenly, evaluations of instructors and courses became more about student satisfaction than about a professor's instructional effectiveness.

When the driving mechanism for faculty evaluations shifts from educating to pleasing, many problems occur. "Student evaluations of their professors are impacted heavily by student perception," states Professor Stanley Fish, dean emeritus at the University of Illinois (2007). "When student experiences in classes do not match their prior expectations, they react in negative ways. Students may begin to boycott classes they're unhappy with, they may write complaint letters to administrators, or they may challenge the academic integrity of their professors. Some students may become so disrespectful of the professor that they circulate their feelings in the press, on the internet, and over the airways." In 1965, for example, students at the University of California–Berkeley generated a review of teacher performance in a manual entitled *The Slate Supplement,* and sold it at the campus bookstore. "Most of the opinions in the manual were ill-informed and mean-spirited," recalls Fish. "The opinions weren't from professionals in the field but transient students with little or no stake in the enterprise who would be free (because they were anonymous) to indulge any sense of grievance they happened to harbor in the full knowledge that nothing they said would ever be questioned or challenged. The abuse would eventually affect the careers and livelihoods of faculty members especially the young, nontenured professors" (Selvin 1991). In addition, with the negative exposure, university officials became alarmed that the dissatisfaction would lead to students dropping their courses or leaving the university altogether. With the mounting anxieties, many instructors countered by lowering the expectations in their courses. A survey of faculty found 70% of professors believe that their grading leniency and course difficulty bias student ratings, and 83% admitted making their course easier in response to student evaluations (Ryan, Anderson, and Birchler 1980).

This was nicely demonstrated when Peter Sacks, a young journalism instructor, was hired on a tenure track at a small northwest college. At the end of the first semester, Sacks, an accomplished writer but not yet an accomplished teacher, found himself in trouble with student evaluations. When he started, Sacks resolved to maintain a high quality in his courses by emphasizing critical thinking about issues. Although he found it extremely difficult, he stuck with his plan for the entire semester, and as a consequence, received terrible student evaluations. Fearing that he would lose his tenure-track appointment after the spring term, he decided to change his tactics and attempt to achieve higher evaluations by deliberately pandering to his students. At the end of his three-year trial, he had dramatically raised his teaching evaluations and gained tenure. Sacks shamelessly admits he became utterly undemanding and uncritical of his students, giving out easy grades, and teaching to the lowest common denominator (1986). Other researchers have confirmed that lenient grading is the most frequently used faculty strategy to counter abusive student assessment (Howard and Maxwell 1982; Greenwald 1997).

Another problem with the business model is that students truly believe they're paying for their credits and not their education. Consumers are used to paying for merchandise that can later be returned for a refund with no questions asked. The student confusion over this probably resides in the way universities charge pupils for the credits they're taking (at least for students attending part time or over the summer). If, for example, a high school biology teacher decided to upgrade his or her knowledge of wildflowers and enrolled in a three-credit course at a local college on spring flora, the teacher would be charged for the three credits. If the teacher decided to continue the learning the following semester on summer wildflowers, he or she would again pay for the three credits. It's not hard, therefore, to see how the idea of paying for credits rather than earning them came about.

A final reason why student evaluations are an unreliable way to assess faculty is that most students simply don't know what good teaching is. Undergraduates generally have a vision of how college teaching is conducted from depictions in movies or hearing tales from former students. The most common view is that professors stand before a class and recite, write on the chalkboard, or use PowerPoint slides to get across the information students should know in the lesson (McKeachie 1992).

I asked my students what they thought made a great instructor and was told the best professors move unhurriedly through their notes, speaking at a slow-to-moderate pace, explaining the information the students need to learn. One student told me that good professors don't get sidetracked by superficial chunks of information and don't waste time off the subject. Some students also suggested that competent professors are entertaining when they lecture and frequently use demonstrations and videos to back up their presentations. Many class members said the best professors repeat several times the items that are the most salient and hold review sessions before each exam to reaffirm the important content.

Most contemporary theorists, however, tell us that top instructors don't do most of those things. According to education leaders, competent teachers seldom lecture to a gallery of passive students, but provide experiences and directions that actively challenge class members to think and discover information (Handelsman et al. 2004). Practiced professors believe understanding is the driving force for learning and spend a great amount of preclass time orchestrating team-based learning situations for the upcoming class. Proponents of student-centered instruction acknowledge that active participation in classes and discovery-based laboratories help students develop the habits of mind that drive science (Udovic et al. 2002). Furthermore, while traditional instructors create factual recall questions for their exams where students reiterate what they were told in class, contemporary teachers challenge students to discover the answers through application, synthesis, or evaluation (Huitt 2004). Quality teachers understand what agronomist George Washington Carver meant in 1927 when he wrote, "I know nothing more inspiring than discovering new information for oneself" (Carver 1998).

Students also believe that the best professors don't expect class members to know information that the professor hasn't covered in lecture. Students don't seem to realize that education is the art of using information, not the art of restating it. College graduates must understand that once they're out of school, they'll depend on their education to get them through life. Often will they have to address unfamiliar questions. As I've stated previously, "Once they're out of college, students can't fall back on the answer, 'I don't know 'cause it wasn't covered by my professor'" (Lord 2007).

Enough has been written on this matter that colleges and universities should justify why they continue to use student evaluations to assess their faculty. "The answer is already known," answers Cahn (1986). "Institutions of higher education provide faculty evaluations to students to assess student satisfaction. Not only are the evaluations easy to grade and inexpensive to administer, but they give the impression of objectivity in comparison with more subjective measures such as letters from observers since student evaluations produce definite numbers."

"The role of the university is leadership, not a servant of consumer demands as the current business model requires," states Wilson (1998). "Universities certainly have a responsibility for the safety, well-being, and satisfaction of the people they serve, but they also have a responsibility to educate the people as well. With their dignity and reputation on the line, the most important responsibility is to certify that their graduates are truly educated. Under the consumer model, the goals of satisfaction and education are sometimes in conflict. It is important, therefore, that the metaphor of students as consumers be replaced by the metaphor of students as apprentices" (Haskell 1997).

References

Cahn, S. 1986. *Saints and scamps: Ethics in academia.* Totowa, NJ: Rowman and Littlefield.

Carver, G.W. 1998. *The all-university celebration.* Iowa City, IA: University Press.

d'Apollonia S., and P. Abrami. 1997. Navigating student ratings of instruction. *American Psychologist* 52 (11): 1198–1208.

Fish, S. 2007. Advocacy and teaching. *Academe* 93 (4): 23–27.

Greenwald, A.G. 1997. Validity concerns and usefulness of student ratings. *American Psychologist* 52 (11): 1182–86.

Handelsman, J., D. Ebert-May, R. Beichner, P. Burns, A. Chang, R. DeHann, J. Gentile, S. Luffefer, J. Stewart, S. Tukgnab, and W. Wood. 2004. Scientific thinking. *Science* 304 (5670): 521–22.

Haskell, R. 1997. Academic freedom, tenure and student evaluation of faculty: Galloping polls in the 21st century. *Education Policy Analysis Archives* 5 (6): 43.

Howard, G., and S. Maxwell. 1982. Linking raters' judgments. *Evaluation Review* 6 (1): 140–46.

Huitt, W. 2004. Bloom et al's taxonomy of the cognitive domain. *Educational Psychology Interactive*. http://chiron.valdosta.edu/whuitt/col/cogsys/bloom.html. Valdosta, GA: Valdosta University Press.

Lord, T. 2007. Putting inquiry to the test: Enhancing learning in college botany. *Journal of College Science Teaching* 36 (7): 56–59.

McKeachie, W. 1992. Student ratings: The validity of use. *American Psychologist* 52 (11): 1218–25

Reisman, D. 1981. *On higher education: The academic enterprise in an era of rising student consumerism.* San Francisco: Jossey Bass.

Remmers, D. *1927.* Experimental data on the Purdue rating scale. In *Student ratings of instructors: Issues for improving practice,* eds. M. Theall and J. Franklin. 1990. San Francisco: Jossey Bass.

Ryan, J., J. Anderson, and A. Birchler. 1980. Student evaluation: The faculty responds. *Research in Higher Education* 12 (4): 395–401.

Sacks, P. 1986. *Generation X goes to college.* LaSalle, IL: Open Court Press.

Selvin, P. 1991. The raging bull at Berkeley. *Science* 251 (4992): 368–71.

Wilson, R. 1998. New research casts doubt on value of student evaluations of professors. *Chronicle of Higher Education* 44 (19): A2–A14.

Udovic, D., D. Morris, A. Dickman, J. Postlethwait, and P. Wetherwax. 2002. Workshop biology: Demonstrating the effectiveness of active learning in an introductory biology course. *Bioscience* 52 (3): 272–81.

Thomas Lord (trlord@grove.iup.edu) *is a professor in the Department of Biology at the Indiana University of Pennsylvania in Indiana, Pennsylvania.*

Notetaking Techniques

In the first edition of *The Curious Researcher,* I confessed to a dislike of notecards. Apparently, I'm not the only one who feels that way. Mention notecards, and students often tell horror stories. It's a little like talking about who has the most horrendous scar, a discussion that can prompt participants to expose knees and bare abdomens in public places.

Although it's true that some writers find notecards useful, I'm convinced that notecards are too small for a good conversation. On the contrary, they seem to encourage "data dumps" rather than dialogue (see Figure 3.2).

But what's the alternative? You've already practiced one approach in the previous exercise, "Listening in, Speaking up." There you used opposing sides of a notebook or Word document to summarize your understanding of an essay and collect relevant passages, and then you told the story of your thinking about the reading. This is *knowledge making* rather than dump truck driving; you are going beyond simply recording and collecting information to actually *doing* something with it. You'll also practice a technique called the "double-entry" journal.

The Double-Entry Journal

The double-entry approach (see Figure 3.3) is basically this: Use opposing pages of your research notebook or opposing columns in a Word document—two columns and one row for each source. At the top of the page for each source,

Figure 3.2
Notecards versus
Notebooks

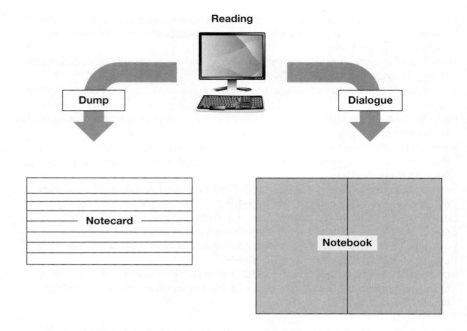

write down the bibliographic information for that source. Then, using the left side or column, compile your notes from a source—paraphrases, summaries, quotes. Put appropriate page numbers in the margin next to borrowed material or ideas. Then on the right side, comment on what you collected from each source. Imagine that the line down the middle of the page—or the spiral binder that divides opposing pages—is a table at which you sit across from an author with something to say about a topic you're interested in. Take care to listen to what the author says through paraphrase, summary, and quotation on the left, and then on the right respond with a fastwrite in which you give your own commentary, questions, interpretations, clarifications, or even feelings about what you heard. Your commentary can be pretty open ended, responding to questions such as the following:

- What strikes you? What is confusing? What is surprising?
- If you assume that this is true, why is it significant?
- If you doubt the truth or accuracy of the claim or fact, what is the author failing to consider?
- How does the information stand up to your own experiences and observations?
- How does it address your research question? Does it support or contradict your thesis (if you have one at this point)?
- How might you use the information in your paper? What purpose might it serve?

Figure 3.3
Double-Entry
Journal Method

Notes from Source **(left page or column)**	**Fastwrite Response** **(right page or column)**

• Direct quotations, paraphrases, and summaries of material from the source:
  • of ideas that are important to project
  • of ideas that are surprising or puzzling or generate some emotional response
• Be careful to:
  • include bibliographic information at the top;
  • include the page number from the source.
	• Focused fastwrite in response to material at left
	• Tips for fastwrite:
	  • Write as long as possible; then look left and find something else to respond to.
	  • Try shifting between stances of believing and doubting.
	  • Use the questions listed on pp. 98-99.

- What do you think of the source?
- What further questions does the information raise that might be worth investigating?
- How does the information connect to other sources you've read?

Refer to this list of questions (and any others that occur to you) as a prompt for the writing on the right side of your journal (or right column of your Word document). There are a variety of ways to approach the double-entry journal. If you're taking notes on the printout of an article or a photocopy from a book, try reading the material first and underlining passages that seem important. Then, when you're done, transfer some of that underlined material—quotes, summaries, or paraphrases—into the left column of your journal. Otherwise, take notes in the left column *as* you read.

While you take notes, or after you've finished, do some exploratory writing in the right column. This territory belongs to you. Here, through language, your mind and heart assert themselves over the source material. Use your notes in the left column as a trigger for writing in the right. Whenever your writing stalls, look to the left. The process is a little like watching tennis—look left, then right, then left, then right. Direct your attention to what the source says and then to what *you* have to say about the source. Keep up a dialogue.

Figures 3.4 and 3.5 illustrate how the double-entry journal works in practice. Note these features:

- Bibliographic information is recorded at the top of the page. Do that first, and make sure it's complete.
- Page numbers are included in the far-left margin, right next to the information that was taken from that page. Make sure you keep up with this as you write.

Figure 3.4
Amanda's Double-
Entry Journal

Here, Amanda
concentrates on
thinking through
the implications
of the summaries
and quotations
she collected from
an article on teeth
whitening.

Prior, Molly. "Bright On: Americans' Insatiable Appetite for Whiter-Than-White Teeth Is Giving Retailers Something to Smile About." Beauty Biz, vol. 1, Sept. 2005, pp. 36–43.

Teeth are no longer just for eating with—their appearance is becoming more important as a factor in a person's image, and they need to be perfectly white. (36)

Cosmetics companies are now entering territory once reserved for dentists as more and more people care mostly about the aesthetics of their teeth and smile. (36)

"Sephora is so enthusiastic about the [tooth-whitening] category, it named 'smile' its fifth retail pillar, joining the four others (makeup, fragrance, skin care and hair care) earlier this year." (37)

"The trend has shed its clinical beginnings and assumed a new identity, smile care. Its new name has been quickly adopted by a growing troupe of retailers, who hope to lure consumers with a simple promise: A brighter smile will make you look younger and feel more confident." (37)

Instead of going to the dentist and taking care of their teeth so they function well, people are investing a cosmetic interest in their teeth. People selling tooth-whitening products hope people associate whiter, more perfect teeth with higher self-esteem and social acceptance. (40)

"What says health, youth and vitality like a great smile?" (40)

I have noticed the increasing amount of importance that people put on the whiteness of their teeth, but this also seems to have increased with the amount of advertising for whitening products on TV and in magazines. I wonder if the whole thing is profit driven: Hygiene companies wanted to make more money, so instead of just selling toothbrushes and toothpaste, they created a whitening product and then worked to produce a demand for it. I almost feel really manipulated, like everyone's teeth were fine the way they naturally existed, and then all of the sudden a big company decided it needed to create a new product and sell it by making us feel bad about our smiles, and thus bad about ourselves.

The whole thing is sad, because once something becomes the societal "norm," we start to become obligated to do it. If everyone's teeth are beige, it's no problem when yours are too. But when everyone has sparkling white teeth, then it looks funny if you let yours stay brown. It either says "I don't have the money to whiten my teeth," or "I don't care about my appearance."

Sometimes it feels people might also judge you as being dirty, because white teeth seem healthier and cleaner than brown teeth, or lazy, for not spending the time to whiten your teeth. All those things are negative, and create a negative cloud around our teeth where we once felt good, or at least ambivalent. I don't like the way I'm being told my smile isn't good enough the way it is. I feel like when I smile it should just be about showing happiness and conveying that to others, not a judgment about me as a person.

Greenbaum, Jessica B. "Training Dogs and Training Humans: Symbolic Interaction and Dog Training." *Anthrozoos*, vol. 23, no. 2, pp. 129–141.

"The 'traditional' dominance-based method of training endorses obedience by using a human-centric approach that places dogs in a subordinate position in order to maintain a space in the family. The 'reward-based' behavior modification method promotes a dog-centric approach that highlights companionship over dominance...." (129)	Article seems to capture the essence of the debate: Is a well-behaved dog a product of dominance or companionship? Why can't it be both? One of the things that always strikes me about these binaries—either/or—is that it ignores both/and. Dogs will always have some kind of unequal relationship with their owners. Right? They have to. And won't they try to sort out, in their own way, the question of who is in charge?
"The methods we use to train our dogs reflect our perceptions of relationships between human and non-human animals. The socially constructed status of dogs, as pet or companion, influences the philosophy, methods, and training skills used." (129)	This seems key: "the socially constructed status of dogs" has an enormous influence on how we construe our relationship with them. Greenbaum draws the distinction as between "pet" and "companion." Behind those general terms is a whole set of ways in which we "socially construct" pets. A pet can be a companion, right? It doesn't necessarily imply subservience? I keep returning to the binaries that theorists draw. This is exactly the same thing that I notice with dog trainers themselves. There is a "right" and "wrong" way, and this divide is typically described as it is here: between positive reinforcement and negative reinforcement.
Mead discounted idea that animals can engage in symbolic communication with humans: "the ability to think was the ability to say." But article, using Sanders, argues that in a sense, pet owners "speak for" their animals. Sanders's research on police dogs, however, also highlighted the "ambiguity" of dog ownership—they are both companions and "tools." Subjective beings and objective things. (130)	This idea that we "speak for animals" strikes home, and I imagine that people like me who constantly give dogs and cats a human voice are more likely to favor "human-centric" methods. How can you put a shock collar on a dog that can talk back? But I never thought about this "ambiguity" between dogs as "tools" and "companions." Though wouldn't this be mostly true of people who train dogs for particular purposes? Is this ambiguity typical of most pet owners who don't?
Fennel argues that while the principle of modeling training on pack behavior makes sense, the method is often misapplied—correction is too harsh or effort to domesticate too extreme. She thinks this is cause of most behavior problems. "Dog guardians have failed as pack leaders." (131)	Must read Fennel's study. Seems like her argument is much like the one I'm thinking about: It may be that dogs do behave in some ways like wild pack animals, but their trainers aren't exactly alpha dogs, either.

Figure 3.5
Double-Entry Journal

Here's a double-entry journal entry that uses Word's Table feature to respond to an article I was reading on theories of dog training. I could copy and paste quotes from the original article, a PDF file, and drop them into the left column. Also notice, however, that I rely on summaries as well. Page numbers in parentheses follow borrowed material.

- Whereas the material from the source in the left column may be quite formal or technical, the response in the right column should be informal and conversational. Try to write in your own voice. Find your own way to say things. And don't hesitate to use the first person: *I*.

- The writers often use their own writing to try to question a source's claim or understand better what that claim might be (e.g., "What the authors seem to be missing here..." and "I don't get this quote at all...").

- Seize a phrase from your source, and play out its implications; think about how it pushes your own thinking or relates to your thesis.

- In Figures 3.4 and 3.5, the writers frequently pause to ask themselves questions—not only about what the authors of the original sources might be saying but also what the writers are saying to themselves as they write. Use questions to keep you writing and thinking.

What I like about the double-entry journal system is that it turns me into a really active reader as I'm taking notes for my essay. That blank column on the right, like the whirring of my computer right now, impatiently urges me to figure out what I think through writing. All along, I've said the key to writing a strong research paper is *making the information your own*. Developing your own thinking about the information you collect, as you go along, is one way to do that. Thoughtful notes are so easy to neglect in your mad rush to simply take down a lot of information. The double-entry journal won't let you neglect your own thinking; at least it will remind you when you do.

The Research Log

The research log is an alternative to the double-entry journal that promotes a similar "conversation" between writer and source but with a few differences. One is that, like a *Tonight Show* host, the researcher starts with a monologue and always gets the last word. The standard format of the research log can serve as a template, that can be retrieved whenever you're ready to take notes on another source. Those notes can then be easily dropped into a draft as needed, using the cut and paste features of your word-processing program.

The basic approach is this:

1. Take down the full bibliographic information on the source—article, book chapter, Web page, or whatever (see Figure 3.6). Then read the source, marking up your personal copy in the usual fashion by underlining, making marginal notes, and so on.

2. Your first entry will be a fastwrite that is an *open-ended response* to the reading under the heading "First Thoughts." For example, you might begin by playing the "believing game," exploring how the author's ideas, arguments, or findings are sensible, and then shift to the "doubting game," looking for gaps, questions, and doubts you have about what the source says.

Project: Belief in Alien Abduction

Source: Kelley-Romano. "Mythmaking in Alien Abduction Narratives." *Communication Quarterly,* vol. 54, no. 3, August 2006, pp. 383–406.

Date: 11 November 2013

First Thoughts:

This article argues that alien abduction stories are essentially myths, and by this she doesn't mean necessarily "untrue," but that they are stories that a growing number of people tell themselves for the same reasons we've always told myths: They are instructive. Through interviews with 130 people who claim to have been abducted, Kelley-Romano identifies four of the most common narratives. These include the "salvation" narrative (aliens are coming to save us from ourselves), the "hybridization" narrative (they need us to reproduce with them and save their own kind). . . . What I find so interesting about this is that instead of dismissing alien abduction stories as tales told by crazy people, the author argues that they are actually mythical stories that can tell us a lot about not only the people who believe them but also the state of our culture. . . .

Notes:

"An examination of this fascinating and significant phenomenon has the potential to inform our understanding of symbolic practices—exploring what it means to believe, and how we come to know. Most importantly, unlike religions and other codified systems of belief, the alien abduction myth—the Myth of Communion—is still developing. Beginning with the supposed crash of a UFO at Roswell in 1947 and fueled by the abduction of Betty and Barney Hill in 1961, believers in the abduction phenomenon have produced a set of narratives that continues to increase in complexity in both form and function." (384)

Unlike religious myth, the "alien abduction myth" is fluid—the narrative "continues to increase in complexity." (384)

The five elements of myth: heroes, "narrative form," "archetypal language," and focus on a particular place and time. (386)

There is a difference between myths and other kinds of stories like folk tales and fairy tales because myths are "accepted as true" by their believers. (387)

. . .

Second Thoughts:

As I think about my research question, this idea of the "myth of communion"—the alien abduction narrative that suggests that aliens are trying to integrate humanity into the "cosmos"—seems the most powerful explanation of why these stories seem to cultivate believers like religions do. As the author points out, believers who embrace this "myth of communion" see something "sacred" about the whole thing. Narrators who embrace the "myth of communion" view other alien abduction stories as relatively unenlightened, even "transcendent." The author really emphasizes how the need for such myths comes during certain times, and in the case of the "communion myth," this seems to be a time when people feel they need to be "rescued" . . . .

Figure 3.6
Research Log

You could write a response to any or all of the questions suggested for the double-entry journal.

3. Next, mine the source for nuggets. Take notes under the heading "Notes." These are quotations, summaries, paraphrases, or key facts you collect from the reading. They are probably some of the things you marked as you read the source initially. Make sure you include page numbers that indicate in the source where the material in your notes came from.

4. Finally, follow up with one more fastwrite under the heading "Second Thoughts." This is a second, *more focused* look at the source in which you fastwrite about what stands out in the notes you took. Which facts, findings, claims, or arguments that you jotted down shape your thinking now? If the writing stalls, skip a line, take another look at your notes, and seize on something else to write about.

Narrative Notetaking

This is the simplest method of all. As you read, mark up or annotate your source in the ways you usually do. After you read through it carefully, you will fastwrite a rapid summary for at least 1 full minute, beginning with the following prompt (see Figure 3.7):

> What I understand this to be saying is....

Skip a line, and begin a second episode of fastwriting. Tell the story of your thinking, a narrative of thought that begins with what you initially might have believed about the topic covered in your source, and then how that thinking was influenced by what you read. This time, scribble (or type) for as long as you can without stopping, beginning with this prompt:

> When I first began reading this, I thought _____, and now I think _____.

Whenever your writing stalls, repeat the prompt again, inserting another discovery from your reading.

Online Research Notebooks

These days, academic researchers frequently work with digital documents, especially PDF files. Although it's always a good idea to print out hard copies of anything you use, it's also convenient to annotate and mark up electronic copies. In addition to highlighting passages, it's also possible with some software to insert comments. These can be much like responses in the double-entry journal.

The problem is that most of the software that can annotate PDF files isn't free. For example, although anyone can download Adobe Reader to read PDF documents, you might need to buy Adobe Acrobat to annotate them. There is, however, some free software that can help you organize your digital research files and attach documents to them. That way, you can attach your notes for each

Figure 3.7
Amanda's
Narrative Notes

Focusing Question: How has cosmetic dentistry changed the way we think of the smile, and what are the repercussions?

Source: Walker, Rob. "Consumed; Unstained Masses." New York Times, 2 May 2004. www.nytimes.com/2004/05/02/magazine/the-way-we-live-now-5-2-04-consumed-unstained-masses.html

Rapid Summary (1 minute):
What I understand this article to be saying is that the American public is getting more and more vain, as evidenced by the fact that tooth whitening is growing in popularity. While only celebrities used to modify the appearance of their teeth, now average people are doing it. Because of the value of appearance in our society, once we realize we can modify the way we look to our advantage, we seem to flock to it quickly. That's what's happening with the whole trend of smile care—we're using whiteners to change the way our teeth look so maybe we will be judged more profitably. And when a large percentage of society decides to buy something, there will always be corporations and retailers standing alongside to reap a profit.

Narrative of Thought (6 minutes):
Before I started reading this article I thought that it was the capitalistic profit motive that had introduced whitening products and created a consumer demand for them. Now I understand that all of us as consumers have an equal responsibility with the companies that make and market such products, because we're the ones that buy them and change our standards of beauty. That makes me think that this is a complicated issue. While it's frustrating to feel like I can never be attractive enough, because the standard of attractiveness to which I'm held keeps getting harder and harder to meet, I'm the one that is interested in meeting it in the first place. While it would be easy to denigrate that as vanity, however, I can also see that being judged by others as attractive does have actual benefits, be it a higher salary or better treatment from strangers. In that case I'm put in a tough spot— I can work against the culture that tells me I don't look the right way, and feel negatively judged, or I can conform to it, and feel disappointed that I folded to social pressure. This isn't just an issue about people whitening their teeth for fun, it's about how society changes its standards and how quickly we assimilate to them—and why.

source to the digital original. The downside, of course, is that these notes aren't keyed to particular passages in the source, but the software is still useful for researchers. Here's a list of a few you might try:

1. **Zotero** (http://zotero.org). This is a favorite software for research because it not only organizes digital documents in project folders but also organizes citation information for each source. Zotero is an add-in that works on the Firefox browser, though there is also a "stand-alone" version.

2. **Evernote** (http://evernote.com). You can organize your research sources and associated notes and then upload them so they're accessible everywhere you have an Internet connection. The program also runs on all kinds of devices—iPads, iPhones, PCs, Androids, and so on. In addition, Evernote has a function that allows you to search your notes by tags or titles.

3. **Google Docs** (http://google.com). Google Docs is the standard for many users who want to organize (and share) documents, and it's even more useful now that it allows documents like PDFs and Word files to remain in their native formats. As with Evernote, you can access your Google Docs wherever you have an Internet connection.

When You're Coming up Short: More Advanced Searching Techniques

During week three of a research project, students often hit a wall. This is the week when students announce, "I can't find anything on my topic! I need to find another one." Their frustration is real, and it often has to do with that moment in a creative process when motivation sinks as the difficulties arise. For student researchers, these difficulties include a lot of things, like trying to remember citation details, worrying about plagiarism, wondering if there's enough time to wait for those interlibrary loan books to come in, and confronting problems with the project's focus or research question. But the problem is rarely that there is not enough information on the topic.

I take that back. Sometimes it *is* a problem, but it's usually one of the easiest to solve: You just need to exploit the many techniques that help researchers to dig more deeply. Here's where advanced searching techniques pay off (see Figure 3.8). We'll look briefly at each of these.

Advanced Library Searching Techniques

These advanced library searching techniques are listed in the order you might try them.

1. **Vary search terms.** Try using some search terms suggested by your research so far. You might, for instance, try searching using the names of people who have published on your topic.
2. **Search other databases.** Okay, so you've tried a general subject database like Academic OneFile and even a specialized database like PsycINFO. But

---

Figure 3.8
More Advanced
Searching
Techniques

Library	Internet	Alternative Sources
• Vary search terms	• Vary search terms	• Search blogs
• Search other databases	• Use advanced search features	• Search images
• Check bibliographies	• Use multiple search engines	• Listen to archived radio and podcasts
• Use interlibrary loan	• Watch videocasts	• Search iTunes U
• Troll government documents		• Visit local organizations or libraries
• Ask a librarian		

have you tried another general database such as Academic Search Premier or another specialized database like InfoTrac Psychology? Broaden your coverage.

3. **Check bibliographies.** Academic books and articles always include a list of references at the end. These can be gold mines. Look at all the sources that you've collected so far and scan the titles in the bibliographies that seem promising. Find these by searching the library databases.

4. **Consider using interlibrary loan services.** Your campus library will get you that article or book it doesn't have by borrowing the materials from another library. This is an incredibly useful service, often available on-line. These days, delivery of requested materials can take as little as a few days!

5. **Troll government documents.** The U.S. government is the largest publisher in the world. If your research question is related to some issue of public policy, then there's a decent chance you'll find some government documents on the subject. Try the USA.gov site, a useful index to the gazillions of government publications and reports.

6. **Ask a reference librarian for help.** If you do, you won't be sorry.

Additional Advanced Internet Searching Techniques

It's more likely that you've tapped out relevant sources on the Internet before you've tapped out those in the library—most of us like to begin with the Internet. But make sure that you've tried some of the following search strategies on the Web.

1. **Vary search terms.** By now, you've gathered enough information on your topic to have some new ideas about terms or phrases that might yield good results. Say you're researching the origins of American blues music, and you discover that among its many traditions is something called the Piedmont style. Try searching using that phrase in quotation marks. Also consider doing Web searches on the names of experts who have contributed significantly to the conversation on your topic.

2. **Use advanced search features.** Few of us use the advanced search page on Google and other search engines. By habit, we just type in a few terms in the simple search window. But advanced searching will allow you to exploit methods that will give you better results—things like phrase searching in conjunction with Boolean operators like AND and OR.

3. **Use multiple search engines.** Don't call for retreat until you've gone beyond Google. Try Yahoo!, Ask.com, and similar search engines. Also try specialized search engines that are relevant to your subject (see Chapter 2).

Thinking Outside the Box: Alternative Sources

Sometimes you need to be creative. Try searching for sources on your research question in places you hadn't thought to look.

1. **Search blogs.** It's easy to dismiss blogs as merely self-indulgent musings of people with nothing better to do, but some blogs are written by people who really know what they're talking about. Bloggers can be vigilant observers of new developments, breaking news stories, and cutting-edge opinion. There are a number of specialized search engines to scour the blogosphere.

2. **Search images.** Another source of material you may not have thought of is images available on the Internet. A photograph of a collapsed school building following the 2008 earthquake in central China will do much to dramatize your essay on the vulnerability of buildings to such a disaster. Or a historical essay on lynching in the South might be more powerful with a picture of a murder from the Library of Congress archives (especially see http://memory.loc.gov/). Your campus library may also have a collection of digital images relevant to your project. Remember that if you use them in your essay, images need to be cited like any other source.

3. **Archived radio or podcasts.** Suppose your research question focuses on Martin Luther King Jr. Why not listen to an interview of Taylor Branch, the man who wrote a three-volume biography of the civil rights leader? You can find it on NPR.org. National Public Radio is a particularly good source for material for academic projects. There are also a variety of search engines that will help you find podcasts on nearly any subject.

4. **Check out YouTube.** It isn't just about laughing babies anymore. YouTube is a rich archive of video that can provide material on many topics. For the project on Martin Luther King Jr., for example, you might watch a video of his last speech

5. **Search iTunes U.** Across the United States, colleges and universities are going online through Apple's iTunes U, putting up video and audio speeches, lectures, and other academic content. You can find iTunes U on iTunes, of course, and you can do a keyword search on multiple sites using "power search." The term *global warming* produced 90 hits, including lectures, opinions, and reports from some of America's top universities.

6. **Local organizations.** The reference librarians on our campus routinely refer students to the state historical society or state law library when relevant to their projects. Local organizations can be rich sources of not only published information but also interviews and artifacts.

Exercise 3.4

BUILDING AN ANNOTATED BIBLIOGRAPHY

Reading to write starts with a very practical motive: *Can I use this source to develop my ideas and argument or to explore my topic?* With this in mind, the most skillful readers intuitively know that there are three kinds of readings they need to do (see Figure 3.9): First, they need to understand what the source is saying (yes, even if they disagree with it); second, they need to try to place what they've read in the context of what they already know about the topic; and finally, they need to imagine how some of the reading might be *used* in their own writing. This is the kind of reading that will help you develop a certain kind of *annotated bibliography*—in this case, a preliminary list of relevant sources, each of which has a brief summary and evaluation attached to it.

Imagine, for instance, that you were researching these questions: What is the relationship between gender and reactions to facial expressions? Do men and women react differently to facial expressions of emotion? The literature—and conventional wisdom— seem to confirm the view that women are more intuitive than men, and that they have a higher "emotional intelligence." Might a partial explanation for this be that women are better at recognizing facial expressions, including subtle ones that communicate feeling? You find an article in an academic database in which the researchers show 133 students in an undergrad course a series of pictures that includes a variety of facial expressions related to anger, contempt, disgust, fear, happiness, sadness, and surprise. Are both men and women equally competent in recognizing the emotions behind these facial expressions, including the subtler emotions? Here are some of what you discover in the article:

1. **Understand.** It's clear that, up to a point, women are better than men at recognizing the feeling behind a facial expression, particularly subtler feelings. But the study also qualifies this finding by suggesting that when it comes to "highly expressive" expressions, there is no difference between women and men.

2. **Contextualize.** Since you had been doing research on this topic, you recognize that this study looks at only a small aspect of what psychologists call "emotional competence." It doesn't

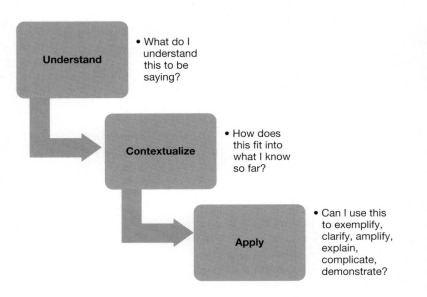

• What do I understand this to be saying?

Understand

• How does this fit into what I know so far?

Contextualize

• Can I use this to exemplify, clarify, amplify, explain, complicate, demonstrate?

Apply

Figure 3.9

Reading Strategy for Building an Annotated Bibliography

fully explain whether women have an advantage over men in this ability. It does seem to confirm, however, your own experience that men can be emotional blockheads until things get really out of hand emotionally.

3. **Apply.** There's a great graph that contrasts how both men and women respond to facial expressions of varying intensity, from mellow to horrified. Why not use it to emphasize the idea that women seem to be better than men at recognizing subtler emotions?

These three readings give you a good start on building a short paragraph annotation of the article that includes all three elements: your summary of what the source says, your comments about how the article fits into a larger understanding of your topic, and a guess about how you might use the article in your essay. For example:

Sample Evaluative Annotation

1. Hoffman, Holger, et al. "Expression Intensity, Gender, and Facial Emotion Recognition: Women Recognize Only Subtle Facial Emotions Better than Men." *Acta Psychologica*, vol. 135, 2010, pp. 278–83.

This article investigates whether there is a "female advantage" over men when it comes to the ability to recognize facial expressions that imply emotion. This question is a part of larger investigations about "emotional competence" and whether it's related to gender. Conventional wisdom and the popular press suggest women are better at feelings than at reason. My research poses the question of whether, if true, this emotional "advantage" might be related to women's sensitivity to emotional facial expressions. This article, which reports on two studies of college students, seems to confirm it: Women who were quickly shown images of actors with a range of six different emotions, from subtle to "full-blown," were much better than men at detecting the less intense expressions. At higher intensities there was no difference between men and women. A graph in the article might be particularly dramatic evidence of this in my essay.

End the week by writing annotations like this for a handful of the best sources you've found so far. Cite the sources as best you can (refer to Chapter 5 and the Appendices for help with this), but focus especially on your annotations.

Chapter 4
The Fourth Week

In this chapter, you'll learn to . . .

- Understand the differences between exploratory and argumentative research essays and how each uses a different logic and structure.

- Refine and revise your inquiry question so that it leads to a judgment rather than simply a report.

- Consider types of "leads" for your draft, and apply some of these to determine which best frame your purpose.

- Learn methods of writing for reader interest, and apply these to the draft.

- Identify some of the moves writers make in researched writing to put information to work, and apply them in your own draft.

- Identify the typical problems—and some solutions—with using quoted material.

Getting to the Draft

How do you know when you're ready to start writing the draft? Actually, you already have. If you've been writing the past few weeks about what you've encountered in your research, what you understand it is saying and how it influences your thinking about your research question, then you *are* drafting. Even if you aren't putting the pieces together yet, you're figuring out what you might want to say.

But there's a deadline. And as it approaches you have new problems to solve:

1. Has the story of your thinking reached any climax? In other words, as you reflect on what you understood at the beginning of the project and

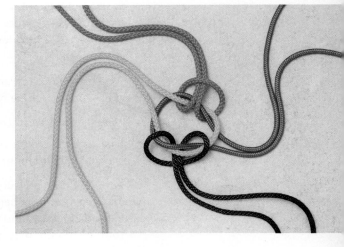

what you understand now about your research question, what is the key thing you've discovered?

2. A few weeks ago, before you knew much about your topic, you had a preliminary research question. What is it now? What does that imply about additional research you might need to do?

3. What shape might this essay take? An argument? An exploratory essay? What does that imply about how the draft should be structured?

Like strands of rope in a tight knot, each of these questions wrap around the others. Your research question is related to what you highlight as your key discovery, and each in turn has implications about how you structure the draft. As you work through this chapter, we'll follow each of these strands, beginning with trying to clarify what kind of essay you might want to write, and focusing your thoughts on what you might want to say in a draft. We'll also spend a time refining your research question and examining what that implies about the structure of your essay.

Exploration or Argument?

After a few weeks of research, have your motives changed? Is your goal to *find out* or is it *to prove*? How you answer this question will determine your approach to the draft.

1. *Argument.* Your discoveries in the past few weeks may have convinced you that a certain answer to your research question is particularly persuasive. Now you want to prove it. Another way to think about this is to ask yourself whether you want your readers to *think* or possibly even *do* something about your research topic.

2. *Exploratory essay.* On the other hand, maybe you're still not ready to make a judgment about the best answer to your research question and you want to use your essay to continue exploring it. You are less concerned with trying to get readers to think or do something than you are with helping them to appreciate what you find interesting or complicated about your topic.

Sometimes your research question will lead you toward one kind of essay or the other. Compare these two questions:

- *What should be done about the problem of smoking on campus?* (Argument)
- *How do smoking bans on college campuses influence social relationships between smokers?* (Exploration)

Although both questions involve open-ended inquiry into the topic of campus smoking, one more naturally leads ultimately to a claim that is supported by reasons and evidence, and the other to an exploration of possible effects.

Your instructor may also give you guidance about whether your draft should be exploratory or argumentative.

What Do I Know?

To investigate a topic that we're curious about is to create a story that we narrate, first to ourselves and then to others. It begins with a question—for example, how *have* online dating sites influenced dating behaviors?—and like any story, there are complications that get in the way of easy answers. But if things go well, there are breakthroughs, and these can be dramatic in their own way. For instance, suddenly you see that you're not asking the right question. It's not just any dating behavior that interests you, but whether digital dating empowers women. The new question opens unexpected doors—you interview your girlfriends about their online dating experience, and you discover a body of behavioral research on dating and gender you never knew existed. Then there are those moments when you make an unexpected connection between two ideas, or maybe have a wonderful moment of clarity (picture the sun bursting through cloud cover) when you discover what you think: Digital dating might empower some women, but it's much more complicated than that!

Telling that story—even if it's still in the making—will help you to narrate your draft. All writing is narrated. Writers, even if they're behind the scenes, are guiding readers through information, directing a reader's gaze, foregrounding certain ideas rather than others, managing the order of things and a reader's experience of them. However, to be that kind of narrator in your research essay, you have to know what you think is important. Let's spend some time trying to sort that out.

Exercise 4.1

DIALOGUE WITH DAVE

STEP 1: Dave is the reader you imagine when you picture the reader of your essay. He's a pretty nice guy and smart, too. But first off, like any reader, he wants to know why he should care about the subject you're writing about. Then, once you've got Dave's interest, he has questions about what you're telling him about your topic. Like any conversation, what he asks about depends on the details of what you tell him. This conversation can't be scripted. Just let it develop as you write.

When you imagine Dave's persona in this exercise, consider some of the stuff Dave might want to know, like

- Why? Where? Who? When? What?
- What do you mean by ____?
- How do most people see this? How do you see it differently?

- Are you kidding? I didn't know that. What else did you find out?
- Can you give me an example?
- Did that surprise you?
- What other questions does this raise?
- Who does this affect, mostly?
- What should we do about this?
- I'm not sure I believe this. Why do you?
- What do you think we should do about it?

Use the Table feature to format a document on your computer, creating two columns—one for Dave's questions and the other for your answers. Start the conversation with Dave's first question—"What's the big deal about this, anyway?"—and take it from there.

If this is going to be useful, try to keep this conversation going for at least a half hour.

STEP 2: Many conversations like this one move toward some kind of conclusion. Reread what you wrote, and finish the exercise by crafting an answer to Dave's final question: *Okay, this is all interesting. But based on everything you've learned so far, what's your point?*

Presenting Research in Alternative Genres

Slide Presentations: Planning and Design

Everybody knows that PowerPoint® can be a bore. Yet slide presentations are the most multimedia genres of the four I'm proposing, combining five modes: writing, visual, audio, gesture, and speech. As a result, well-done presentations can be extremely effective ways of presenting research. Though PowerPoint® is the best-known slideware, there are plenty of alternatives, including Prezi, which uses a less linear approach. The key is to imagine that slides are *supplementary* to talk, reinforcing a limited number of key ideas from your research. Slide content is not meant to stand alone. Plan your speech carefully, and decide what points you'd like to visually dramatize on slides.

Rhetorical Considerations
- Most effective with audience that is already interested in topic.
- Good way to communicate a lot of information, especially if supplemented by handouts.
- Particularly effective way to present hierarchically organized information.
- Vulnerable to being more speaker oriented than audience oriented.

Design Tips
- Minimize text. Avoid long bulleted lists or dense text. Consider combining spare text with a relevant image or graphic that reinforces a point.
- One point per slide.
- If you can, use slide titles to tell a story, not to describe content (e.g., "The Turning Point")
- Use graphs or pie charts, not tables, which are difficult to read.
- Minimize distracting animation.
- Always choose good-resolution images and graphics. Avoid clip art.
- Use font, background color, images, and graphics to create a consistent theme.

Say One Thing

Many years ago, I was lucky enough to go to graduate school where a wonderful writer and teacher named Donald Murray taught, and he became both a friend and mentor. One of Don's endearing habits was to take a saying about which he was particularly fond and print it out on cardboard, which he would then distribute to his students. *"Nulla dies sine linea"*—never a day without a line—was one of these. Another was "S.O.F.T." This was an acronym for Say One Fricking Thing. Don believed that every piece of writing should say one fricking thing; it may deal with many ideas, but the writer's job is to find the *one* thing he or she wants most to say about an essay topic.

More formally, we often understand this to mean that writing— especially academic writing—should have a thesis, a point, a theme, and a main idea. Too often, I'm afraid, writers arrive at this too early in their research—ending the inquiry process prematurely—or they don't arrive at it at all, and the essay or paper seems pointless.

In Exercise 4.1 you moved toward finding your S.O.F.T., and when you did, several things might have happened.

1. You discovered a point, and maybe it was one you didn't expect. Hallelujah! This one might need some fine-tuning but it seems to reflect your understanding of the topic at this point.

2. You arrived at a point, but it doesn't seem quite right. You feel like you're still groping toward a thesis—an answer to your research question—and this one seems forced or too general.

3. You have no clue what might be the S.O.F.T. All you have is more questions. Or perhaps you realize that you simply don't know enough yet to have any idea what you want to say.

If you find yourself in the first situation—you discovered a thesis that seems right—then maybe your draft should be an argumentative essay in which you attempt to prove your point. The second situation might invite you to continue your investigation by writing an exploratory research essay, and the third probably means that you haven't done nearly enough research yet. Actually, you probably need to do more research in every case, and you will as you continue the process.

Organizing the Draft

How you approach writing your first draft this week depends on what you decide about which kind of research essay you think you want to write: an argument or an exploratory essay. Let's look at how the two might differ.

But first, the five-paragraph theme. Like a lot of schoolkids, I learned to write something called the "five-paragraph theme": introduction with thesis; five body paragraphs, each with a topic sentence and supporting details; and conclusion. This was the container into which I poured all of my writing back then. Though it didn't produce particularly interesting writing, the five-paragraph structure was a reliable way to organize things. It was well suited to outlines. I vaguely remember this one from sixth grade:

I. China is a really big country.
   A. The population of China is really big.
   B. The geographic size of China is really big.
   C. The economic dreams of China are really big.

What's useful about thinking of structure this way is the notion of hierarchy: Some ideas are subordinated to others, and each idea has some information subordinated under it. A problem with it, however, is the assumption that hierarchy is *always* the best way to organize information. For instance, essays can often make relevant digressions, or they might play with one way of seeing the topic and then another.

Perhaps a more basic problem with forms like the five-paragraph theme is the idea that structure is this kind of inert container that stands apart from the things you put into it and from your particular motives in writing about something.

Yet structure is important. It's especially important when you've got a lot of information. (If you haven't done enough research, you'll be forced to use everything you have, which usually means an unfocused essay no matter what structure you choose).

I'd like to encourage you, as you start drafting this week, to avoid thinking about the structure of your essay as something set in concrete before you begin. Instead, think of form rhetorically: Who is your audience and what does the assignment say and what is your purpose in writing about your topic? But an even more basic question to consider as you plan the organization of your research essay is motive. Do you want to narrate the story of your thinking on your research question or do you want to prove a point? Each relies on a different logic and structure.

Following Narrative Logic

One day I gave my students packets of 60 cards that each contained a range of facts about topics like health care, environmental issues, energy use, personal relationships, technology, and race relations. I asked my students to organize the cards in any way that made sense to them. The result was predictable. They organized the cards in categories—every fact relating to health care went in one pile, and every fact related to the environment went in another, and so on. Topic categories like this are typically hierarchical; you come up with an overriding concept to which you can subordinate information. This is a sensible, powerful way of organizing things. But what's always interesting to me is that my students never thought of ways to organize the fact cards that *cut across* these conventional categories. In other words, a card with a fact on the problem of obesity (usually tucked under "health care") was never organized in relationship with a card on, say, energy use, though in my mind both could be related.

One day, I asked students to start over again, and organize the cards around what I called "narrative logic." What's narrative logic? One of the main reasons that we tell stories is to examine causes and effects. Something happened, and we try to figure out why or what the consequences might be. At the heart of narrative logic, then, is an interest in causal relationships. But because stories always live in some relationship to time (and often place), that's part of narrative logic, too: Not only what happened, but when (and often where). So when my students returned to the card packets, they suddenly saw the facts in a new way. For example, one group combined cards from the education, relationships, and technology categories and rearranged the statistics to basically tell this story: First you have bad approaches to sexual education in schools, then you have bad sexual relationships, and then you turn increasingly to sex online, and before long you feel ugly and alone. Another group took all the cards with statistics about American obesity and ordered the findings chronologically, dramatizing the problem.

In narrative logic, you are more likely to *coordinate* information rather than *subordinate* it; in other words, rather than using information to support a claim or serve as examples of a concept or category, you see information as *exhibits* that can be considered, at least initially, as equally valid and in relationship to each other. You also see information in the context of particular times (and often places). In the end, then, whatever point you make in narrative logic is qualified: *This is what I understand now that seems true in this particular context.* "Theories of Intelligence," the essay on page 000 of *The Curious Researcher*, uses narrative logic to explore what I learned about various views on intelligence and how that complicated my own views of how "smart" I am. Like most exploratory essays, the thesis or main idea comes at the end rather than the beginning. It's a "delayed thesis" paper.

Narrative logic is a method in all kinds of academic research, particularly when investigating people and cultures in particular places and times. Anthropologists, for example, use narrative logic to write ethnographies about tribal cultures, nursing scholars might use case studies to examine doctor–nurse relationships at a particular local hospital.

Narrative reasoning checklist. As you consider whether your own inquiry project might use narrative logic, ask yourself the following questions:

- Is my main motive to *find out* what I think?
- Do I want to tell the story of what I've come to understand about my research question?
- Am I writing about a problem in a particular time or place? Am I reluctant to claim that whatever answers I come up with to my research question might also be true in other contexts?
- Am I interested exploring causes and effects or reasons or consequences? If so, am I uncertain about what they are? Is exploring this the focus of my project?

If narrative logic seems relevant to your research project, consider writing an exploratory essay, one that uses the Three-Act Structure described in Figure 4.1. But also consider the alternative—argumentative logic.

Following Argumentative Logic

Undoubtedly, you're much more familiar with the logic of argument, which is the form that much academic writing uses. It's a powerful and important method of thinking, particularly when your motive is to prove a point, perhaps

Figure 4.1
The Three-Act
Structure of
the Exploratory
Research Essay

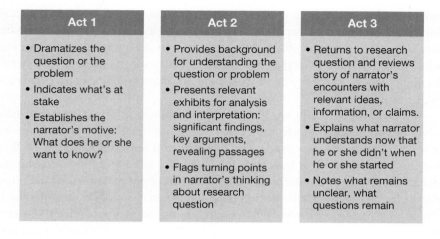

Act 1	Act 2	Act 3
• Dramatizes the question or the problem • Indicates what's at stake • Establishes the narrator's motive: What does he or she want to know?	• Provides background for understanding the question or problem • Presents relevant exhibits for analysis and interpretation: significant findings, key arguments, revealing passages • Flags turning points in narrator's thinking about research question	• Returns to research question and reviews story of narrator's encounters with relevant ideas, information, or claims. • Explains what narrator understands now that he or she didn't when he or she started • Notes what remains unclear, what questions remain

one you arrived at following the discovery phase of your research. Typically, argumentative logic dispenses with what went on behind the scenes, the process that led you to deciding what you think is the best answer to your research question. Instead, fairly early on, you billboard your thesis, and use the body of your essay to offer both reasons and supporting evidence that establish why that thesis makes sense. Actually, it's a little more complicated than that. Even in an argument, the thesis isn't Teflon-coated, impervious to findings that might complicate the claim. You might start, say, arguing that climate change denial is more a psychological than political problem. Although you may not waiver from that basic point, at the end of your essay you revisit it, and suggest that there are ways the psychological and political are also linked.

Unlike narrative logic, in argumentative reasoning you're much more likely to subordinate—rather than coordinate—information and ideas. The facts you gather from your research are often deployed in support of reasons that serve to validate your thesis. But this isn't necessarily a steady march: Here's what I think is true, here's why, and this is evidence that supports those reasons. It's a bit messier than that, which is no surprise because, well, interesting things are always complicated. For one thing, you should entertain—and analyze—points of view that depart from your own. This can happen anywhere in the argumentative research essay. These turns to look at points of view that differ from yours aren't perfunctory; they might complicate your thinking and even qualify your thesis. After all, the point of argument isn't to make a point, but to get to the truth of things.

Argumentative Logic Checklist. Should your research project make an argument? To decide, consider the following questions:

- Do I think I want *to prove* a point? Is there an answer to my research question to which I'm strongly drawn?

- Is there something that readers should do about the problem I'm writing about, and would I like to persuade them to do it?

- Can I see compelling *reasons* for believing what I do? Have I encountered significant evidence that convinces me and might convince others?
- Can I actually articulate a thesis statement at this point, even if I revise it later on?

There is no formula for organizing an argumentative research paper, but like most written compositions it has a beginning, middle, and end, and each of these typically do different work (see Figure 4.2). The beginning establishes the significance of the problem and helps readers understand what stake they might have in it. It also billboards the writer's big idea. The middle, which is typically about half of the paper, is where you get down to work using your research to slowly build a convincing case that your big idea makes sense. This can be structured in a lot of ways, though often in middle begins with a summary of what the debate is all about, who are key players, and what they believe. In more formal academic essays, this is sometimes called a *literature review*. It might also be helpful to provide background and key definitions. From there, you might start building a case for your thesis, offering reasons and evidence that you think are convincing. But there's other content, too: counterarguments, difficult questions, unsettled research, and helpful explanations. Finally, the end of an argumentative research essay often revisits the thesis, not to merely restate it, but to *add* to it.

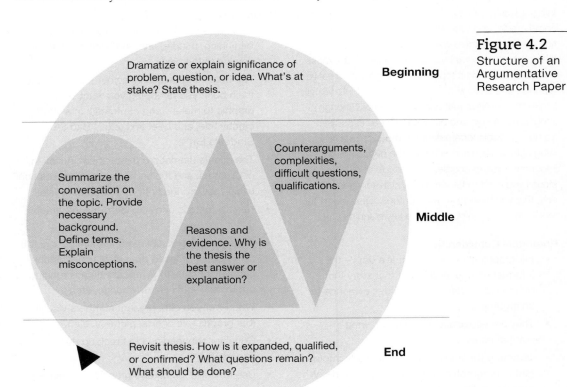

Figure 4.2
Structure of an Argumentative Research Paper

Dramatize or explain significance of problem, question, or idea. What's at stake? State thesis.

Beginning

Summarize the conversation on the topic. Provide necessary background. Define terms. Explain misconceptions.

Counterarguments, complexities, difficult questions, qualifications.

Reasons and evidence. Why is the thesis the best answer or explanation?

Middle

Revisit thesis. How is it expanded, qualified, or confirmed? What questions remain? What should be done?

End

In the end, are there qualifications, elaborations, and uncertainties about the big idea you initially offered as an answer to your research question?

However you choose to organize it, your research essay will have certain characteristics. For example, nearly any academic research paper includes the following items:

1. A S.O.F.T.—a point, a claim, a thesis—one main thing you are trying to say about the research question
2. A review of what has already been said by others about your topic
3. Specific information—the evidence or data on which your interpretations, conclusions, assertions, and speculations are based
4. A method of reasoning through the question, some pattern of thought—usually narrative or argument—that writer and reader find a convincing way to try to get at the truth of things

Presenting Research in Alternative Genres

Infographic: Planning and Design

Infographics are everywhere—newspapers, magazines, social media, and Web sites. In an age of information overload, readers want to quickly see the *story* that facts tell. Infographics do this by taking the most compelling data on a topic, combining it with creative graphics and snappy writing, and turning it into visually interesting narrative that catches the eye. Although infographic design and production takes expertise, it's now possible for amateurs to produce simple infographics using free software like piktochart or infogr.am. First, of course, you need to decide what stories you want to tell visually, and this means, naturally, that you have to know your topic. Drawing a rough mock-up of your infographic is a key planning step.

Rhetorical Considerations
- Infographics focus on *selective* data—the information that lends itself to a story that dramatizes, informs, or provides evidence for an argument.
- They are especially useful for drawing comparisons.
- Targeting the audience is particularly important if infographics are used to persuade. Who exactly needs to take action on the problem?

Design Tips
- Like any story, infographics often have a beginning, middle, and end, with each section flowing to the next.
- The beginning establishes your purpose—the main point you're hoping you want your infographic to make—and captures it in a short, catchy title, and brief text (e.g., "Bad Stuff Students Eat").
- The middle dramatizes the problem, question, or dilemma, and the end introduces the solution, usually toward the bottom of the visual field.
- Usually there is one "big idea" the infographic communicates.
- Consider using visual metaphors (e.g., a graph using beer bottles to dramatize college drinking, a clock face to symbolize time is running out to deal with climate change, etc.)
- Whenever you can, present numbers visually (bar graphs, pie charts, pictures, etc.).
- Consider subheadings to break up the infographic.
- Use font size, color, and graphics to create a visual hierarchy of information.

Exploring or Arguing: An Example

Susan was writing an exploratory research essay on the relationship between attendance at preschool and academic success in elementary school. She decided to introduce her topic by describing her own dilemma with her son, Sam. She wanted to send him to preschool, but as a working college student, she wasn't sure she could afford it. Her personal anecdote highlighted the problem many parents face and the question behind her research: Will children who don't attend preschool be at a disadvantage in primary school? In the middle section of her essay, Susan reported on several studies that looked at a range of skills that were affected by preschool experience and discussed which of these she found most significant, particularly in the context of her personal interviews with several local teachers. In the second-to-last section of her draft, Susan concluded that preschool does indeed make a difference, particularly in the areas of reading and reasoning.

Imagine that Susan wanted instead to write an argumentative research paper, a more conventional form for academic research. Would it be organized differently? Although she still might begin with a personal anecdote as a way to dramatize the problem, Susan might choose instead to begin with information, highlighting the statistics and arguments that establish the importance of the problem. How many children in the United States attend preschool? How many don't? What are the trends? Are more parents struggling to find affordable preschools? Are fewer preschools available in disadvantaged areas? Is there a shortage of teachers? A significant difference would be where in the paper Susan puts her thesis. In the argumentative paper, the thesis usually appears toward the beginning and is stated explicitly: "I will argue in this essay that the growing number of children in the United States who are being denied a preschool experience will be at a serious disadvantage in reading and reasoning skills when they enter elementary school." Her essay would then go on to methodically establish the truth of this claim using her research. Susan might end her essay by suggesting how elementary teachers could address the learning deficits these children bring into their classrooms or how more children could be given access to preschool.

Preparing to Write the Draft

If research is a little like soup making, then you want to make something hearty, not thin; that's nearly impossible to do unless you have a lot of information. If you slacked on developing focused knowledge last week and didn't do enough research on your question, then you'll find that you have to use almost everything you *do* have to write the first draft. If that happens, your essay will be unfocused and uninformative. Scanty research is one of the most common problems I see in student work at this stage in the process. Your first decision before beginning the draft is whether you've got what it takes to make at least decent soup.

Refining the Question

But you can't really judge the quality of your information until you feel comfortable with your research question. Are you asking the right question? Is it the question that you find most interesting? Is it focused enough? Did you refine it as you learned more about your topic? Does it incorporate the language or terms you may have learned in your reading? Typically, research questions evolve, especially if you are tackling a topic that you initially didn't know much about.

For these kinds of topics, the research questions we often ask initially are broadly informative or questions of definition:

- *What are the theories of dog training?*

As we learn more about our research topic, the questions frequently become more specific—which is far more helpful in guiding research—and reflect our new understandings of the topic. The next generation of questions often moves beyond questions of fact or definition and reflects a *particular* interest in the topic: Is it any good? What does it mean? What should be done? What might be true? What are important causes? (See Figure 4.3.)

For example, this rewrite of the original research question is a little more specific and also implies value:

- *What are the best theories of dog training?*

The following question is more specific still and incorporates some of the language in the literature:

- *Is there evidence that "dog-centric" approaches to training that reward behavior work better than approaches that emphasize the trainer's dominance over the dog?*

And the following question is even more specific:

- *What is the relationship between the use of shock collars and dog aggression or submission?*

Revisit your research question before you begin your draft. In light of what you've learned about your topic so far, can you rewrite the question so that it provides you with stronger guidance about your purpose in the draft? When you've rewritten your research question, write it on a notecard or sticky note, and put it somewhere on your computer monitor where you can see it as you're writing the draft. Your research question (or thesis) is the anchor that will keep you from going adrift.

Refining the Thesis

If you're writing an argumentative essay, then you need to settle on a tentative thesis. It may change as you continue doing the writing and research, but for now you should have a pretty specific statement of what you think. Exercise 4.1 might have helped nudge you in this direction. Now work with your thesis a bit more.

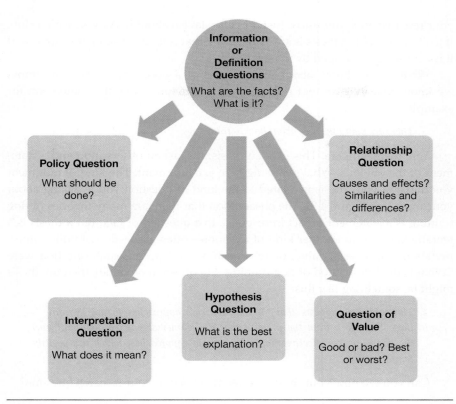

Figure 4.3 Categories of Questions.

Usually our initial research questions are questions of fact or definition: What is known about this topic? What is it? But a strong research essay needs *to do* something with the facts. One way to think about what a question is trying to do is to place it in one of these additional categories: questions of policy, interpretation, hypothesis, value, or relationship. Before you begin your draft, rethink your question. Can it be more specific? Can you rewrite your question so that it gives you a stronger sense of what you're trying to do with your research?

There is considerable talk about thesis statements. Sometimes it seems like a thesis (or S.O.F.T., main point, central claim, organizing idea, etc.) is a kind of club required to beat an essay into submission, forcing every part of the work into obedience. In this view, there is no room for digression, contrary evidence, opposing views, or uncertainty. Much writing—like the world that writers attempt to explore in that writing—is much messier than that, and that complexity is what makes inquiry interesting.

And yet, when writers discover what they want to say—the answer to the question, the realization about what should be done, or the interpretation that makes the most sense—it's essential that they say it clearly, first for themselves and then for their readers. At this stage in the research process, your thesis is tentative, but if you spend some time refining it, it will reward you later. A well-stated thesis gives you a sense of direction and can help you to organize both your research and your essay. Just don't be slavish about it. A thesis isn't a club. It isn't even a tool. A thesis is a way of seeing that is made of sand, not stone, and it is continually reshaped by what you learn.

What do we know about the qualities of a good thesis? For one thing, we know that they are not overly broad or obvious. Take this statement, for example:

> *There are many theories about how to train dogs.*

Yep, there sure are. This is not a thesis; it's just an observation and a statement of the obvious. What's missing here is a judgment. The kind of judgment you make in your thesis is related to the kind of question you're asking about your topic (see Figure 4.3). The observation that there are many theories of dog training is a statement of fact in response to a question of fact. But a thesis is a tentative answer to another kind of question—often a question of policy, interpretation, hypothesis, value, or relationship. So if my research question were "What is the *best* method of dog training?" (a question of value), then my thesis might be something like this:

> *The evidence suggests that "human-centric" approaches to dog training— those that work from the premise that the trainer should be dominant over the dog—are less effective than "dog-centric" approaches, which use positive reinforcement.*

Can you see how your thesis is directly related to your research question?

Exercise 4.2

SHARPENING YOUR POINT

Even if you're writing an exploratory essay, it's helpful to think about what your thesis might be at this stage in the inquiry process. This is a kind of reality check: What do I think *right now* based on what I've learned? You are invited to change your mind later. If your essay is argumentative, then it's even more important to establish a tentative thesis. The following templates, each based on the kind of question you're asking, might help:

Thesis from a Question of Value

Based on _____, the evidence strongly suggests that _____ is (better/worse, more effective/less effective) than _____.

EXAMPLE: Based on recent studies comparing how well disciplines teach critical thinking to college students,

the evidence suggests that business programs are failing to do a good job of teaching reasoning skills to their undergraduates.

Thesis from a Question of Policy

In the debate over _____, I'm persuaded that the most important thing to do is _____.

EXAMPLE: In the debate over what to do with the overpopulation of wild horses in western rangelands, it's clear that the only effective solution is for the federal agencies to cull the herds.

Thesis from a Question of Interpretation

The pattern in _____ that is most (significant/interesting/obvious) is _____.

EXAMPLE: Throughout Ken Kesey's *One Flew Over the Cuckoo's Nest*, the character of Nurse Ratched represents everything that sexist men fear: the threat of emasculation by a woman.

Thesis from a Hypothesis Question

Based on my research, the assumption that _____ appears to be (true/false, qualified/unqualified, accurate/inaccurate, difficult to determine/impossible to determine).

EXAMPLE: My research on Facebook and social intimacy appears to confirm my impression that "friending" can promote connection but can also be used to manipulate and divide.

Thesis from a Relationship Question

There is a (strong/weak) relationship between _____ and _____.

EXAMPLE: There is a strong relationship between dog owners' views about the need for dominance over their pet and their choice of either "human-centric" or "dog-centric" training methods.

These templates are a bit crude, but try to use them as a starting point to craft a one- or two-sentence thesis that *reflects your current understanding of your topic*. Write this on a sticky note or notecard and, along with your research question, put it on your computer monitor as a reminder when you write the draft.

Deciding Whether to Say *I*

If you're writing an exploratory research essay, you'll likely write in the first person. After all, you're telling the story of your experience thinking through possible answers to a research question. Argumentative research papers may or may not be written in first person. If your instructor doesn't give you guidance on this, how do you decide? This is always a question about rhetorical situation and not some presumed "rule" about never using first person in academic writing. As I noted previously, all writing is narrated, even in the absence of the first person. Someone is always the "man (or woman) behind the curtain?," guiding readers through the work and orchestrating their experience. When should that narrator reveal himself or herself? Here are a few rhetorical considerations.

- **Relationship with readers.** First person promotes—and impersonal approaches diminish—the sense that writer and reader are relative equals. "I think that …" and "This paper will argue that …" imply two different identities; one gets its authority from the sense that the writer is in a conversation with the reader, and the other establishes authority by suggesting that the writer's absence minimizes bias.

- **Research conventions.** Writers in the sciences often avoid first-person writing because they want to direct readers' gaze to the data not the researcher. It also *sounds* more objective. In qualitative research, the kind often done in fields like business, nursing, anthropology, and English, the researcher often plays a more visible role, orchestrating the study and interpreting the results.

There are actually good reasons to consider writing this essay in the first person. For one thing, you're likely not doing empirical research. But the most important reason is this: When writers stop pretending that the *text* talks instead of the *author* (e.g., "This paper will argue that…") and actually enters into their

Presenting Research in Alternative Genres

Photographic Essay

Photographs are our most accessible visual language. Many of us take pictures incessantly, especially now that smartphones make it easy to do. The photographic essay exploits the visual language of pictures, which are thoughtfully composed and then later arranged to tell a story or make an argument. As a genre for presenting research writing, the photo essay has limitations—you can't use much text, and images are often more effective at communicating feeling rather than facts. But good photos are also saturated with meanings that can be more powerful than just words. To present your findings in a photo essay, imagine taking—or finding (perhaps in archival sources online)—images that dramatize the problem you're writing about. For example, the San Francisco Bicycle Coalition, arguing for more space on trains for bikes, took contrasting shots of a bike-filled train car at various times during the day and paired it with the near-empty passenger cars on those same trains. The message was clear: Free up some passenger cars for bikes. You can use free photo software to create your essay (Picassa, iPhoto, Flickr, etc.), use Microsoft Photo Story 3, or even slideware like Prezi or PowerPoint®.

Rhetorical Considerations

- Images often embody pathos—they evoke feelings—and can be particularly effective for dramatizing a problem.

- The arrangement of photos should have a narrative logic—beginning, middle, and end.
- Combine images with brief text so that each is in *conversation* with the other.
- Focus your photo essay on one key idea or theme.

Design Tips

- Decide if you'll use existing images or shoot new ones to develop your theme.
- If taking new shots, collect multiple images of each subject, varying distance, angle, and light.
- Depending on your research topic, consider finding archival photos online at sites like the Library of Congress.
- Review images, and rank them, looking for shots relevant to the theme.
- Play with order, exploiting story structures: cause and effect, problem/solution, change over time, movement through space and place, action/reaction, etc.
- Combine long shots to set scenes, and close ones for examining details.
- Incorporate text to tie image back to theme, add essential information, or move the story forward.
- Consider how the text will work with images: Captions? Superimposed over image? Appearing after image dissolves? Voice narration?

text, they are much more likely to initiate a genuine conversation with their readers *and* with their sources. This dialogue might well lead to some new ways of seeing her topic—which is, after all, the purpose of inquiry.

Starting to Write the Draft: Beginning at the Beginning

John McPhee, whom I mentioned previously as one of the masters of the research-based essay, gave a talk some years back about beginnings, which vex many writers.

The first part—the lead, the beginning—is the hardest part of all to write. I've often heard writers say that if you have written your lead you have written 90 percent of the story. You have tens of thousands of words to choose from, after all, and only one can start the story, then one after that, and so forth. And your material, at this point, is all fresh and unused, so you don't have the advantage of being in the middle of things. You could start in any of many places. What will you choose? Leads must be sound. They should never promise what does not follow.

As McPhee said in his talk, "Leads, like titles, are flashlights that shine down into the story."[*]

Flashlights or Floodlights?

I love this: *"Leads … are flashlights that shine down into the story."* An introduction, at least the kind I was taught to write in high school, is more like a sodium vapor lamp that lights up the whole neighborhood. I remember writing introductions to research papers that sounded like this:

> There are many critical problems that face society today. One of these critical problems is environmental protection, and especially the conservation of marine resources. This paper will explore one of these resources—the whale—and the myriad ways in which the whale-watching industry now poses a new threat to this species' survival. It will look at what is happening today and what some people concerned with the problem hope will happen tomorrow. It will argue that new regulations need to be put into effect to reduce boat traffic around our remaining whales, a national treasure that needs protection.

This introduction isn't that bad. It does offer a statement of purpose, and it explains the thesis. But the window it opens on the paper is so broad—listing everything the paper will try to do—that readers see a bland, general landscape. What's to discover? The old writing formula for structuring some papers—"Say what you're going to say, say it, and then say what you said"—breeds this kind of introduction. It also gets the writer started on a paper that often turns out as bland as the beginning.

Consider this alternative opening for the same paper:

> Scott Mercer, owner of the whale-watching vessel *Cetecea*, tells the story of a man and his son who decide that watching the whales from inside their small motorboat isn't close enough. They want to swim with them. As Mercer and his passengers watch, the man sends his son overboard with snorkel and fins, and the boy promptly swims toward a "bubble cloud," a mass of air exhaled by a feeding humpback whale below the surface. What the swimmer doesn't know is that, directly below that bubble cloud, the creature is on its way up, mouth gaping. They are both in for a surprise. "I got on the P.A. system and

---

[*]McPhee, John. University of New Hampshire, 1977.

told my passengers, just loud enough for the guy in the boat to hear me, that either that swimmer was going to end up as whale food or he was going to get slapped with a $10,000 fine. He got out of the water pretty fast."

I think this lead accomplishes nearly as much as the bland version but in a more compelling way. It suggests the purpose of the paper—to explore conflicts between whale lovers and whales—and even implies the thesis—that human activity around whales needs more regulation, a point that might follow the anecdote. This lead is more like McPhee's "flashlight," pointing out the direction of the paper without attempting to illuminate the entire subject in a paragraph. An interesting beginning will also help launch the writer into a more interesting paper, for both reader and writer.

It's probably obvious that your opening is your first chance to capture your reader's attention. But how you begin your research paper will also have a subtle yet significant impact on the rest of it. The lead starts the paper going in a particular direction; it also establishes the *tone*, or writing voice, and the writer's relationships to the subject and the reader. Most writers at least intuitively know this, which is why beginnings are so hard to write.

Writing Multiple Leads

One thing that will make it easier to get started is to write three leads to your paper, instead of agonizing over one that must be perfect. Each different opening you write should point the "flashlight" in a different direction, suggesting different trails the draft might follow. After composing several leads, you can choose the one that you—and ultimately, your readers—find most promising.

Writing multiple openings to your paper might sound hard, but consider all the ways to begin:

- **Anecdote.** Think of a little story that nicely frames what your paper is about, as does the lead about the man and his son who almost became whale food.

- **Scene.** Begin by giving your readers a look at some revealing aspect of your topic. A paper on the destruction of tropical rain forests might begin with a description of what the land looks like after loggers have left it.

- **Profile.** Try a lead that introduces someone who is important to your topic. Amanda's essay on the relationship between the popularity of tooth whitening and our changing notions of beauty might begin, for example, by describing Dr. Levine, the man who determined with mathematical precision the dimensions of the "perfect smile."

- **Background.** Maybe you could begin by providing important and possibly surprising background information on your topic. A paper on steroid use might start by citing the explosive growth in use by high school athletes in the last 10 years. A paper on a novel or an author might begin with a review of what critics have had to say.

- **Quotation.** Sometimes, you encounter a great quote that beautifully captures the question your paper will explore or the direction it will take. Heidi's paper on whether *Sesame Street* provides children with a good education began by quoting a tribute from *U.S. News and World Report* to Jim Henson after his sudden death.

- **Dialogue.** Open with dialogue between people involved in your topic. Dan's paper on the connection between spouse abuse and alcoholism began with a conversation between himself and a woman who had been abused by her husband.

- **Question.** Pointedly ask your readers the questions you asked that launched your research or the questions your readers might raise about your topic. Here's how Kim began her paper on adoption: "Can you imagine going through life not knowing your true identity?"

- **Contrast.** Try a lead comparing two apparently unlike things that highlight the problem or dilemma the paper will explore. Dusty's paper "Myth of the Superwoman" began with a comparison between her friend Susan, who grew up believing in Snow White and Cinderella and married at 21, and herself, who never believed in princes on white horses and was advised by her mother that it was risky to depend on a man.

- **Announcement.** Sometimes the most appropriate beginning *is* one like the first lead on whales and whale watchers mentioned previously, which announces what the paper is about. Though such openings are sometimes not particularly compelling, they are direct. A paper with a complex topic or focus may be well served by simply stating in the beginning the main idea you'll explore and what plan you'll follow.

Exercise 4.3

THREE WAYS IN

STEP 1: Compose three different beginnings, or leads, to your research paper. Each should be one or two paragraphs (or perhaps more, depending on what type of lead you've chosen and on the length of your paper). Think about the many different ways to begin, as mentioned previously, and experiment. Your instructor may ask you to write the three leads in your research notebook or print them out and bring them to class. (For an example, see Figure 4.4.)

STEP 2: Get some help deciding which opening is strongest. Circulate your leads in class, or show them to friends. Ask each person to check the one lead he or she likes best and that most makes him or her want to read on.

Figure 4.4
Amanda's Three
Leads*

Here are three openings that Amanda crafted for her draft on our cultural obsession with the "perfect smile." Which do you think is strongest?

1. I haven't felt much like smiling recently. It isn't that I've been particularly melancholy or deprived of necessary joy. I've actually been hesitant to smile because lately I've felt insecure about my teeth. I brush and floss every day and see my dentist twice a year, just like any responsible hygiene patient does—but that doesn't seem to be enough anymore. My teeth need to be white. Now when I feel the corners of my mouth pucker upwards and I start to grin at someone, I can't stop thinking about my teeth. What once was a simple visual expression of happiness has become a symptom of my overall doubts about my appearance.

2. Julie Beatty wants people to look at her as a more confident, strong person, so she's doing the only logical thing. She's shelling out over $12,500 for an overhaul on her teeth. While it sounds completely ridiculous to change a person's oral structure to create a different persona, Julie is a member of a booming group of people who are looking to change their smiles to change their lives. Whether or not Julie's straightening, whitening, and tooth reshaping will change her success as an executive is still unknown, but the popularity of cosmetic dentistry and smile care is an undeniable new phenomenon.

3. I can feel individual molecules of air battering at my teeth. It's the middle of the night, but I can't sleep because of the constant pain in my mouth. Even the weight of my lips pressing down on my teeth is agonizing, like I've spent the day being hit in the mouth with a hammer and have exposed nerves protruding throughout. I haven't been beaten up, though. The cause of all my agony is a 10 percent peroxide gel I've been smearing into trays and putting on my teeth for the past week to whiten them. All this pain is due to my vanity and desire for a bit more pearliness in my pearly whites. As I watch the numbers of the clock roll from 2:00 to 4:00, I wonder why I'm putting up with such dental distress just for a more gleaming smile.

*These excerpts are reprinted with permission of Amanda Stewart.

STEP 3: Choose the lead you like (even if no one else does). To determine how well it prepares your readers for what follows, ask a friend or classmate to answer these questions: Based on reading only the opening of the paper: (a) What do you predict this paper is about? What might be its focus? (b) Can you guess what central question I'm trying to answer? (c) Can you predict what my thesis might be? (d) How would you characterize the tone of the paper?

It's easy to choose an opening that's catchy. But the beginning of your paper must also help establish your purpose in writing it, frame your focus, and perhaps even suggest your main point or thesis. The lead will also establish the voice, or tone, the paper will adopt.

That's a big order for one or two paragraphs, and you may find that more than a couple of paragraphs are needed to do it. If you did Exercise 4.3, tentatively select the one opening (or a combination of several) you composed that does those things best. I think you'll find that none of the leads you composed will be wasted; there will be a place for the ones you don't use somewhere else in the paper. Keep them handy.

Writing for Reader Interest

You've tentatively chosen a lead for your paper. You've selected it based on how well you think it frames your tentative purpose, establishes an appropriate tone or voice, and captures your readers' attention. Once you've gotten your readers' attention, you want to keep it. Consider the following:

1. Give your readers a sense of purpose *throughout* the essay, not just at the beginning.
2. Find ways that your topic intersects with readers' own knowledge of the topic. Build your essay from there.
3. Put a face on your topic—not just how it affects people but *How did it affect a person*?
4. Write an ending that *adds* something rather than tells readers what they already know.
5. Emphasize what's less known about a topic, what may be surprising.

Who's Steering and Where to?

Imagine that reading is like pedaling a bike up a hill, only the writer is steering the thing while you do all the work. You will not keep pedaling if you think the writer isn't taking you somewhere, and you have to be confident of this within the first few paragraphs of an essay. That's why a strong lead is so important: It gives your readers a sense of direction, a sense of *purpose*. They read an introduction about the rise of the Tea Party in U.S. politics and know that what interests the writer is the Tea Party's constitutional arguments about national health care. Or they read the beginning of an essay on the disgusting habits of ticks, and within a couple paragraphs readers know why the writer is sharing this—to make the argument that climate change is affecting tick-borne illnesses in moose. In each case, if readers know that the bike is headed in a particular direction, they might keep pedaling.

But readers must sense this not just at the beginning but throughout the essay. One way to help readers continue to sense this direction is to keep returning to the question (or thesis) that is driving the essay. This might look something like this:

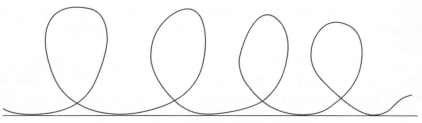

Question, Hypothesis, or Thesis

Figure 4.5
Keep looping back to your opening question, hypothesis, or thesis.

In other words, look for opportunities to return again and again *throughout your essay* to the question (or thesis) that opened it, and then arc away by examining the relevance of each source before arcing back to how the source advances your thinking or supports (and maybe complicates) your thesis.

Working the Common Ground

You're writing about the dangers of genetically modified food, and you also know that everyone eats. You're writing about the hemorrhaging economy of Detroit, and you also know that many of us drive cars that were made there. You're writing about the influence of Mississippi delta blues, and you also know that there are traces of that music in Elvis' "Blue Suede Shoes." There are what you know about your topic and what your readers know about your topic, and one way to engage them in what you have to say is to begin with the common ground. Ask yourself this:

- *What are my readers' own experiences with my topic?*
- *Is there some way in my paper that I can help them see that it's relevant to them?*
- *How can I help them see what they may already know?*

Putting People on the Page

Essayist E. B. White once advised that when you want to write about humankind, you should write about a human. The advice to look at the *small* to understand the *large* applies to most writing, not just the research paper.

Ideas come alive when we see how they operate in the world we live in. Beware, then, of long paragraphs with sentences that begin with phrases such as *in today's society*, where you wax on with generalization after generalization about your topic. Unless your ideas are anchored to specific cases, observations, experiences, statistics, and especially, people, they will be reduced to abstractions and lose their power for your reader.

USING CASE STUDIES   Strangely, research papers are often peopleless landscapes, which is one of the things that can make them so lifeless to read. Lisa wrote about theories of child development, citing studies and schools of thought about the topic yet never applying that information to a real child, her own daughter, two-year-old Rebecca. In his paper decrying the deforestation of the Amazon rain forest, Marty never gave his readers the chance to hear the voices of the Indians whose way of life is threatened. *Ultimately, what makes almost any topic matter to the writer or the reader is what difference it makes to people.*

Candy's paper on child abuse and its effect on language development, for example, opened with the tragic story of Genie, who, for nearly 13 years, was bound in her room by her father and beaten whenever she made a sound. When Genie was finally rescued, she could not speak at all. This sad story about a real girl makes the idea that child abuse affects how one speaks (the paper's thesis) anything but abstract. By personalizing the problem, Candy gave her readers reason to care about what she learned about it.

Sometimes, the best personal experience to share is your own. Have you been touched by the topic? Kim's paper about the special problems of women alcoholics included anecdotes about several women gleaned from her reading, but the paper was most compelling when she talked about her own experiences with her mother's alcoholism.

USING INTERVIEWS   Interviews are another way to bring people to the page. Heidi's paper on *Sesame Street* featured the voice of a school principal, a woman who echoed the point the paper made about the value of the program. Such research essays are filled not just with information about the topic but also with people who are touched by it in some way.

As you write your paper, look for opportunities to bring people to the page. Hunt for case studies, anecdotes, and good quotes that will help your readers see how your topic affects how people think and live their lives.

Writing a Strong Ending

Readers remember beginnings and endings. We already explored what makes a strong beginning: It engages the reader's interest, it's more often specific than general, and it frames the purpose of the paper, defining for the reader where it is headed. A beginning for a research paper should also state its thesis (as in an argumentative essay) or state the question (as in an exploratory essay).

We haven't said anything yet about endings, or "conclusions" as they are traditionally labeled. What's a strong ending? That depends. If you're writing a formal research paper in some disciplines, the basic elements of your conclusion might be prescribed. For example, you might need to summarize major findings and suggest directions for further research. But often, especially if you're writing a less formal research essay, you'll be able select from a wide range of options. For example, in an argumentative research essay, you might end by emphasizing what readers should do about the problem and why it matters. Exploratory essays might end with an anecdote, one that illuminates the understandings the writer has discovered. An ending for either kind of essay might suggest new questions, other avenues for research, or a reconsideration of an initial thesis.

ENDINGS TO AVOID   The ending of your research paper could be a lot of things, and in a way, it's easier to say what it should *not* be.

- Avoid conclusions that simply restate what you've already said. This is the "kick-the-dead-horse" conclusion some of us were taught to write in school on the assumption that our readers probably aren't smart enough to get our point, so we'd better repeat it. This approach annoys most readers, who *are* smart enough to know the horse is dead.

- Avoid endings that begin with *in conclusion* or *thus*. Words such as these also signal to your reader what she already knows: that your essay is ending.

And they often lead into a general summary, which gets you into a conclusion such as the one mentioned previously: dead.

- Avoid endings that don't feel like endings—that trail off onto other topics, are abrupt, or don't seem connected to what came before them. Prompting your readers to think is one thing; leaving them hanging is quite another.

In some ways, the conclusion of your research paper is the last stop on your journey; the reader has traveled far with you to get there. The most important quality of a good ending is that it adds something to the paper. If it doesn't, cut it and write a new one.

What can the ending add? It can add a further elaboration of your thesis that grows from the evidence you've presented, a discussion of solutions to a problem that has arisen from the information you've uncovered, or perhaps a final illustration or piece of evidence that drives home your point.

"Looking for Utopia," Laura Burn's argumentative research paper in Appendix B, examines the Jonestown tragedy. Nearly 40 years ago, 900 members of a religious group led by a charismatic leader, Jim Jones, were found dead in the Guyana compound where they had arrived a few years before, escaping what they believed was religious persecution in the United States The victims had all apparently drunk poisoned Kool-Aid. The tragedy shocked Americans, and the group, the "People's Temple," was widely described as a cult led by a deranged leader. Its members were largely viewed as dupes. Burn's thesis, however, was that the rise and tragic fall of the People's Temple was "more complex," and that the movement Jones inspired at least began in earnest idealism. Here's the ending of her paper:

> "The people who died in Jonestown were sweet, altruistic people," stated Timothy Stoen. "One of the tragedies of Jonestown is that people haven't paid enough attention to that" (Hatfield, 1998). It was not only Jones's sweet talking that convinced the Temple members to "drink the Koolaid." The people of Jonestown were idealist building a utopia, following a man they thought would lead them there. They loved their children, and feared for their futures. They cared for each other, and stayed together, even in death. They believed in a better world, and dedicated their lives, and deaths, to making it a reality. "As a society we fail to take serious the very strong and powerful desire, or hunger, for community, a community of people working for social change," stated Rebecca Moore, whose sisters Carolyn Layton and Annie Moore, died in Jonestown. "At times I despair we've learned nothing" (Hatfield, 1998).

Unlike the dreary conclusions that simply restate the thesis, the final paragraph of "Looking for Utopia" is a poignant reminder of another casualty of the Jonestown tragedy: the death of the ideals that started the movement. By bringing in the voices of a survivor and a sister of two of the victims, Burns returns to the thesis but makes it personal, and therefore poignant.

Using Surprise

The research process—like the writing process—can be filled with discovery for the writer if he or she approaches the topic with curiosity and openness. When I began researching lobsters, I was constantly surprised by things I didn't know: Lobsters are bugs; it takes 8 years for a lobster in Maine to grow to the familiar 1-pound size; the largest lobster ever caught weighed about 40 pounds and lived in a tank at a restaurant for a year, developing a fondness for the owner's wife. I could go on and on. And I did, in the book, sharing unusual information with my readers on the assumption that if it surprised me, it would surprise them, too.

As you write your draft, reflect on the surprising things you discovered about your topic during your research and look for ways to weave that information into the rewrite. Later, after you have written your draft, share it with a reader and ask for his or her ideas about what is particularly interesting and should be further developed. For now, think about unusual specifics you may have left out.

However, don't include information, no matter how surprising or interesting, that doesn't serve your purpose. For example, Christine's survey on the dreams of college freshmen had some fascinating findings, including some accounts of recurring dreams that really surprised her. She reluctantly decided not to say much about them, however, because they didn't really further the purpose of her paper, which was to discover what function dreams serve. On the other hand, Bob was surprised to find that some politically conservative politicians and judges actually supported decriminalization of marijuana. He decided to include more information in his revision about who they were and what they said, believing it would surprise his readers and strengthen his argument.

Writing with Sources

The need for *documentation*—that is, citing sources—distinguishes the research paper from most other kinds of writing. And let's face it: Worrying about sources can cramp your style. Many students have an understandable paranoia about plagiarism and tend, as mentioned previously, to let the voices of their sources overwhelm their own. Students are also often distracted by technical details: Am I getting the right page number? Where exactly should this citation go? Do I need to cite this or not?

As you gain control of the material by choosing your own writing voice and clarifying your purpose in the paper, you should feel less constrained by the technical demands of documentation. The following suggestions may also help you weave reference sources into your own writing without the seams showing.

Synthesizing Sources and the Moves Writers Make

Imagine that a well-made research essay is a woven piece of fabric made of five colors of thread. Four of the five represent key sources of information from your research: reading, interview, observation, and experience. The fifth thread is the most important of all: your own commentary. This fifth thread is largely missing from a research report, of course, but in a research essay it should be woven throughout the piece, adding color to the beginning and end of the paper, surrounding quotations, wrapping around key arguments and counterarguments, and emerging emphatically as you return again and again to the questions that interest you.

What does this mean, practically speaking? Think of it this way: You have your research question (or thesis), and you have your research. It is the collision of the two that creates the occasion for writers to *do* something with the information they've gathered. But what exactly do you do? In Figure 4.6, I list some of the moves that research writers make when they work with information. Of course, all of these moves are used to explore the research question or make a convincing argument, so always keep those purposes in mind.

Figure 4.6
Moves Research
Writers Make

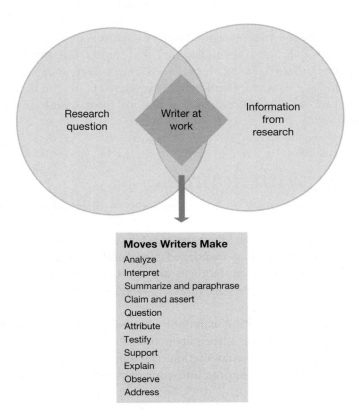

Moves Writers Make
Analyze
Interpret
Summarize and paraphrase
Claim and assert
Question
Attribute
Testify
Support
Explain
Observe
Address

Keep in mind that like a fleet-footed boxer, a writer can make these moves in quick succession as he or she puts information to work to explain, explore, and argue. That's obvious from the following example. In just the first three paragraphs of Rachel Gallina's research essay excerpted ("Seeing Beyond Fear" in Appendix A), she asserts, attributes, questions, testifies, supports, and addresses. These are scenes of writing in which a writer is in constant motion, actively engaged in putting her research to work for her.

Assert	Martin Luther King, Jr. once said, "To return hate for hate does nothing but intensify the existence of evil in the universe." We live in an era of hate. We see it all around us.
Attribute	According to Bruce Riedel of the Brookings Institution, the 21st century brought with it massive technological innovation, the expansion of the internet, and *terrorism*.
Testify	Spending large portions of my life in "danger zones" I've seen what terrorism has the power to do with my own eyes.
Question	But if terrorism is the expression of hate and hate fuels only more hate, what is to be done about it?
Assert and Support	Unrestrained fear, though, distorts our reasoning. Trevin Wax, writing for *The Washington Post* puts it this way, "Terrorism thrives on fear, and fear—if left unchecked—can spread in the deepest darkest corners of our hearts and lead to decisions and choices that, in normal times, would be unthinkable" (Wax).
Address	Well, let me ask you a few questions: Do you think Islam is set in its ways and unable to adapt to new realities? Do you think it has no common values with other major world religions, say the Western ones like Christianity and Judaism? Have you ever thought Islam is inferior to Western thinking, that it's somehow outdated, barbaric, and irrational? Do you think Islam is violent and supportive of terrorism?

As you draft your essay, keep these moves in mind. This is especially important whenever you have an inclination to import some of your research into your essay. The least effective research essays sometimes feel like "data dumps" where a writer simply deposits information without doing anything with it. This can be especially true with quoted material. In the section that follows, we'll look more closely at how to handle quotations effectively.

Handling Quotes

The seams in a research essay often show most when a writer is using quotations. Understandably, we love to use quotations. Sometimes a source just says it better than you can. But just as often, the quotation is the default choice because it is simply *easier*. You don't have to paraphrase, and you can dodge the danger of plagiarism.

In the section that follows, we'll look at some of the most common problems that arise when quoting sources and how to solve them.

PROBLEM #1: STOP AND PLOP QUOTATION   The stop and plop quotation is when you suddenly insert a quotation, especially one that might be paraphrased, into the middle of your own prose without any attribution. An example of this

Presenting Research in Alternative Genres

Poster

The "poster session" is a mainstay at academic conferences, including those that showcase undergraduate research. Posters are typically around 36 × 48 inches that highlight key findings from a research project. They're designed to be visually appealing, incorporating brief blocks of text (no more than 300 to 800 words) that are organized to flow, storylike, from one section to the next. Arresting images and tables often break up the text. Posters in the sciences are often organized around conventional structure of articles: introduction, methods, results, etc. But because your project isn't experimental, consider making your inquiry question the headline. Column sections may present information on things like "The Problem," "Case Studies," "Thesis," "Causes and Effects," "Solutions," and so on. Typically, posters are designed to be presented by the researcher who highlights key claims, questions, and findings and uses the poster for emphasis and explanation. But the poster should also be able to stand alone. There are conference poster templates online. Also search .edu sites for instructional how-to pages on developing posters.

Rhetorical Considerations

- Of the four suggested alternative genres, the poster can present the most information on your research.
- Assume an audience of non-experts.
- Posters are designed to trigger conversation by getting message across quickly and persuasively.
- Citations are often included.

Design Tips

- Mock up poster with pen and paper.
- Title should highlight either major finding or inquiry question.
- Use columns to structure blocks of information and a hierarchy of subheadings that guide viewers gaze from one section to the next.
- Always use high-resolution images that can be enlarged without degradation.
- Poster should be readable from 5 feet away (heads 48 pt. or larger, and text 24 pt. or larger).
- Use consistent fonts and colors.
- Some universities have printing services that will print your poster.

kind of passive blending of sources into your writing and a version that is far more active and takes control of the information follow.

Passive Blending:

> It's anyone's guess how many people believe in alien abduction. "One of the earliest studies of abductions found 1700 claimants, while contested surveys argued that 5–6 percent of the general population might have been abducted" (Wallace 4).

A much stronger version would paraphrase the information (it isn't that quotable anyway) and thread it into your paraphrase.

Active Blending:

> It's anyone's guess how many people believe in alien abduction, but initial findings were that 1,700 people claimed to have been abducted. Several "contested" surveys suggested that the number of

abductees' claims might total more than 5 percent of the population (Wallace 4).

PROBLEM #2: BREADLESS SANDWICH QUOTATION   The breadless sandwich quotation is another passive approach to using quotations. In this case, the meat (sorry, vegetarians)—the quoted material—is served up without any surrounding commentary or analysis from the writer. Typically you should introduce a quotation with some statement of intention—*why this voice is relevant*—and follow it with interpretation or analysis—*this is what this seems to be saying* or *here's how it addresses the inquiry question or thesis*. Here's what I mean:

Passive Blending:

> It's easy to dismiss the widespread belief in alien abduction as a simple delusion suffered by people who are not quite right. But here's another view:

>> That the abduction phenomenon is frequently discussed in popular culture, but is largely ignored by establishment sources[,] is not socially healthy. By generally refusing even to acknowledge the fact that many people are suffering from the abduction phenomenon, much less to fund research to reveal its cause, establishment leaders invite the paranoid fringe to conclude that the "government" is not only covering up an alien presence, but worse still is somehow in league with it. Even the non-paranoid may ask why this phenomenon is not examined more closely by those in a position to provide a satisfactory explanation of it. The present essay is in part an attempt to answer that question (Zimmerman 235).

> Mississippian Calvin Parker Jr. is someone who reported an alien encounter 40 years ago, and he regretted reporting it until the day he died....

Active Blending: Sandwich a quoted passage—particularly a longer one—between a brief discussion of your reason for bringing it in (or to direct readers' attention toward something) and a follow-up commentary that clarifies, summarizes, analyzes, interprets, or otherwise uses the quotation to move your essay forward.

> It's easy to dismiss the widespread belief in alien abduction as a simple delusion suffered by people who are not quite right. But even scholars in reputable journals think that's too narrow a view because it feeds people's suspicions that there actually might be something to the claims. For instance, Michael Zimmerman in *Philosophy Today* argues that it's not "socially healthy" to ignore the abduction experience.

>> That the abduction phenomenon is frequently discussed in popular culture, but is largely ignored by establishment sources[,] is not socially healthy. By generally refusing even to acknowledge the fact that many people are suffering from the abduction phenomenon, much less to fund research to reveal its cause, establishment leaders invite the paranoid fringe to conclude that the "government" is not only covering up an alien presence, but worse still is somehow in league with it. Even the non-paranoid may ask why this phenomenon is not

examined more closely by those in a position to provide a satisfactory explanation of it (235).

Belief in alien abduction, no matter how crazy it seems, is a cultural phenomenon, and it's also a belief that Zimmerman observes is widely shared. To be dismissive of the claims not only might reinforce the "paranoid fringe" that believes in a cover-up but also is a missed opportunity to study the phenomenon itself—how is it that so many people can hold beliefs that seem utterly irrational?

Mississippian Calvin Parker Jr. is someone who reported an alien encounter 40 years ago, and he regretted reporting it until the day he died....

PROBLEM #3: THE KITCHEN SINK QUOTATION   The easiest thing to do with a quote you like is to use it all, to throw it all in your essay, kitchen sink and everything. But it's often far better to pare off the strongest and most relevant lines and passages and blend them into your own writing. To see how this might work, contrast the use of quotes in this paragraph and in the reworked paragraph that follows. I've underlined the quoted material so that you can visualize the difference between a passage that selectively uses a quotation and one that does not.

Passive Blending:

> Black Elk often spoke of the importance of the circle to American Indian culture. "You may have noticed that everything an Indian does is in a circle, and that is because the Power of the World always works in circles, and everything tries to be round.... The sky is round, and I have heard that the earth is round like a ball, and so are all the stars." He couldn't understand why white people lived in square houses. "It is a bad way to live, for there is not power in a square."

Here the quotes stand out, separate from the writer's own text, but in the revised paragraph they are worked smoothly into the writer's own prose:

Active Blending:

> Black Elk believed the "Power of the World always works in circles," noting the roundness of the sun, the earth, and the stars. He couldn't understand why white people live in square houses: "It is a bad way to live, for there is not power in a square."

Although long quotes, especially if unintegrated, should usually be avoided, occasionally it may be useful to include a long quotation from one of your sources. A quotation that is longer than four lines should be *blocked*, or set off from the rest of the text by indenting it an inch from the left margin. Like the rest of the paper, a blocked quotation is typed double-spaced. For example:

> According to Robert Karen, shame is a particularly modern phenomenon. He notes that in medieval times people pretty much let loose, and by our modern tastes, it was not a pretty sight:
>
> > Their emotional life appears to have been extraordinarily spontaneous and unrestrained. From Johan Huizinga's *The Waning of the Middle*

Ages, we learn that the average European town dweller was wildly erratic and inconsistent, murderously violent when enraged, easily plunged into guilt, tears, and pleas for forgiveness, and bursting with psychological eccentricities. He ate with his hands out of a common bowl, blew his nose on his sleeve, defecated openly by the side of the road, made love, and mourned with great passion, and was relatively unconcerned about such notions as maladjustment or what others might think.... In post-medieval centuries, what I've called situational shame spread rapidly....(61)

Note that quotation marks are dropped from a blocked quotation. In this case, only part of a paragraph was borrowed, but if you quote one or more full paragraphs, indent the first line of each a quarter inch in addition to the inch the block is indented from the left margin. Note, too, that the writer has introduced this long quote in a way that effectively ties it to his own paper.

We'll examine *parenthetical references* more fully in the next section, but notice how the citation in the blocked quotation is placed *after* the final period. That's a unique exception to the usual rule that a parenthetical citation is placed *before* the period of the borrowed material's final sentence.

Other Quick Tips for Controlling Quotations

From our discussion so far, you've seen the hazards and the benefits of using quotations. Quotations from your sources can definitely be overused, especially when they seem dumped into the draft, untouched and unexamined, or used as a lazy substitute for paraphrase. But when it's appropriate, bringing the voices of others into your own writing can bring the work to life and make readers feel as though there is a genuine conversation going on.

You've also seen some basics on how to handle quotes. Here are some specific tips for doing this effectively.

GRAFTING QUOTES Frequently, the best way to use quoted material is to graft it onto your own prose. Sometimes you just use a word or phrase:

Some words for hangover, like ours, refer prosaically to the cause: the Egyptians say they are "still drunk," the Japanese "two days drunk," the Chinese "drunk overnight."*

In other situations, especially when you want to add emphasis to what a source has said, you might give over parts of several sentences to a source, like this:

The makers of NoHang, on their Web page, say what your mother would: "It is recommended that you drink moderately and responsibly." At the same time, they tell you that with NoHang "you can drink the night away."*

*Acocella, Joan. "A Few Too Many." *The New Yorker,* 26 May 2008, pp. 32–37.

BILLBOARDING QUOTES   Another way you can control quotations is by adding emphasis to billboard parts of a particular quote. Typically you do this by italicizing the phrase or sentence. Here is an example, taken from the end of a block quotation:

> For the sake of Millennials—and, through them, the future of America—the most urgent adult task is to *elevate their expectations.* (Emphasis added) (Howe and Strauss 365)*

Notice that the parenthetical note signals that the original quote has been altered to add emphasis.

SPLICING QUOTES   Sometimes you want to prune away unnecessary information from a quotation to place emphasis on the part that matters most to you or to eliminate unnecessary information. Ellipsis points, those three dots (…) you sometimes see at the beginning, middle, or end of a sentence, signal that some information has been omitted.

Take this passage, for example:

> During the Gen-X child era, the American family endured countless new movements and trends—feminism, sexual freedom, a divorce epidemic, fewer G-rated movies, child-raising handbooks telling parents to "consider yourself" ahead of a child's needs, gay rights, Chappaquiddick, film nudity, a Zero Population Growth ethic, *Kramer vs. Kramer,* and *Roe v. Wade.* A prominent academic in 1969 proclaimed in the *Washington Post* that the family needed a "decent burial."

That's a pretty long list of movements and trends, and the reader could get a taste without being served up the whole thing. Ellipsis points can help:

> During the Gen-X child era, the American family endured countless new movements and trends—feminism, sexual freedom, a divorce epidemic…, [and a] prominent academic in 1969 proclaimed in the *Washington Post* that the family needed a "decent burial."

When you have to slightly reword the original text or alter the punctuation for a smoother splice, put the alteration in brackets. In the preceding example, for instance, I turned what was a separate sentence in the original into a compound sentence using the conjunction *and*.

HANDLING INTERVIEW MATERIAL   The great quotes you glean from your interviews can be handled like quotations from texts. But there's a dimension to a quote from an interview that's lacking in a quote from a book: Namely, you participated in the quote's creation by asking a question, and in some cases, you were there to observe your subject saying it. This presents some new choices. When you're quoting an interview subject, should you enter your essay as a

---

*Howe, Neil, and William Strauss. *Millennials Rising.* Vintage, 2000.

participant in the conversation, or should you stay out of the way? That is, should you describe yourself asking the question? Should you describe the scene of the interview, your subject's manner of responding, or your immediate reaction to what she said? Or should you merely report what was said and who said it? Either can work. Setting the scene for your interview by describing the situation in which it took place is often effective in exploratory essays, especially those that follow the narrator's journey investigating a question. Entering the essay as the questioner often makes sense in that kind of essay, too. But more often, what's important is what the interviewee said rather than the questioner's presence in the scene.

TRUSTING YOUR MEMORY   One of the best ways to weave references seamlessly into your own writing is to avoid the compulsion to stop and study your sources as you're writing the draft. I remember that writing my research papers in college was typically done in stops and starts. I'd write a paragraph of the draft, then stop and reread a photocopy of an article, then write a few more sentences, and then stop again. Part of the problem was the meager notes I took as I collected information. I hadn't really taken possession of the material before I started writing the draft. But I also didn't trust that I'd remember what was important from my reading.

If, during the course of your research and writing so far, you've found a sense of purpose—for example, you're pretty sure your paper is going to argue for legalization of marijuana or analyze the symbolism on old gravestones on Cape Cod—then you've probably read purposefully, too. You *will* likely know what reference sources you need as you write the draft, without sputtering to a halt to remind yourself of what each says. Consult your notes and sources as you need them; otherwise, push them aside, and immerse yourself in your own writing.

Citing Sources to Tell a Story

Writers of popular articles often use research, and they don't have to cite their sources; so why do academic writers? The simple answer is that scholarly researchers attempt to *build knowledge*, and this involves establishing who has said what before them on a topic. A more interesting way of looking at it is that through citation, academic writers tell a story, one that enlists some of the relevant actors on a research topic—who they were, what they said, what they found, where they agreed and disagreed—and from this, academic writers add their own narratives, extending the story these others started. In a way, then, citations are like the screen credits in a movie, except, of course, they don't come just at the end.

You'll be citing sources *in* your essay next to material that you borrowed, and these are keyed to references at the end of your essay.

There are three or four major citation systems, but the big two are the APA and the MLA. APA is the system of choice in the social sciences, whereas MLA is associated with the humanities. The big difference between the two is that APA emphasizes *when* something was published whereas MLA highlights *who* said it.

Before you begin writing your draft, go to Appendix A or B and read the sections under "Citing Sources in Your Essay." These will describe in some detail when and where you should put parenthetical references to borrowed material in the draft of your essay. Don't worry too much about the guidelines for preparing the final manuscript, including how to do the bibliography. You can deal with that next week.

Driving through the First Draft

You have an opening, a lot of material in your notes—much of it, written in your own words—and maybe an outline. You've considered some general methods of development, looked at ways to write with sources, and completed a quick course in how to cite them. Finish the week by writing through the first draft.

Writing the draft may be difficult. All writing, but especially research writing, is a recursive process. You may find sometimes that you must circle back to a step you took before, discovering a gap in your information, a new idea for a thesis statement, or a better lead or focus. Circling back may be frustrating at times, but it's natural and even a good sign: It means you're letting go of your preconceived ideas and allowing the discoveries you make *through writing* to change your mind.

It's too early to worry about writing a research paper that's airtight, with no problems to solve. Too often, student writers think they have to write a perfect paper in the first draft. You can worry about plugging holes and tightening things up next week. For now, write a draft, and if you must, put a reminder on a piece of paper and post it on the computer next to your thesis statement or research question. Look at this reminder every time you find yourself agonizing over the imperfections of your paper. The reminder should say, "It Doesn't Count."

Keep a few other things in mind while writing your first draft:

1. *Focus on your tentative thesis or your research question.* In the draft, consider your thesis a theory you're trying to prove but are willing to change. If your paper is more exploratory than argumentative, use your focusing question as a reminder of what you want to know. Remember, your question and thesis can change, too, as you learn more about your subject.
2. *Vary your sources.* Offer a variety of different sources as evidence to support your assertions. Beware of writing a single page that cites only one source.
3. *Remember your audience.* What do your readers want to know about your topic? What do they need to know to understand what you're trying to say?
4. *Write with your notes.* If you took thoughtful notes during the third week— carefully transforming another author's words into your own, flagging good quotes, and developing your own analysis—then you've already written at

least some of your paper. You may only need to fine-tune the language in your notes and then plug them into your draft.

5. *Be open to surprises.* The act of writing is often full of surprises. In fact, it should be, because *writing* is *thinking,* and the more you think about something, the more you're likely to see. You might get halfway through your draft and discover the part of your topic that *really* fascinates you. Should that happen, you may have to change your thesis or throw away your outline. You may even have to re-research your topic, at least somewhat. It's not necessarily too late to shift the purpose or focus of your paper (though you should consult your instructor before totally abandoning your topic at this point). Let your curiosity remain the engine that drives you forward.

Chapter 5
The Fifth Week

Learning Objectives

In this chapter, you'll learn to...

- Identify problems in your draft that involve purpose, thesis, question, or structure and apply revision strategies to address those problems.

- Learn techniques to find quick facts on the Web, and use those facts to fill factual gaps in your essay.

- Understand persona as a rhetorical concept, and analyze the persona in your draft.

- Identify problems with integrating sources, organizing paragraphs, and writing strong sentences, and apply techniques for rewriting and copyediting that address these problems.

- Analyze the appearance of your essay, and consider approaches to make it have a more reader-friendly design.

Seeing the "Triangleness" of the Draft

Nearly everyone who looks at this image immediately sees a triangle, a shape that is largely defined by black dots that anchor each corner. In the absence of the triangle, those dots would just be Pac-men figures or partially eaten pies. In other words, it is the "triangleness" of the image that influences how we interpret the dots: The whole helps us to see the parts. Written compositions work the same way. Readers should sense the triangleness of the draft—the idea, question, or claim that unites the piece and helps them to see the significance and relevance of all the parts—down to each paragraph and each sentence. Revision begins with making sure that triangle is what readers see.

But that's not usually how many of us revise. Instead, we become obsessed with focusing on the parts of a draft, tinkering with paragraphs, maybe cutting a sentence here and there. At best, we might reorder a few paragraphs. We often lose sight of the whole altogether.

In writing, we have ways of describing the triangleness of our drafts. We might talk about the controlling idea, thesis, or inquiry question around which the essay revolves. Or we might talk about the purpose of the essay: what it is trying to encourage readers to think, feel, or do. Knowing these things, writers go back to the parts of the draft and ask themselves whether the parts contribute in tangible ways to a reader's understanding of the whole.

This week we'll begin by focusing on the whole of your draft—your purpose, thesis, or research question—to see if the parts help your readers to see it clearly.

Revising for Readers: Writer- to Reader-Based Prose

Writing theorist Linda Flower distinguishes between "writer-based prose" and "reader-based prose." When we first start writing about something in notebooks, journals, and sometimes first drafts, we are our own audience. Sure, we might have a vague sense that someone else will be reading what we write, but often our energies are focused on whether it makes sense to us. "Writer-based prose" like this often works from the tacit assumption that readers and writers share the same understanding and knowledge about a topic. As a result, writers may assume that certain things that should be explained don't need to be. Writers may also assume that the things they find interesting or relevant will also be interesting or relevant to their readers. In "reader-based prose," writers have confronted these assumptions. They have revised their work with their readers in mind.

Reading anything is work. Most of us are willing to do the work if we sense that an author is taking us somewhere interesting. More specifically, readers must trust that writers know what they're doing, that the writers have a destination in mind, that they are reliable guides, and that the journey will likely yield something worth knowing or thinking about.

One way to see if your draft research essay is sufficiently "reader-based" is to determine whether it does three things that all essays must do (see Figure 5.1):

- **Have a clear purpose:** What exactly did you want to find out in this investigation of your topic? What is your research question?

- **Establish why the question (and its answer) are significant:** What stake might readers have in your inquiry?

- **Say one main thing:** Among the possible answers to the question you pose, which one seems most persuasive, most significant, or most revealing?

Figure 5.1 Three Things the Essay Must Do

As you revise your draft, first focus on the whole by asking the following global questions: *Is the question I'm asking clear and sufficiently limited? Have I answered the "So what?" question? Is there one most important thing I'm trying to say?* If your draft explicitly answers each of these, then the boat at least will float and have a clear destination.

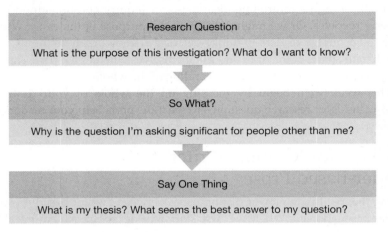

IS IT ORGANIZED AROUND A CLEAR PURPOSE? Purpose, like a torch, lights the way in the darkness. It illuminates one part of your subject, helping to guide your readers in the direction you want them to go. You should determine whether the purpose of your essay is clear and examine how well the information is organized around that purpose.

Presumably, by now you know the purpose of your essay. You know, for instance, whether you're exploring or arguing. But what exactly are you exploring or arguing? Your ability to state this purpose as clearly as you can is a great foundation for revision this week. Try completing one of the following sentences:

For an exploratory essay: The main purpose of my essay on _____ is to explore _____. In particular, I will consider the questions raised by _____ and _____ as well as _____.

For an argument essay: Because of _____ and _____ as well as _____, in this essay I am arguing _____.

Another way of getting at purpose is to clarify your research question, something that you were working on last week. Is it time to revise it again? For example, Amanda's piece on tooth whitening began with this research question: *How has cosmetic tooth-whitening changed the way Americans feel about their teeth?* After a few clarifications she made as she learned more, Amanda had this question: *How does the tooth-whitening trend reflect our culture's quickly changing definitions of beauty, and what does that mean for people who don't fit that definition?*

Go back to the beginning. What was your initial research question? What is it now? If you're struggling with this, revisit "Refining the Question" in Chapter 4, page 000.

Yet another way of checking purpose is to see whether in your draft your sources are all serving your purpose. Writing with research is a wrestling match. You're the 120-pound weakling who may not have written many college research essays before, trying to take on the heavyweight experts on your topic. You're fighting for your life, trying to use what these authorities say or think for your own purpose without getting slammed to the floor for meekly submitting a report rather than an essay. The challenge is to get control of the information, to muscle it to the ground using the strength of your purpose. Establishing this control is one of the hardest parts of drafting research papers. Two extreme responses to this problem are giving up entirely and turning your paper over to your sources (letting them do all the talking) and pretending that you're not really wrestling with anyone and writing a paper that includes only your own opinions. Neither option is what you want.

Who won the wrestling match in your draft? To what extent did you have a coherent purpose and succeed in using other people's ideas and information in the service of your purpose? One way to see who is getting the upper hand in the draft is to mark it up, noting where you've given control to your sources and where you've taken it back. Exercise 5.1 can graphically illustrate who is winning the wrestling match. To what extent is your purpose in the essay enabling you to *use* the information you've gathered to explore your research question or prove your point? The exercise will also reveal how well you've managed to surround your research with your own analysis, interpretations, arguments, and questions.

DOES IT ESTABLISH SIGNIFICANCE?   So what? That's the blunt question here. Any reader will need a *reason* to care about what you have to say. So what reasons might there be for someone to care about a research essay on theories of intelligence, or an investigation of video game addiction, or an argument about what should be done about dog poop in city parks? In other words, what stake might readers have in the question you are exploring? Your mother will think nearly anything you write is significant. But what might make someone else consider that you have important things to say? Here are five possible reasons. Do any apply to your draft and, if so, do you emphasize the significance of your inquiry enough?

Readers may find your discussion of a topic significant if:

1. **It raises questions they want to know the answers to.** As a pet owner, I'm interested in theories of dog training because Fred digs in the garden.
2. **It helps them to see what they've seen before in a way they haven't seen it.** Is the destruction of jack pines in Yellowstone National Park really being caused by global warming and not the drought, as I had assumed?

Exercise 5.1

WRESTLING WITH THE DRAFT*

For this exercise you'll use two highlighters, each a different color.

1. Choose a random page or two of your draft, somewhere in the middle.
2. First mark the parts in which you're a less active author. As you read the page, highlight every sentence that reports facts, quotes sources, or otherwise presents information or ideas that belong to someone else.
3. Now, using the other highlighter, mark the parts in which you're a more active author. Read the same page or pages again, but this time highlight every sentence or paragraph that represents *your* ideas, analysis, commentary, interpretation, definition, synthesis, or claims.

4. Repeat the previous steps with two more pages of your draft.

Which color dominates? Are you turning over too much of the text to your sources? Are you ignoring them and rattling on too much about what you think? Or does your source use seem appropriate to support your purpose?

In addition, look at the pattern of color. What do you notice about this pattern? Are you taking turns paragraph by paragraph with your sources, or is your own analysis and commentary nicely blended *within* paragraphs so that the information is always anchored to your own thoughts? Do you surround quoted passages with your own voice and analysis? Who wins the wrestling match? See Figure 5.2 for an example of this exercise.

Figure 5.2
Amanda Wins the Wrestling Match

The sections of text highlighted in blue are passages from Amanda's sources, and the sections highlighted in blue are passages in which she is commenting, clarifying, asserting, or interpreting. Notice the balance between white and blue. Clearly Amanda has a strong authorial presence. Also notice how quotations are surrounded by her commentary. By controlling quotations like this, she is also using rather than being used by her sources.

Our tooth whiteners are safer, and a study by James W. Curtis, DMD, discovered that bleaching through carbamide peroxide actually decreases the amount of plaque on teeth, but we're still doing it for beauty reasons rather than health ones (Nuss 28).

In her article "Bright On," Molly Prior notes that Procter & Gamble and Colgate-Palmolive revolutionized the whitening industry by bringing over-the-counter whiteners to drugstores everywhere at the turn of the twenty-first century (39). No longer did people have to pay high prices for professional whitening—they could do it themselves, at home, for a reasonable cost. In the past, a patient had to eat a bill of $1,000 for a laser whitening treatment, or $10,000 for a full set of veneers; now a package of Crest Whitestrips retails for only $29.99 (Gideonse). Suddenly, whiter teeth were available to everyone. While a shining smile once indicated wealth and the ability to splurge on cosmetic dentistry, it became affordable to the dentally discolored masses eager to emulate the lifestyles of the people they saw in magazines and on television.

Companies didn't create whitening products to fill a demand created by the public for whiter teeth. While Hollywood glitterati did pay high prices for iconic smiles, most people seemed happy with functional teeth. However, companies saw money to be made in creating a whiter norm for teeth, so they barraged the airwaves with advertisements featuring people complaining about the dullness and imperfection of their teeth. Natural teeth were denigrated as ugly. Crest and Colgate-Palmolive wanted to make money, so they appealed to the American obsession with beauty to secure a financial reason to smile. As Jonathan Levine, DDS, notes, "It's lately seeming much harder to go broke by overestimating the vanity of the American public" (Walker). The companies succeeded in making mouthfuls of money, netting $450 million and getting 45 percent of Americans to try some form of whitening (Prior 42). In effect, they appealed to our egos to get to our pocket books.

* This exercise is adapted from one I borrowed from my colleague Dr. Mike Mattison, who borrowed it from his former colleagues at the University of Massachusetts–Amherst. Thanks to all.

3. **It amplifies what they may already know and care about, leading to new learning.** I play video games and know they're habit forming, but I didn't know the effects on my brain of my playing them.

4. **It moves them emotionally.** The story of the Syrian refugee crisis and its impact on children is heartbreaking. Something should be done about it. But what?

5. **It takes a surprising point of view.** The research leads you to believe that decriminalizing marijuana will actually reduce its use.

You should be able to read your draft and see exactly where you establish the significance of your project to your readers, perhaps touching on one or more of the five reasons listed. Is this content sufficient or is there more you might say?

DOES IT SAY ONE THING?   When I write an exploratory essay, I'm essentially in pursuit of a point and, not infrequently, it playfully eludes me. Just when I think I've figured out exactly what I'm trying to say, I have the nagging feeling that it's not quite right—it's too simplistic or obvious, it doesn't quite account for the evidence I've collected, or it just doesn't capture the spirit of the discoveries I've made. A thesis is often a slippery fish—just when I think I've figured out what I think, I start to think something else.

A thesis can present different problems in an argumentative essay. As we saw in the last chapter, it can become a club—rigid and unyielding—that we use to beat a draft into submission. Yet, the reason to do research is to *test* your ideas about things, and as your draft evolves, so should your thesis.

Now is a good time to consider revising your thesis again. Does it accurately capture what you're trying to say—or *think* you're trying to say? Is it specific enough? Is it interesting? If you need to, return to "Refining the Thesis" on page 000 in Chapter 4 to rework your main idea.

USING A READER   One writer described revision as "conversation repair." When you rewrite to make your ideas clear to others, you look to see how well you're holding up your end of a dialogue with someone who you hope will be as interested as you are in your subject. You can make this conversation real rather than imagined by inviting feedback on your draft.

Your instructor may be that reader, or you might exchange drafts with someone else in class. You may already have someone whom you share your writing with—a roommate, a friend. Whomever you choose, try to find a reader who will respond honestly *and* make you want to write again.

What will be most helpful from a reader at this stage? Comments about your spelling and mechanics are not critical right now. You'll deal with those factors later. For now, the most useful feedback will focus on whether there's a disconnect between what you *intend* in your draft and how a reader understands those intentions.

Exercise 5.2

DIRECTING THE READER'S RESPONSE

Consider two approaches to getting feedback. The first invites readers to identify what they think is the draft's purpose and point. The other gauges your readers' interest in what you have to say.

Feedback on Purpose and Point

After reading your draft, invite readers to address the following questions. You might consider asking them to fastwrite their first thoughts about each question before discussing it with you.

1. After reading the draft, what would you say is the main question the paper is trying to answer or focus on?
2. In your own words, what is the main point?
3. What did you learn about the topic after reading the paper that you didn't fully appreciate *before* you read it? Is this something you find significant or interesting? If so, why?

How your reader responds to the first two questions will tell you a lot about how well you've succeeded in making the purpose and thesis of your paper clear. The answer to the third question will too, but it may also tell you whether you've established the significance of your project.

Feedback on Reader Interest

Wouldn't it be helpful to know how the parts of your draft are working to keep readers engaged in what you're trying to say? For this exercise, number each paragraph in the draft, and then download a template for graph paper into Word. You'll find these online. Next, create a graph like the one that follows.

The vertical axis is a measure of reader interest, with "1" being low and "5" being high. The horizontal axis corresponds to the paragraph numbers in your draft. While you read the draft to your peer reviewers (or they read it to themselves), ask them to rate each paragraph based on how interesting they find the information or the ideas.

What might this tell you? Consistent patterns in reader interest tell you which parts of the draft are working and which aren't working, at least in terms of reader engagement with your writing. This is particularly valuable if you can actually ask your readers why they found some parts better than others. But even if you can't have a conversation, you at least have an idea about what parts to focus on first in revision.

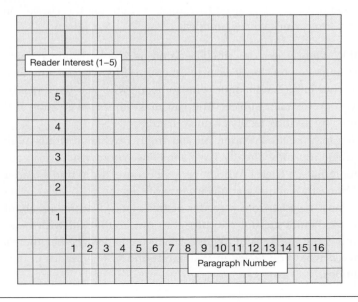

Reviewing the Structure

In addition to focusing on your paper in terms of its purpose, thesis, and reader interest, this global revision is also about focusing on structure. If you did Exercise 5.1, you've already begun to take a closer look at the structure of your essay. There are various other ways of focusing on structure, including using your thesis.

USING YOUR THESIS TO REVISE   The payoff for crafting a stronger thesis is huge. As you will see in Exercise 5.3, a thesis can help you decide what to put in your essay and what to leave out, and in research-based writing, this is a decision that comes up again and again.

Examining the Wreckage   In Exercise 5.3, you will wield your scissors on your draft, breaking it into pieces. Now you can see how the parts relate to the whole and the whole to the parts.

To your horror, you may find that your "reject" pile of paragraphs is bigger than your "save" pile. If that's the case, you won't have much left to work with. You may need to reresearch the topic (returning to the library or going online this week to collect more information) or shift the focus of your paper. Perhaps both. But even if your cut-and-paste goes well, you will likely need to do more research this week to fill the gaps you found. That's perfectly normal.

Exercise 5.3

THE FRANKENSTEIN DRAFT

Try this cut-and-paste revision exercise (a useful technique inspired by Peter Elbow and his book *Writing with Power**):

1. On a notecard or sticky note, write your focusing question, thesis, or main idea. Make sure that it is plainly stated and fully captures what you think you're trying to say or explore in your research essay. Set it aside.
2. Photocopy or print two copies of your first draft (one-sided pages only). Save the original; you may need it later.
3. Cut apart a copy of your research paper, paragraph by paragraph. (You may cut it into even smaller pieces later.) Once the draft has

been completely disassembled, shuffle the paragraphs—get them wildly out of order so the original draft is just a memory.

4. Retrieve the notecard or sticky note with your thesis on it, and set it before you. Now work your way through the stack of paragraphs and make two new stacks: one of paragraphs that are relevant to your thesis or question and one of paragraphs that don't seem relevant, that don't seem to serve a clear purpose in developing your main idea or question. Be as tough as a drill sergeant as you scrutinize each scrap of paper. What you are trying to determine is whether each piece of information, each paragraph, is there for

* Elbow, Peter. *Writing with Power*. Oxford University Press, 1981.

a reason. Ask yourself this question as you examine each paragraph:

> *Does this paragraph (or part of a paragraph) develop my thesis or address my question and further the purpose of my paper, or does it seem an unnecessary tangent that could be part of another paper with a different focus?*

For example,

- Does it provide important *evidence* that supports my main point?
- Does it *explain* something that's key to understanding what I'm trying to say?
- Does it *illustrate* a key concept?
- Does it help establish the *importance* of what I'm trying to say?
- Does it raise (or answer) a *question* that I must explore, given what I'm trying to say?

You might find it helpful to write on the back of each relevant paragraph which of these specific purposes it serves. You may also discover that *some* of the information in a paragraph seems to serve your purpose whereas the rest strikes you as unnecessary. Use your scissors to cut away the irrelevant material, pruning back the paragraph to include only what's essential.

5. You now have two stacks of paper scraps: those that seem to support your thesis or research question and serve your purpose and those that don't. For now, set aside your "reject" pile. Begin to reassemble a rough draft using what you've saved. Play with order. Try new leads, new ends, new middles. As you spread out the pieces of information before you, see if a new structure suddenly emerges. *But especially, look for gaps—places where you should add information.* On a piece of paper, jot down ideas for material you might add; then cut up this paper as well and insert these in the appropriate places. You may rediscover uses for information in your "reject" pile as well. Mine that pile, if you need to.

6. As a structure begins to emerge, reassemble the draft by taping together the fragments of paper, including the ideas for new information and any rejects you've decided to use after all. Don't worry about transitions; you'll deal with those later. When you're done with the reconstruction, the draft might look totally unlike the version you started with.

To your satisfaction, you may discover that your reconstructed draft looks familiar. You may return to the structure you started with in the first draft. If that's the case, it might mean your first draft worked pretty well; breaking it down and putting it back together confirmed that and showed you where you might need to prune and fine-tune.

When Jeff cut up his essay "The Alcoholic Family," he discovered immediately that much of his paper did not seem clearly related to his point about the role outsiders can play in helping the family of an alcoholic. His "reject" pile had paragraph after paragraph of information about the roles that other family members take on when there's an alcoholic in the house. Jeff asked himself, What does that information have to do with the roles of outsiders? He considered changing his thesis to say something about how each family member plays a role in dealing with the drinker. But Jeff's purpose in writing the paper was to discover what *he*, as an outsider, could do to help.

As Jeff played with the pieces of his draft, he began to see two things. First of all, he realized that some of the ways members behave in an alcoholic family make them resistant to outside help; this insight allowed him to salvage some information from his "reject" pile by more clearly connecting the information to his main point. Second, Jeff knew he had to go back to the well: He needed to return to the library and recheck his sources to find more information on what family friends can do to help.

When you slice up your draft and play with the pieces, you are experimenting with the basic architecture of your essay. If the result is going to hold up, certain fundamentals must be in place. You need to be transforming your draft in a direction that is making it more reader based, with a clear purpose, significance, and point.

OTHER WAYS OF REVIEWING THE STRUCTURE Exercise 5.3, "The Frankenstein Draft," invited you to experiment with the organization of your draft by disassembling and then rebuilding your essay, imagining different ways to order information. Its starting point was the thesis. There are other starting points for an examination of structure. A few of these alternative starting points follow.

Type of Essay. The structure of a research essay is partly a function of the type of essay—of whether you are writing an exploratory or an argumentative essay. Depending on the type of essay you're writing, return to Figure 4.2 or 4.3 in the last chapter for an idea about how to organize your paper.

Lead. How you begin your paper has a huge influence on how it develops from there. As we discussed in Chapter 4, a lead or introduction should not only draw readers in but also dramatize or introduce the dilemma, problem, question, or argument that is the focus of your inquiry. You might find a stronger lead buried in the middle of your draft. Try it as an alternative introduction and follow it from there.

Logical Structure. In a general sense, most writing can be said to be structured by either narrative or argumentative logic, something we looked at in the last chapter. But there are other descriptions of patterns of development, too, including the following:

- Thesis to proof
- Problem to solution
- Question to answer
- Comparison and contrast
- Cause and effect, or effect and cause
- Known to unknown or unknown to known
- Simple to complex

Review your draft with these possible structures in mind. You may see a way to strengthen it by reshaping its structure to better fit one of these structures. Remember that although your research essay might generally use one of the logical structures, often a piece of writing that generally uses one structure uses others as microstructures. For example, an essay that has a comparison-and-contrast structure might have elements of narrative.

Reresearching

I know. You thought you were done digging. But as I said last week, research is a recursive process. (Remember, the word is *research,* or "look again.") You will often find yourself circling back to the previous steps as you get a clearer sense of where you want to go. I want to emphasize this. It's actually *unusual,* after you've written a draft, to discover that you're done with research. This means returning to the library databases, trying a different Google Scholar search, going back to interview someone, or returning to the field for more observations. You've got the skills now to do this. Make time for it.

As you stand back from your draft, looking again at how well your research paper addresses your research question or thesis, you'll likely see holes in the information. They may seem more like craters. Jeff discovered he had to reresearch his topic, returning to the library to hunt for new sources to help him develop his point. Because he had enough time, he repeated some of the research steps from the third week. This time, though, he knew exactly what he needed to find.

You may find that you basically have the information you need but that your draft requires more development. Candy's draft on how child abuse affects language included material from some useful studies from the *Journal of Speech and Hearing Disorders,* which showed pretty conclusively that abuse cripples children's abilities to converse. At her reader's suggestion, Candy decided it was important to write more in her revision about what was learned from the studies because they offered convincing evidence for her thesis. Though she could mine her notes for more information, Candy decided to recheck the journal databases to look for any similar studies she may have missed.

Finding Quick Facts

If you're lucky, the holes of information in your research paper draft will not be large at all. What's missing may be an important but discrete fact that would really help your readers understand the point you're making. For example, when Janabeth looked over her draft on the impact of divorce on father–daughter relationships, she realized she was missing an important fact: the number of marriages that end in divorce in the United States. This single piece of information could help establish the significance of the problem she was writing about. And Janabeth could obtain it by simply looking online.

One of the Internet's greatest strengths is its usefulness in searching for specific facts. What are the ingredients in a Big Mac? How high is the Great Wall of China? How many high school kids in Illinois go on to college? What does a map of Brazilian deforestation look like? A quick click or two and the Web can yield a rich harvest of facts and information. Google and similar search engines are naturally where we start looking for that kind of information, and because what you want to know is pretty specific, there's a good chance you'll find what you're looking for. But there are some particularly useful statistical references on the Web that you might want to check out as well.

Facts on the Web

General

- *American Factfinder* (http://factfinder2.census.gov). A rich site maintained by the U.S. Bureau of the Census. It includes data on population and economic trends, both national and local.
- *FedStats* (https://fedstats.sites.usa.gov/). A superstore of statistical resources that allows users to find information from all U.S. government agencies.
- *STATS America* (http://www.statsamerica.org). Search page allows users to find a range of data for states and counties in the United States, including facts on demographics, economics, education, and the workforce.

Subject Specific

Crime

- *National Criminal Justice Reference Service* (http://www.ncjrs.gov). Allows keyword searches to find not just facts but articles on crime, drug abuse, corrections, juvenile justice, and more.

Education

- *National Center for Educational Statistics* (http://nces.ed.gov). The U.S. Department of Education site includes statistics on everything related to schooling in the United States and also features an annual report on the state of education.

Economics

- *Bureau of Economic Analysis* (http://www.bea.gov/). This U.S. Department of Commerce site includes statistics on key economic indicators, trade, corporate profits, and much more.

Energy

- *U.S. Energy Information Administration* (http://www.eia.doe.gov/). Includes use forecasts, environmental impacts, reserves, alternative energy information, and much more.

Health

- *National Center for Health Statistics* (http://www.cdc.gov/nchs). Offers information about injuries, diseases, lifestyles, death rates, and more provided by the Centers for Disease Control.

International

- *U.N. Food and Agricultural Organization* (http://www.fao.org/corp/statistics/en/). The Food and Agricultural Organization site allows users to search not just for statistics on food and hunger but also for information on such topics as world forestry practices and water issues.
- *NationMaster* (http://www.nationmaster.com). Drawing in part from the *CIA Factbook* and United Nations information, Nation-Master will also generate interesting maps and graphics on a wide range of subjects.

In addition to these Web resources, the standard print texts for researchers hunting down facts and statistics are still quite useful. They include the *Statistical Abstracts of the United States,* the *Information Please Almanac, Facts on File,* and the *World Almanac Book of Facts*—all published annually. A number of these are now available on the Web.

Like the online sources mentioned, these fact books can be especially valuable resources when you need to plug small holes in your draft. But even if you're not sure whether you can glean a useful statistic from one of these sources, they might be worth checking anyway. There's a good chance you'll find something useful.

Local Revision: Revising for Language

Most of my students have the impression that revision begins and ends with concerns about language—that it's about *how* they say it rather than *what* they say. Revising for language is really a tertiary concern (though an important one) to be addressed after the writer has dealt with global revision: clear purpose, significance, and thesis as well as structure.

Once you're satisfied that your paper's purpose is clear, that it provides readers with the information they need to understand what you're trying to say, and that it is organized in a logical, interesting way, *then* focus your attention on the fine points of *how* it is written. Begin with voice.

Who Are You in Your Draft?

Yesterday was Halloween here in Boise, Idaho, and I made numerous costume sightings on campus: a yellow dog, a Red Sox player, and a weird guy with a sword. This is a holiday that celebrates alternate personas, masking our usual identities and trying out others. To some extent we do this when we write, too. We imagine the kind of person we're supposed to be in a piece of writing, assumptions that may arise from our understanding of what's expected in the genre we're writing in or the audience we're writing for. But just as often, we adopt personas in writing purely out of habit: "This is how I write for school." Of all the writing assignments in college, the research paper might be the most plagued by unexamined assumptions about how it's "supposed to" sound.

However, persona in writing is a rhetorical choice, just like deciding to write a letter instead of a memo to a close friend. How do you decide on the persona that's appropriate for this essay?

1. Ask your instructor.
2. Consider your purpose. What are you trying *to do* and *to whom* are you trying to speak?
3. How much does your intended audience know about your topic? Typically, more expert audiences expect a more formal tone and treatment than do less knowledgeable audiences.
4. Consider the genre. Are there established conventions on persona that you might need to follow?

Managing Persona Through Diction and Style

If you have a Facebook account, you already know how to manage a persona. In school writing, it's not all that different—you may not be able to post a new profile pic, but you can control your diction and your point of view. We've already talked about point of view in the last chapter (see page 000): Will you write your essay in the first-person singular? The decision to write, "I'm convinced that professional cycling is a corrupt sport" is different from the decision to write, "This paper argues that it's corrupt" or "One believes that it's corrupt." The latter two variations create a more distanced, "objective" persona. But there are also somewhat subtler ways of managing persona in your writing. Consider, for example, the following different ways the same sentence might be written by controlling word choice and style:

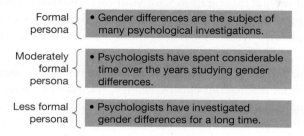

You might notice the following differences in each version:

1. **Passive or active voice:** "Gender differences are the subject of investigations" vs. "*Psychologists* have investigated gender differences." Passive voice is more formal. (See page 162 for more discussion of active voice in writing.)
2. **Level of style:** The phrase "have spent considerable time" is more formal than the phrase "for a long time."
3. **Verb choice:** "Investigated" is a slightly livelier (and less formal) verb than "studied."

Beware, though, of a voice that calls more attention to itself than to the substance of what you're saying.

Sometimes, in an attempt to sound natural, a writer will take on a folksy or overly colloquial voice, which is much worse than sounding dry and flat. What impression does the following passage have on you?

> The thing that really blew my mind was that marijuana use among college students had actually declined in the past ten years! I was psyched to learn that.

Tightening the Seams Between What You Say and What They Say

One of the basic challenges of writing with sources is integrating them seamlessly. In the past, you may have practiced the "data dump" strategy, or simply dropped factual information into your papers in little or big clumps. Of course, this won't do. Not only does it make the writing horribly dull, but it means that you're not *making use* of the information you worked so hard to find. Surrounding your sources with your own prose and according to your own purposes is an important skill you need to learn, and it's something we discussed at length in Chapter 4 (see "The Weave of Research Writing" on page 126) and looked at in Exercise 5.1 previously in this chapter.

In particular, think about the following points:

- **Find your own way of saying things.** This is one of the best ways to take possession of information.
- **Surround factual information with your own analysis.** Provide a context for any quotation you use. Comment on the significance of a fact or statistic. Look for ways to connect any information to your research question or thesis.
- **Make analogies or comparisons.** Is something like something else? Advocates for addressing climate change, for example, have used an extended analogy of a bathtub to illustrate how easy it is to ignore a problem until it's too late. You start the water running, get involved in, say, a computer game, and then have to decide when to check whether the tub is full. How long do you wait? What goes into this calculation?

VERBAL GESTURES Remember Burke's metaphor for the knowledge-making process (see pages 000–000)? He imagined a parlor full of people having an ongoing conversation about what might be true—arguing, agreeing, raising questions, suggesting new ideas, critiquing old ideas, everyone trying to push the conversation along. Any roomful of people in a conversation about things that cause disagreement is also a roomful of gestures. People wave off a point. They nod in assent. They raise a single finger to raise a new question or make a new point. They invite someone to step forward to speak and ask another to step aside.

Similarly, an essay that is a writer's conversation with others about a question that matters to all of them also includes words and phrases that serve as verbal gestures. Some are gestures that invite some people in the room to provide *background* on the question so that everyone understands what has already been said. Other gestures signal *analysis,* or a closer examination and critique of something someone said. Sometimes these verbal gestures signify *speculation;* the writer isn't quite sure what to think for sure, but maybe....Or they might indicate *agreement* or *disagreement*—the writer is taking sides with a particular idea, position, or way of seeing.

Consider whether verbal gestures like these will help you manage the conversation about your topic. Go through your draft, and identify those moments in which you seem to be providing background, analyzing something, agreeing or disagreeing, or speculating. Might some of the following language help you signpost that material?

Background

Among the most important voices on _____, the most relevant to this inquiry are _____.

Most people _____.

The major sources of controversy are _____.

One idea emerges again and again, and it's _____.

Like most people, I believed that _____.

The unanswered questions are _____.

This much is clear: _____.

_____'s most important contribution is _____.

Most relevant is _____.

Analysis

The most relevant point is _____.

In comparison,...

In contrast,...

What is most convincing is _____.

What is least convincing is _____.

What's most interesting is _____.

The surprising connection is _____.

Paradoxically,...

Actually,...

What isn't clear is _____.

Speculation

Perhaps...

Maybe...

It's possible that _____.

Agreement and Disagreement

Indeed,...

Obviously,...

Alternatively,...

Although others have argued that _____, I think _____.

On balance, the most convincing idea is _____.

What _____ has failed to consider is _____.

The more important question is _____.

Based on my research, _____.

A better explanation is _____.

It's hard to argue with _____.

What I understand now that I didn't understand before is _____.

Scrutinizing Paragraphs

IS EACH PARAGRAPH UNIFIED?   Each paragraph should be about one idea and organized around that idea. You probably know that already. But applying this notion is a particular problem in a research paper, where information abounds and paragraphs sometimes approach marathon length.

If any of your paragraphs seem too long (say, over a page or even verging on a page), look for ways to break them up into shorter paragraphs. Is more than one idea embedded in the long version? Are you explaining or examining more than one thing?

Even short paragraphs can lack unity, so look at those, too. Do any present minor or tangential ideas that belong somewhere else? Are any of the ideas irrelevant? In other words, should the information in the paragraph be moved into another paragraph of your paper, or should the paragraph just be cut? The cut-and-paste exercise (Exercise 5.3) may have helped you with this already.

Scrutinizing Sentences

USING ACTIVE VOICE   Which of these two sentences seems more passive, more lifeless?

Steroids are used by many high school athletes.

or

Many high school athletes use steroids.

The first version, written in the passive voice, is clearly the limper of the two. It's not grammatically incorrect; in fact, you may have found texts written in the passive voice to be pervasive in the reading you've done for your research paper. Research writing is plagued by passive voice, and that's one of the reasons it can be so mind-numbing to read.

Passive voice construction is easy to understand: The subject of the sentence is not the thing *doing the action* of the verb but, rather, the thing *acted upon* by the verb. For instance, in the following pair, the *active voice* sentence has as its subject Clarence, who does the action of kicking, but the passive sentence has the dog as the subject, which was kicked:

Clarence kicked the dog.

versus

The dog was kicked by Clarence.

Sometimes in passive sentences, the subject of the corresponding active sentence may be missing altogether, as in:

The study was released.

Who or *what* released it?

If you have passive sentences, you can remedy the problem by using *active voice* to place the doer of the action up front in the sentence or adding a doer if one is missing. For example:

> Many high school athletes use steroids.

A telltale sign of passive voice is that it usually requires a form of the verb *to be* (*is, was, are, were, am, be, being, been*). For example:

> Alcoholism among women <u>has been</u> extensively studied.

Search your draft for *be's,* and see if any sentences are written in the passive voice. (Some word-processing programs will search for you.) Unless this is a sentence that is more appropriate in passive voice, make the passive sentence active. To make a sentence active, move its doer from after the verb into the subject position or supply the appropriate doer if the sentence doesn't have one.

USING STRONG VERBS   Though this may seem like nitpicking, you'd be amazed how much writing in the active voice can revitalize research writing. The use of strong verbs can have the same effect.

As you know, verbs make things happen. Some verbs can create the difference between a sentence that crackles and one that merely hums. Instead of this:

> The study *suggested* that the widespread assumption that oral sex is common among American teenagers might be wrong.

write this:

> The study *shattered* the common belief that American teens increasingly indulge in oral sex.

Just because you're writing about other people's ideas doesn't mean you can't use strong verbs. See the box "Verbs for Discussing Ideas" on the following page, which was compiled by a colleague of mine, Cinthia Gannett. If you're desperate for an alternative to *says* or *argues,* check out the 135 alternatives this box offers.

VARYING SENTENCE LENGTH   Here's part of a research essay on the promise of wind energy. When you read it, I think you'll find the writing choppy. What's going on? One way to understand the problem is to count the number of syllables in each sentence. That's the number in the parentheses.

> The idea of alternative energy is sweeping the country and numerous other developed nations. (29) People are beginning to recycle more plastic and metals. (16) They are also more interested in energy efficiency. (16) Wind energy is among the renewable resources sprouting up around the United States. (25) Wind energy affects the environment, wildlife, society, humans, and politics. (23)

It's not hard to see that the sentence length, measured by syllables, doesn't vary much. There are three sentences in the passage that run between

23 and 29 syllables, and the others both have 16. In addition, the structure of these sentences doesn't vary much. Each has just one main clause. Prose that doesn't vary much in sentence length or structure is invariably boring to read. So what can you do about it?

Verbs for Discussing Ideas			
accepts	critiques	implies	refutes
acknowledges	declares	infers	regards
adds	defends	informs	rejects
admires	defies	initiates	relinquishes
affirms	demands	insinuates	reminds
allows	denies	insists	repudiates
analyzes	describes	interprets	resolves
announces	determines	intimates	responds
answers	diminishes	judges	retorts
argues	disagrees	lists	reveals
assaults	disconfirms	maintains	reviews
assembles	discusses	marshals	seeks
asserts	disputes	narrates	sees
assists	disregards	negates	shares
believes	distinguishes	observes	shifts
buttresses	emphasizes	outlines	shows
categorizes	endorses	parses	simplifies
cautions	enumerates	perceives	states
challenges	exaggerates	persists	stresses
claims	experiences	persuades	substitutes
clarifies	experiments	pleads	suggests
compares	explains	points out	summarizes
complicates	exposes	postulates	supplements
concludes	facilitates	praises	supplies
condemns	formulates	proposes	supports
confirms	grants	protects	synthesizes
conflates	guides	provides	tests
confronts	handles	qualifies	toys with
confuses	hesitates	quotes	treats
considers	highlights	ratifies	uncovers
contradicts	hints	rationalizes	urges
contrasts	hypothesizes	reads	verifies
convinces	identifies	reconciles	warns
criticizes	illuminates	reconsiders	

SOURCE: Reproduced with permission of Cinthia Gannett.

- **Vary sentence length.** Do a syllable count on a paragraph in your draft that seems clunky, and you'll probably find that you need to vary sentence length. Develop the instinct to follow a long sentence, for example, with a short, punchy one from time to time.

- **Combine sentences.** This often works wonders. Can you use punctuation or conjunctions like *or, but,* and *and* to join separate sentences together? For example, you might take this sequence of sentences in the passage on wind energy:

  People are beginning to recycle more plastic and metals. (16) They are also more interested in energy efficiency. (16)

  and revise it through sentence combining to read like this:

  People are beginning to recycle more plastic and metals, and they're also more interested in energy efficiency. (32)

Notice that you now have a compound sentence. In varying length, you'll often also be varying structure.

EDITING FOR SIMPLICITY   Somewhere, many of us got the idea that simplicity in writing is a vice—that the long word is better than the short word, that the complex phrase is superior to the simple one. The misconception is that to write simply is to be simpleminded. Research papers, especially, suffer from this mistaken notion. They are often filled with what writer William Zinsser calls *clutter.*

AVOIDING STOCK PHRASES   A place to begin cutting unnecessary clutter in your essay is to hack away at stock phrases. Like many types of writing, the language of the college research paper is littered with words and phrases that find their way to the page as inevitably as drinking root beer prompted my 12-year-old daughter and her friends to hold burping contests. In each case, the one just

Exercise 5.4

CUTTING CLUTTER

The following passage is an example of cluttered writing at its best (worst?). It contains phrases and words that often appear in college research papers. Read the passage once. Then take a few minutes and rewrite it, cutting as many words as you can without sacrificing the meaning. Look for ways to substitute a shorter word for a longer one and to say in fewer words what is currently said in many. Try to cut the word count by half.

The implementation of the revised alcohol policy in the university community is regrettable at the present time due to the fact that the administration has not facilitated sufficient student input, in spite of the fact that there have been attempts by the people affected by this policy to make their objections known in many instances.
(55 words)

seems to inspire the other. Following is a list of stock phrases that I often find in research papers. There is nothing grammatically wrong with these. It's simply that they are old, tired phrases, and you can say the same thing more freshly and with fewer words. Look for them in your draft and then edit them out.

Tired Phrases	Better Alternatives
Due to the fact that ...	Because ...
At this point in time, ...	Now ...
In my opinion, ...	(Unnecessary. We know it's your opinion.)
A number of ...	Many ... / Some ...
A number of studies point to the fact that ...	Many/Some researchers conclude (or argue) ...
In the event of ...	If ...
In today's society ...	Today we ...
In conclusion, ...	(Omit. If you're at the end of the paper, you're probably concluding.)
Until such time as ...	Until ...
Referred to as ...	Called ...
It should be pointed out that ...	(Omit. You are pointing it out.)
Is in a position to ...	Can
It is a fact that ...	(Omit. Just state the fact, ma'am.)
It may be said that ...	(Omit. Just say it.)
There can be little doubt that ...	It's likely ...
It is possible that ...	Perhaps ...

Preparing the Final Manuscript

I wanted to title this section "Preparing the Final Draft," but it occurred to me that *draft* doesn't suggest anything final. I always call my work a draft because until it's out of my hands, it never feels finished. You may feel that way, too. You've spent 5 weeks on this paper—and the last few days, disassembled it and put it back together again. How do you know when you're finally done?

For many students, the deadline dictates that: The paper is due, say, tomorrow. But you may find that your paper really seems to be coming together in a satisfying way. You may even like it, and you're ready to prepare the final manuscript.

Considering a "Reader-Friendly" Design

As consumers of texts these days—especially online—we are constantly influenced by visual rhetoric even if we aren't aware of it. "Eye-tracking" studies, for example, suggest that there is a sequence in how we look at a Web page: Most readers typically read a Web page in an upside-down "L" pattern, reading across the top of the page and then down the left side. Print advertisers are also acutely aware of visual rhetoric for obvious reasons; text works better with images if they are designed to work together.

A research essay like the one you're working on right now would seem to have little to do with visual rhetoric. The form of an academic paper, particularly if the emphasis is on the text—and it usually is—seems largely prescribed by the Modern Language Association or the American Psychological Association. Some papers in the social sciences, for example, require certain sections (abstract, introduction, discussion of method, presentation of results, and discussion of results), and these sections need to be clearly defined with subheadings, making it easy for readers to examine the parts they're most interested in. You probably discovered that in your own reading of formal research. You'll likely learn the formats research papers should conform to in various disciplines as you take upper-level courses in those fields.

Although you should document your paper properly, you may have some freedom to develop a format that best serves your purpose. As you consider format in revising, keep readers in mind. How can you make your paper more readable? How can you signal your plan for developing the topic and what's important? Some visual devices might help, including:

- Subheadings
- Bulleted lists (like the one you're reading now)
- Graphs, illustrations, tables
- Block quotes
- Underlining and paragraphing for emphasis
- White space

Long, unbroken pages of text can appear to be a gray, uninviting mass to the reader. All of the devices listed help break up the text, making it more reader friendly. Subheadings, if not overused, can also cue your reader to significant sections of your paper and how they relate to the whole. Long quotes, those over four lines, should be blocked, or indented one inch from the left margin, so that they're distinct from the rest of the text. (See "Writing with Sources" in Chapter 4, for more on blocking quotes.) Bullets—dots or asterisks preceding brief lines of text—can be used to highlight a list of important information. Graphs, tables, and illustrations also break up the text but, more importantly, they can also help clarify and explain information. (See Section 2.1.5, "Placement of Tables, Charts, and Illustrations," in Appendix B or Section 2.1.8, "Tables and Figures," in Appendix C.)

Using Images

Thanks to digital imaging, it's easier than ever to find pictures and use them in papers. As you probably know, Google allows users to do keyword searching specifically for images. You're writing an essay on the nutritional problems with fast food? You won't have any trouble finding a picture of a Big Mac that you can drop into your essay. Even better, perhaps you're writing your essay on a historical event, a local controversy, or perhaps a profile. With a few clicks you may find a less generic and more relevant image: a photograph of your profile subject or of the Civil War battle that you're analyzing.

You can do this. But should you?

That's up to your instructor, of course. But if she allows it, any visual addition to your essay—and especially an image—needs to do much more than take up space or break up gray text. It must do some work. What kind of work can an image do?

- **Pictures can dramatize a moment, situation, or outcome that you emphasize in your text:** a photograph of the space shuttle's missing insulation in a paper arguing for an end to funding space exploration programs; a picture of the shootings of students on the Kent State campus in 1970 in a paper exploring campus violence.

- **Pictures can help clarify difficult explanations:** Like a well-crafted analogy, an image can help readers to see more clearly what you're trying to explain. To explain quantitative data, you typically turn to tables and charts. But how can you use pictures? Use images that don't simply reinforce what you say in words but that also amplify what you say. An obvious example: If you're writing about a painting, then surrounding an image of the work with your textual explanations will bring your words to life. Readers will simply have more to work with to understand what you want them to see.

- **A sequence of pictures can tell a story or illustrate a process:** A disturbing example of this is a series of photos of a meth addict—usually police booking shots—that tell the story of addiction to the drug in the steady deterioration of the user's face. Pictures of Brazilian rain forests before and after logging can help make an argument about loss of biodiversity.

Following MLA Conventions

I've already mentioned that formal research papers in various disciplines may have prescribed formats. If your instructor expects a certain format, he has probably detailed exactly what that format should be. But in all likelihood, your essay for this class doesn't need to follow a rigid form. It will, however, probably adhere to the basic Modern Language Association (MLA) guidelines, described in detail in Appendix A. There, you'll find methods for formatting your paper and instructions for citing sources on your "Works Cited" page. You'll also find a sample paper in MLA style by Rachell Gallina, "Seeing Past Fear." In 2016, the MLA style changed dramatically, so you'll really want to study Appendix A. The American Psychological Association (APA) guidelines for research papers, the primary alternative to MLA guidelines, are described in Appendix B. You'll find a sample paper in APA style by Laura Burns, titled "Looking for Utopia."

Proofreading Your Paper

You've spent weeks researching, writing, and revising your paper. You want to stop now. That's understandable, no matter how much you were driven by your curiosity. But before you sign off on your research paper, placing it in someone else's hands, take the time to proofread it.

I was often so glad to be done with a piece of writing that I was careless about proofreading it. That changed about 10 years ago, after I submitted a portfolio of writing to complete my master's degree. I was pretty proud of it, especially an essay about dealing with my father's alcoholism. Unfortunately, I misspelled that word—*alcoholism*—every time I used it. Bummer.

PROOFREADING ON A COMPUTER   Proofreading used to necessitate gobbing on correction fluid to cover up mistakes and then trying to line up the paper and type in the changes. Writing on a computer, you're spared from that ordeal. The text can be easily manipulated.

Software programs can, of course, also help with the actual job of proofreading. Most word-processing programs, for example, come with spelling and grammar checkers. These programs will count the number of words in your sentences, alerting you to particularly long ones, and will even point out uses of passive voice. Although these style-checkers may not be all that helpful because of their dubious assumptions about what constitutes "good" style, spell-checkers are an invaluable feature. You probably already know that.

Some writers proofread on screen. Others find they need to print out their paper and proofread the hard copy. They argue that they catch more mistakes if they proofread on paper than if they proofread on screen. It makes sense, especially if you've been staring at the screen for days. A printed copy of your paper *looks* different, and I think you see it differently—maybe with fresher eyes and a more energetic attitude. You might notice things you didn't notice before. Decide for yourself how you want to proofread.

LOOKING CLOSELY   You've already edited the manuscript, pruning sentences and tightening things up. Now proofread for the little errors in grammar and mechanics that you missed. Aside from misspellings (usually typos), some pretty common mistakes appear in the papers I see. For practice, see if you can catch some of them in the following exercise.

10 COMMON THINGS TO AVOID IN RESEARCH PAPERS   The following is a list of the ten most common errors (besides misspelled words) made in research papers that should be caught in careful proofreading. A number of these errors occurred in Exercise 5.5.

1. Commonly confused words, such as *your* instead of *you're*. Here's a list of others:

their/there/they're	advice/advise
know/now	lay/lie
accept/except	its/it's
all ready/already	passed/past

Exercise 5.5

PICKING OFF THE LINT

I have a colleague who compares proofreading to picking the lint off an outfit, which is often your final step before heading out the door. Examine the following excerpt from a student paper. Proofread it, catching as many mechanical errors as possible. Note punctuation mistakes, agreement problems, misspellings, and anything else that seems off.

> In an important essay, Melody Graulich notes how "rigid dichotomizing of sex roles" in most frontier myths have "often handicapped and confused male as well as female writers (187)," she wonders if a "universel mythology" (198) might emerge that is less confining for both of them. In Bruce Mason, Wallace Stegner seems to experiment with this idea; acknowledging the power of Bo's male fantasies *and* Elsa's ability to teach her son to feel. It is his strenth. On the other hand, Bruces brother chet, who dies young, lost and broken, seems doomed because he lacked sufficient measure of both the feminine and masculine. He observes that Chet had "enough of the old man to spoil him, ebnough of his mother to s-often him, not enough of either to save him (*Big Rock*, 521)."

If you did this exercise in class, compare your proofreading of this passage with that of a partner. What did each of you find?

2. Possessives. Instead of *my fathers alcoholism,* the correct form is *my father's alcoholism.* Remember that if a singular noun ends in *s,* still add *'s: Tess's laughter.* If a noun is plural, just add the apostrophe: *the scientists' studies.*

3. Vague pronoun references. The excerpt in Exercise 5.5 ends with the sentence *He observes that Chet....* Who's *he*? The sentence should read, *Bruce observes that Chet....* Whenever you use the pronouns *he, she, it, they,* and *their,* make sure each clearly refers to someone or something.

4. Subject and verb agreement. If the subject is singular, its verb must be, too:

> The perils of climate change are many.

What confuses writers sometimes is the appearance before the verb of a noun that is not really the subject. Exercise 5.5 begins, for example, with this sentence:

> In an important essay, Melody Graulich notes how "rigid dichotomizing of sex roles" in most frontier myths have "often handicapped and confused male as well as female writers."

The subject here is not *frontier myths* but *rigid dichotomizing,* a singular subject. The sentence should read:

> In an important essay, Melody Graulich notes how "rigid dichotomizing of sex roles" in most frontier myths has "often handicapped and confused male as well as female writers."

The verb *has* may sound funny, but it's correct.

5. Punctuation of quotations. Note that commas belong inside quotation marks, not outside. Periods belong inside, too. Colons and semicolons are exceptions—they belong *outside* quotation marks. Blocked quotes don't need quotation marks at all unless there is a quote within the quote.

6. Commas. Could you substitute periods or semicolons? If so, you may be looking at *comma splices* or *run-on sentences*. Here's an example:

> Since 1980, the use of marijuana by college students has steadily declined, this was something of a surprise to me and my friends.

The portion after the comma, *this was . . .*, is another sentence. The comma should be a period, and *this* should be capitalized.

7. Parenthetical citations. In MLA style, there is no comma between the author's name and page number: (*Marks 99*).

8. Dashes. Though they can be overused, dashes are a great way to break the flow of a sentence with a related bit of information. You've probably noticed that I like them. In a manuscript, type dashes as *two* hyphens (--), not one. Most word-processing programs will automatically turn the hyphens into a solid em dash, which is what you want.

9. Names. After mentioning the full name of someone in your paper, you should normally use his or her *last name* in subsequent references. For example, this is incorrect:

> Denise Grady argues that people are genetically predisposed to obesity. Denise also believes that some people are "programmed to convert calories to fat."

Unless you know Denise or for some reason want to conceal her last name, change the second sentence to this:

> Grady also believes that some people are "programmed to convert calories to fat."

One exception to this is when writing about literature. It is often appropriate to refer to characters by their first names, particularly if characters share last names (as in Exercise 5.5).

10. Colons and semicolons. A colon is usually used to call attention to what follows it: a list, quotation, or appositive. A colon should also follow an independent clause. For example, this won't do:

> The most troubling things about child abuse are: the effects on self-esteem and language development.

In this case, eliminate the colon. A semicolon should be used as a period, separating two independent clauses. It simply implies that the clauses are closely related. Semicolons should *not* be used as if they were colons or commas.

USING THE "FIND" OR "SEARCH" FUNCTION Use the "Find" or "Search" function in your word-processing program to help you track down consistent problems. You simply tell the computer what word or punctuation to look for, and it will locate all occurrences in the text. For example, if you want to check for comma

Presenting Research in Alternative Genres

Reflecting

You take a writing course like this one because you want to apply what you've learned about composing, research, rhetoric, and genre to other situations—certainly other classes but also into your personal and professional life after college. Research on how to transfer knowledge from one situation to another highlights the importance of so-called "metacognitive" thinking. This means taking time to think about *how* you think about accomplishing a task: how you assess your strengths and weaknesses, how you approach problems and how you try to solve them, as well as what worked and what didn't. You can do this kind of reflection before a task, during it, and after. Take some time to evaluate your experience adapting your research to an alternative genre. Consider the following questions:

1. How well did it go? What are some key things I learned about myself and working with an unfamiliar genre? What do I know now that I didn't when I started the project?
2. What problems arose? How did I solve them? If I could start over, what would I do differently?
3. How can I use what I learned about presenting research in alternative genres in other classes and in other professional situations?

splices, search for commas. The cursor will stop on every comma, and you can verify if you have used it correctly. You can also search for pronouns to locate vague references or for words (like those listed in item 1) that you commonly confuse.

AVOIDING SEXIST LANGUAGE   One last proofreading task is to do a *man* and *he* check. Until recently, sexism wasn't an issue in language. Use of words such as *mankind* and *chairman* was acceptable; the implication was that the terms applied to both genders. At least, that's how use of the terms was defended when challenged. Critics argued that words such as *mailman* and *businessman* reinforced the idea that only men could fill these roles. Bias in language is subtle but powerful. And it's often unintentional. To avoid sending the wrong message, it's worth making the effort to avoid sexist language.

If you need to use a word with a *man* suffix, check to see if there is an alternative. *Congressperson* sounds pretty clunky, but *representative* works fine. Instead of *mankind,* why not *humanity*? Substitute *camera operator* for *cameraman.*

Also check your use of pronouns. Do you use *he* or *his* in places where you mean both genders? For example:

> The writer who cares about his topic will bring it to life for his readers.

Because a lot of writers are women, this doesn't seem right. How do you solve this problem? You can ask your instructor what she prefers, but here are some guidelines:

1. Use *his or her, he or she,* or the mutation *s/he.* For example:

> The writer who cares about his or her topic will bring it to life for his or her readers.

This is an acceptable solution, but using *his or her* repeatedly can be awkward.

2. Change the singular subject to plural. For example:

    Writers who care about their topics will bring them to life for their readers.

    This version, which also avoids discriminatory language, sounds much better.

3. Alternate *he* and *she, his* and *hers* whenever you encounter an indefinite person. If you have referred to writers as *he* in one discussion, refer to them as *she* in the next. Alternate throughout.

Looking Back and Moving On

This book began with your writing, and it also will end with it. More than a month ago, you began your inquiry project, and even if you're still not happy with your essay, you probably learned some things that influenced the way you think about yourself as a writer, about the nature of research in a university, and how to solve typical problems that arise when you're writing research-based papers.

In this final exercise, you'll do some thinking about all of this in your journal, or perhaps on a class blog or discussion board.

Exercise 5.6

ANOTHER DIALOGUE WITH DAVE

You may remember Dave from Chapter 4 (see Exercise 4.1, "Dialogue with Dave"). He's back and has some things to ask you about your experience with this project. Draw a line down the middle of a blank page in your journal, or create two columns in a Word document. Ask each of Dave's questions by writing them in the left column, and then fastwrite your response in the right column. Spend *at least* 3 minutes with each question.

Dave	You
1. "Hey, you, I think you can't really say that one opinion is better than another one. Don't you agree?"	
2. "There's all this stuff in the book about research as a process of discovery. What did you discover?"	
3. "What do you figure was the most challenging problem you had to solve while working on this research project? How did you solve it?"	
4. "After all this work, what do you take away from this experience? What have you learned that you can *use*?"	

Appendix A
Guide to the New MLA Style

Every once awhile, even in the arcane world of academic citation, there's a change in how things are done. This is rarely a revolution. But the new documentation guidelines for the Modern Language Association, published in 2016, come pretty close. A lot of people who have an interest in such things say a change was overdue. The difference between print and online sources has blurred over the years, and now a source may be found in a range of media—print, videos, images, audio—and a range of formats—article, Web page, podcast, cartoon, e-book, and so on. As the publication formats changed and expanded, the MLA's list of rules for citing sources got bigger and bigger—models for how to cite a YouTube video, a tweet, an Instagram post. This was the problem that the new MLA guidelines most wanted to address. The new approach comes down to two key concepts:

1. **What's important in a citation is not the "delivery method" or publication format—online, print, whatever—but the "core elements" that most sources share.** Those "core elements" include:

    * Author
    * Title
    * Name of "container" (more on this later)
    * Other contributors (if any)
    * Version
    * Number
    * Publisher
    * Publication date
    * Location

2. **Writers may adapt some rules depending on the project they're working on.** To anyone who has used the MLA citation format in the past—or any academic citation system, for that matter—this sounds positively revolutionary. Dutifully following the rules has always seemed like the only way to avoid getting kicked off the playground during recess. Although it's true that there still *are* rules, the MLA gives writers more discretion to make decisions about how to cite a source and what information to include, based on the focus of the writing they are doing. And the new guidelines acknowledge that students aren't just writing research papers anymore: They are producing PowerPoints, posters, podcasts, and a range of other kinds of research-based work that challenges the familiar format of the Work Cited page parked at the end of written work.

Therefore, the same citation might have more or less information depending on why a writer is using it and for what purpose. Here's what the *MLA Handbook*, 8th edition, has to say about this:

> Different situations call for different solutions. A writer whose primary purpose is to give credit for borrowed material may need to provide less information than a writer who is examining the distinguishing features of particular editions (or even specific copies) of source texts. Similarly, scholars working in specialized fields may need to cite details about their sources that other scholars making more general use of the resources do not. (4)

Practically speaking, what does this mean for an undergraduate who writes research essays? First, two principles should always guide his or her decisions about citation: providing *appropriate credit* to sources and *enough information* so that readers can track them down if they want to. Beyond that, it may not always be necessary to provide every detail about a source in an effort to conform to rigid citation rules. Different information may be required, for example, depending on the format you are using, and the audience for whom you are writing. (For more about this, you may want to visit the *MLA Style Center* at style.mla.org.)

In building a source citation, research writers should start with the most basic "core" elements. The most important information to initially collect, no matter what format the source is in, is the name of the author(s), title, publication source, where the source was found, and when it was published. Let's use as our model a citation for an article from a scholarly journal:

> Volk, Jennifer S., et al. "Tenants with Additional Needs: When Housing First Does Not Solve Homelessness." *Journal of Mental Health*, vol. 25, no. 1, 2015, pp. 169–175. *Academic Search Premier*, doi: 10.3109/09638237.2015.1101416.

1. **Author(s).** List the first author: last name, first name. If there is a second author, list that name following the first author and *and:* first name last name. If there are more than two authors, the first author's name is followed by the Latin *et al.*, which means "and others." The author name is followed by a period.
2. **Title.** Titles of works, like the one in our model, that are part of a larger work are in quotation marks. Stand-alone sources like books are italicized. The title is followed by a period.
3. **Title of Container.** The MLA uses the word *container* to represent a larger whole in which the specific source resides—and there can be more than one. There are two containers in our model—the journal (*Journal of Mental Health*) in which the article appears, and the database (*Academic Search Premier*) in which the journal was accessed. Containers are always italicized. The container name is followed by a comma.
4. **Volume and Issue Number.** The volume and issue numbers are listed, separated by a comma. Use the abbreviations *vol.* and *no.* for these.
5. **Publication date.** The date of publication is included in the series of publication information, nestled between commas. All months except May, June, and July are abbreviated. The publication date is followed by a comma.

6. **Location.** "Location" means where you found the specific information you are using in your research—the page numbers in a print source, or the URL or DOI for an online source. In this case, you need to provide locations within two containers—the journal and the database—so you need to include both page numbers and a "doi" number. Often the location of an article in a database will be a URL, but sometimes you will see a digital object identifier (doi) listed in the article. These are always better than URLs because they don't change. Do not include *http* in URLs, and make sure to end this final piece of information with a period.

The citation gurus at MLA, who earnestly hope these changes will simplify things, encourage research writers to think about basic "slots" of information that a citation might include. However, all the slots might not be filled depending on the type of source and how it's being used by the writer. Here's a "practice template" that the MLA includes in the 8th edition of the *Handbook* that should help you visualize what they mean.

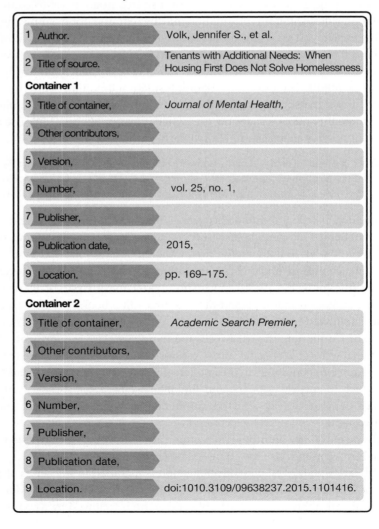

1	Author.	Volk, Jennifer S., et al.
2	Title of source.	Tenants with Additional Needs: When Housing First Does Not Solve Homelessness.

Container 1

3	Title of container,	*Journal of Mental Health,*
4	Other contributors,	
5	Version,	
6	Number,	vol. 25, no. 1,
7	Publisher,	
8	Publication date,	2015,
9	Location.	pp. 169–175.

Container 2

3	Title of container,	*Academic Search Premier,*
4	Other contributors,	
5	Version,	
6	Number,	
7	Publisher,	
8	Publication date,	
9	Location.	doi:1010.3109/09638237.2015.1101416.

As you can see, I've inserted the relevant information for our sample citation in each slot, but in the absence of some of the publication data a number of slots remain unfilled. Apply this template whenever you build citations, filling in relevant (and available) information for each source. Keep in mind that in some cases there will be more than two containers; in those cases, simply add another set of slots with that information.

So far, I've introduced you to the basics of the new MLA guidelines when you list sources in a Works Cited page. In a later section (see p. 000), we'll look more closely at each of these elements, exploring some of the many variations. But let's look next at how to cite sources *in the text* of your essay or other research project.

Directory of MLA Style

Part One: Citing Sources in Your Work

1.1 When to Cite

Before examining the details of how to use parenthetical citations, remember when you must cite sources in your paper:

1. Whenever you quote from an original source
2. Whenever you borrow ideas from an original source, even when you express them in your own words by paraphrasing or summarizing
3. Whenever you borrow from a source factual information that is *not common knowledge*

THE COMMON KNOWLEDGE EXCEPTION The business about *common knowledge* causes much confusion. Just what does this term mean? Basically, *common knowledge* means facts that are widely known and about which there is no controversy.

Sometimes, it's really obvious whether something is common knowledge. The fact that the Super Bowl occurs in late January or early February and pits the winning teams from the American Football Conference and the National Football Conference is common knowledge. The fact that President Ronald Reagan was once an actor and starred in a movie with a chimpanzee is common knowledge, too. But what about Carolyn's assertion that most dreaming occurs during rapid eye movement (REM) sleep? This is an idea about which all of her sources seem to agree. If you find that four or more sources cite the same information, then you can probably assume that it's common knowledge. But if you have any doubt, cite it!

1.2 The MLA Author/Page System

The Modern Language Association (MLA) uses the author/page parenthetical citation system. As you can see in Appendix B, the American Psychological Association (APA) uses the author/date system.

THE BASICS OF USING PARENTHETICAL CITATION The MLA method of in-text parenthetical citation is fairly simple: As close as possible to the borrowed material, you indicate in parentheses the original source (usually, the author's name) and the page number in the work that the borrowed material came from. For example, here's how you'd cite a book or article with a single author using the author/page system:

> When the umpire Marianna Alves kept calling Serena William's serves out of bounds when they clearly weren't, tennis commentator John McEnroe "was shocked that Serena was able to hold it together" (Rankine 27).

The parenthetical citation here tells readers two things: (1) This information about Serena William's composure does not originate with the writer but with someone named Rankine, and (2) readers can consult the original source for further information by looking on page 27 of Rankine's book or article, which is cited fully at the back of the paper in the Works Cited. Here is what readers would find there:

Works Cited

Rankine, Claudia. *Citizen: An American Lyric.* Graywolf Press, 2014.

Here's another example of a parenthetical author/page citation, from another research paper. Note the differences from the previous example:

> "One thing is clear," writes Thomas Mallon, "plagiarism didn't become a truly sore point with writers until they thought of writing as their trade…. Suddenly his capital and identity were at stake" (3–4).

The first thing you may have noticed is that the author's last name—Mallon—was omitted from the parenthetical citation. It didn't need to be included because it had already been mentioned in the text. *If you mention the author's name in the text of your paper, then you need to parenthetically cite only the relevant page number(s).* This citation also tells us that the quoted passage comes from two pages rather than one.

Placement of Citations. Place the citation as close as you can to the borrowed material, trying to avoid breaking the flow of the sentences, if possible. To avoid confusion about what's borrowed and what's not—particularly if the material you're borrowing spans more than a sentence—when possible mention the name of the original author *in your paper* in a way that clarifies what you've borrowed. Note that in the next example, the writer simply cites the source at the end of the paragraph, not naming the source in the text. As a result, it is hard for the reader to figure out whether Blager is the source of the information in the entire paragraph or just in part of it:

Citations That Go with the Flow

There's no getting around it: Parenthetical citations can be like stones on the sidewalk. Readers stride through a sentence in your essay and then have to step around the citation at the end before they resume their walk. Yet citations are important in academic writing because they help readers know who you read or heard that shaped your thinking. And you can write your citations in such a way that they won't trip up readers. As a result, your essay will be more readable. Try these techniques:

- Avoid lengthy parenthetical citations by mentioning the name of the author in your essay. That way, you usually have to include only a page number in the citation.

- Try to place citations where readers are likely to pause anyway—for example, at the end of the sentence or right before a comma.
- Remember you *don't* need a citation when you're citing common knowledge or referring to an entire work by an author.
- If you're borrowing from only one source in a paragraph of your essay and all of the borrowed material comes from a single page of that source, don't repeat the citation over and over again with each new bit of information. Just put the citation at the end of the paragraph.

> Though children who have been sexually abused seem to be disadvantaged in many areas, including the inability to forge lasting relationships, low self-esteem, and crippling shame, they seem advantaged in other areas. Sexually abused children seem to be more socially mature than other children of their same age group. It's a distinctly mixed blessing (Blager 994).

In the following example, notice how the ambiguity about what's borrowed and what's not is resolved by careful placement of the author's name and parenthetical citation in the text:

> Though children who have been sexually abused seem to be disadvantaged in many areas, including the inability to forge lasting relationships, low self-esteem, and crippling shame, they seem advantaged in other areas. According to Blager, sexually abused children seem to be more socially mature than other children of their same age group (994). It's a distinctly mixed blessing.

In this latter version, it's clear that Blager is the source for one sentence in the paragraph and that the writer is responsible for the rest. When you first mention authors in your essay, use their full names, and when you mention them again, use only their last names. Also note that the citation is placed *before* the period of the sentence (or last sentence) that it documents. That's always the case, except at the end of a blocked quotation, where the parenthetical reference is placed *after* the period of the last sentence. The citation can also be placed near the author's name, rather than at the end of the sentence, if it doesn't unnecessarily break the flow of the sentence. For example:

> Blager (994) observes that sexually abused children tend to be more socially mature than other children of their same age group.

1.2.1 When There Are No Page Numbers Non-print sources like Web pages, e-books, YouTube videos, and other sources often lack page numbers. There are a range of solutions for this when handling in-text citations, and the most common is to simply cite the author's last name. For example, here's a citation for a Web site:

> According to critics, the Food and Drug Administration's move to regulate e-cigarettes will have a negative impact on the many small vape shops scattered throughout the U.S. (Humer and Polke).

Although some e-books may use the pagination from a print version, many don't. My Kindle, for example, uses something called a "position number," and this may vary from device to device. Unless these page numbers are stable, don't use them. On the other hand, sometimes you can help readers locate the original passage you're citing by using a section or chapter number that is stable.

> Lawrence Anthony describes how in recent years he has had to be ever more vigilant about elephant poaching in his reserve (ch. 1).

1.2.2 When You Mention One Author It's generally good practice in research writing to identify who said what. The familiar convention of using attribution tags such as "According to Fletcher,..." or "Fletcher argues..." and so on helps readers attach a name with a voice or an individual with certain claims or findings. As just discussed, when you mention the author of a source in your sentence, the parenthetical citation includes only the page number. For example,

> Robert Harris believes that there is "widespread uncertainty" among students about what constitutes plagiarism (2).

As was also discussed, the page number could come directly after the author's name.

> Robert Harris (2) believes that there is "widespread uncertainty" among students about what constitutes plagiarism.

Here's another example from a critical review on a Web site that lacks page numbers.

> Beyonce's recent video "Lemonade" is a mixed-genre masterpiece in which she "has to rewrite all the rules" (Bale).

1.2.3 When You Mention More Than One Author Often your sources will have more than one author. If the book or article has two authors, list both their last names in the parenthetical citation, with *and* before the final author; for example:

> (Oscar and Leibowitz 29)

Sources that don't have page numbers would simply list the authors:

> (Humer and Polke)

If your source has more than two authors, use the first author and et al.

> (Kemp et al. 199)

1.2.4 When There Is No Author Occasionally, you may encounter a source whose author is anonymous—that is, who isn't identified. This isn't unusual with pamphlets, editorials, government documents, some newspaper articles, online sources, and short filler articles in magazines. If you can't parenthetically name the author, what do you cite?

Most often, cite the title (or an abbreviated version, if the title is long) and, if you can, the page number. If you abbreviate the title, begin with the word under which it is alphabetized in the Works Cited list. For example:

> Economists were disappointed by the number of jobs added in May, 2016, which complicates the political debate ("US Adds 160,000 Jobs").

Here is how the publication would be listed at the back of the paper:

Works Cited

"US Adds 160,000 Jobs in April." *YT Wochit Business*, 6 May 2016, www
.youtube.com/watch?v=_WBSLXFpUd0.

As with other sources, for clarity, it's often helpful to mention the original source of the borrowed material in the text of your paper. Refer to the publication or institution (e.g., the American Cancer Society or Department of Defense) you're citing or make a more general reference to the source. For example:

An article in *Cuisine* magazine argues that the best way to kill a lobster is to plunge a knife between its eyes ("How to Kill" 56).

or

According to one government report, with the current minimum size limit, most lobsters end up on dinner plates before they've had a chance to reproduce ("Size" 3–4).

Note the abbreviations of the article titles; for example, the full title for "How to Kill," listed in the Works Cited, is "How to Kill a Lobster." Typically, you would abbreviate a title if it is longer than a single noun phrase. Note also that article titles are in quotation marks and book titles are italicized.

1.2.5 Works by the Same Author Suppose you end up using several books or articles by the same author. Obviously, a parenthetical citation that merely lists the author's name and page number won't do because it won't be clear *which* of several works the citation refers to. In this case, include the author's name, an abbreviated title (if the original is too long), and the page number. For example:

The thing that distinguishes the amateur from the experienced writer is focus; one "rides off in all directions at once," and the other finds one meaning around which everything revolves (Murray, *Write to Learn* 92).

The Works Cited list would show multiple works by one author as follows:

Works Cited

Murray, Donald M. *Write to Learn*. 8th ed. Heinle, 2004.

---. *A Writer Teaches Writing*. Heinle, 2004.

It's obvious from the parenthetical citation which of the two Murray books is the source of the information. Note that in the parenthetical reference, no punctuation separates the title and the page number, but a comma follows the author's name. If Murray had been mentioned in the text of the paper, his name could have been dropped from the citation.

How to handle the Works Cited list is explained more fully later in this appendix, but for now, notice that the three hyphens used in the second entry signal that the author's name in this source is the same as in the preceding entry.

1.2.6 Works by Different Authors with the Same Name How do you distinguish between different authors who have the same last name? Say you're citing a piece by someone named Lars Anderson as well as a piece by someone named Kelli Anderson. The usual in-text citation, which uses the last name only (Anderson 2), wouldn't help the reader much. In this situation, add the author's first initial to the citation: (L. Anderson 2) or (K. Anderson 12).

1.2.7 Indirect Sources Whenever you can, cite the original source for material you use. For example, if an article on television violence quotes the author of a book and you want to use the quote, try to hunt down the book. That way, you'll be certain of the accuracy of the quote and you may find some additional usable information.

Sometimes, however, finding the original source is not possible. In those cases, use the term *qtd. in* to signal that you've quoted or paraphrased material that was quoted in your source and initially appeared elsewhere. In the following example, the citation signals that the quote from Bacon was in fact culled from an article by Guibroy, rather than from Bacon's original work:

> Francis Bacon also weighed in on the dangers of imitation, observing that "it is hardly possible at once to admire an author and to go beyond him" (qtd. in Guibroy 113).

1.2.8 Personal Interviews If you mention the name of your interview subject in your text, no parenthetical citation is necessary. If you don't mention the subject's name, cite it in parentheses after the quote:

> The key thing when writing for radio, says one journalist, is to "write to the sound if you've got great sound, and read your stuff aloud" (Tan).

Regardless of whether you mention your subject's name in your text, you should include a reference to the interview in the Works Cited. In this case, the reference would look like this:

Works Cited

Tan, Than. Personal interview, 28 Jan. 2011.

1.2.9 Several Sources in a Single Citation Suppose two sources both contributed the same information in a paragraph of your essay. Or, even more likely, suppose you're summarizing the findings of several authors on a certain topic—a fairly common move when you're trying to establish a context for your own research question. How do you cite multiple authors in a single citation? Use author names and page numbers as usual, and separate them with a semicolon. For example,

> A whole range of studies have looked closely at the intellectual development of college students, finding that they generally assume "stages" or "perspectives" that differ from subject to subject (Perry 122; Belenky et al. 12).

SAMPLE PARENTHETICAL REFERENCES FOR OTHER SOURCES MLA format is pretty simple, and we've already covered some of the basic variations. You should also know the following four additional variations:

1.2.10 An Entire Work If you mention an author's name and his or her work in the text but don't refer to specific details, no citation is necessary. The work should, however, be listed in the Works Cited. For the following example, Beyonce's video would be listed in the Works Cited.

> Beyonce's video "Lemonade" is considered to be a masterpiece by some critics.

1.2.11 A Volume of a Multivolume Work If you're working with one volume of a multivolume work, it's a good idea to mention which volume in the parenthetical reference. The citation that follows attributes the passage to the second volume, page 3, of a work by Baym and other authors. The volume number is always followed by a colon, which is followed by the page number:

> By the turn of the century, three authors dominated American literature: Mark Twain, Henry James, and William Dean Howells (Baym et al. 2: 3).

1.2.12 A Literary Work Because so many literary works, particularly classics, have been reprinted in so many editions, and readers are likely using different editions, it's useful to give readers information about where a passage can be found regardless of edition. You can do this by listing not only the page number but also the chapter number—and any other relevant information, such as the section or volume—separated from the page number by a semicolon. Use arabic rather than roman numerals.

> Izaak Walton warns that "no direction can be given to make a man of a dull capacity able to make a Flie well" (130; ch. 5).

When citing poems or plays, instead of page numbers, cite line numbers for poems and act, scene, and line numbers, separated with periods, for plays. For example, (*Othello* 2.3.286) indicates act 2, scene 3, line 286 of that play.

Part Two: Building Citations for the Work Cited Page

The first few pages of this Appendix introduced you to the new MLA conventions for developing full citations of the sources you used in your project. Here we'll look a little more closely at the core elements of a Works Cited citation, and some of the ways to handle the peculiarities of different kinds of sources.

2.1 Author

2.1.1 The Basics In the MLA system, sources appear in the Works Cited in alphabetical order, listed with the last name of the author first, then first name and initial. If there is a single author, this is followed by a period. For example,

> Newsome, Phillip R. "The Role of the Mouthguard in the Prevention of Sports-related Dental Injuries." *International SportMed Journal,* vo. 4, no. 1, 2003, pp. 1–4.

Two authors? Then the first author is listed in the usual style—last name first—followed by *and* and then the name of the second author, whose name is written first name and then last name. The entry ends in a period.

> Broglio, Steven, and Kevin Guskiewcz. "Concussion in Sports: The Sidelines Assessment." *Sports Health,* vol. 1, no. 5, 2009, pp. 326–350. *Article First,* www.ncbi.nlm.nih.gov/pmc/articles/PMC3445181.

For three or more authors, use the "et al." convention following the first author's name, which is reversed in the usual fashion:

> Schiff, Melissa et al. "Injury Prevention in Sports." *American Journal of Lifestyle Medicine,* vol. 4, no. 2, 2012, pp. 275–278.

For names that appear in online sources like Twitter and other social platforms, list the author by his or her username.

> @jonthanstray. "A Rough Guide to Spotting Bad Science." *Twitter,* 10 May 2016.

2.1.2 When No Author Is Listed Online sources sometimes have no author, or have institutional or corporate authors. In that case, you generally begin with the title of the source.

> "Voting Rights Act." *History,* 10 May 2016, www.history.com/topics/ black-history/voting-rights-.
>
> "Flesh Fly." *Wikipedia,* 27 Jan. 2016.

2.1.3 Other Kinds of Contributors Sometimes people don't author a source in the traditional sense but contribute to it in other ways. The most common example would be someone who edits a collection of work by other writers. But you might also cite translators, creators, producers, performers, and so on. If this is the case, MLA style recommends that you spell out the nature of the contribution

> Freedman, Diane P, and Olivia Frey, editors. *Autobiographical Writing Across the Disciplines,* Duke UP, 2003.
>
> Griffith, D.W, director. "Birth of a Nation." David W. Griffith Corporation, 1915.

2.2 Title

2.2.1 The Basics The title typically isn't hard to find in nearly any source. But should the title be italicized, or should it be in quotation marks? MLA instructs us to italicize a title if it's a stand-alone work, like a book, television show,

Web site, etc. The title should be put in quotation marks when it's *part* of a larger work. For example, if you're citing a whole Web site, it would be italicized, but if you're citing an article *in* a Web site, the title would be in quotation marks. The same is true, naturally, of an article within a periodical, an essay in a collection, an episode of a television show, or a song on an album.

For example, here's a citation for a stand-alone work where the title is italicized:

> Biewen, John, and Alexa Dilworth, editors. *Reality Radio: Telling True Stories in Sound*. Center for Documentary Studies, 2010.

And here's the citation for an essay that is part of that same work. The title of the essay is in quotation marks.

> Carrier, Scott. "That Jackie Kennedy Moment." *Reality Radio: Telling True Stories in Sound*, edited by John Biewen and Alexa Dilworth, Center for Documentary Studies, 2010, pp. 27–35.

As you can see in the examples, the subtitle of the work is also included, placed after a colon that ends the main title. Unlike APA conventions (see Appendix B), all but the connecting words in a title are capitalized.

2.2.2 When There Is No Title In rare cases, a source might not have an obvious title. For example, you might be citing a tweet or an e-mail message without a title in the subject line. In some cases, you can provide a general description, like this:

> Kelley, Karen. E-mail message on plastic bag ordinance. Received by Bruce Ballenger, 11 May 2016.

When citing a tweet, use the whole message as a title, enclosed in quotation marks.

> @ninarota. "T. S. Eliot's name was an anagram for toilets @Frank Delaney via #EzraPound #unconfirmed." *Twitter*, 11 May 2016, 10:00 pm,twitter.com/ninarota/status/730231821896548352.

2.3 Container

2.3.1 The Basics The idea that sources can be located in one or more "containers" is probably the biggest change in the new MLA guidelines, and at first, it's a bit hard to imagine. Understanding the motive behind this change helps. In the old days, sources largely stood alone—the source was a book, article, movie, album, and so on. Now, of course, a book might not only exist in print but also as part of a database like GoogleBooks. An article appears in the print journal and is also part of an online database. A television show may be viewed on a network or through a service like Netflix or AmazonPrime. Because there might be differences among these versions, it's important to signal exactly where you found the source you used. To do this, you flag each of these containers in your citations. In many cases, this is really straightforward. For example, if you cite an article in a print magazine, you're only dealing with one container: the title of the magazine. But if you found the magazine on your library database, you have two containers: the title of the magazine, and the title of the database. Both of these would be italicized.

One thing to keep in mind is that the MLA is not concerned with the kind of *device* on which you may be reading your source. If you read a book on your Kindle or a tablet, for example, you need only provide the same publication information you would provide if you were reading it in print—the author, title, publisher, and date of publication. If, however, you access the book through an online database—say, GoogleBooks or Project Gutenberg—then you need to include that database as part of your citation.

For example, here's how you'd cite a journal article you found in the print version:

> Durst, Russell. "British Invasion: James Britton, Composition Studies, and Anti-Disciplinarity." *College Composition and Communication*, vol. 66, no. 3, Feb. 2015, pp. 384–401.

Here's how you'd cite the same article that you found online:

> Durst, Russell. "British Invasion: James Britton, Composition Studies, and Anti-Disciplinarity." *College Composition and Communication*, vol. 66, no. 3, Feb. 2015, pp. 384–401. *ProQuest Central*, search.proquest .com/docview/1661792839/abstract/7126439A769B4BD3PQ/1?acco untid=9649.

As you can see, in the second citation, two containers were listed—the journal *College Composition and Communication*, and the database *ProQuest Central*. In addition, the URL of the article was included (note the "http://" prefix is omitted). Typically, sources have one or sometimes two containers, but they can have more.

2.3.2 Other Kinds of Containers Citing an essay in a book of essays, or an article in a journal that is nested in a database is pretty straightforward, really. So let's look at some other kinds of containers that are a bit more unusual. We'll start with an easy one—an article on a Web site. In this case, you're working with one container.

> Snyder, Marjorie A. "Girls Suffer Sports Concussions at a Higher Rate Than Boys. What is That Overlooked?" *The Washington Post*, 10 Feb. 2015, www.washingtonpost.com/posteverything/wp/2015/02/10/ our-effort-to-reduce-concussions-in-youth-sports-overlooks-the-biggest-victims-girls.

Here's a citation of a TED Talk video on YouTube, which has two containers, each of which is included in the citation.

> Levitin, Daniel. "How to Stay Calm When You Know You'll Be Stressed." *TED Talks*, 23 Nov. 2015. *YouTube*, www.youtube.com/watch?v= 8jPQjjsBbIc.

A citation of an e-book typically involves two containers—the title of the book and the name of the e-book service, followed by the book's online location. That address can be long and cumbersome like the one that follows.

> Yamaguchi, Mitsutsune. *Climate Change Mitigation: A Balanced Approach to Climate Change.* Springer London, 2012. *Ebook Library,* reader.eblib.com/(S(cagfgcxqibd5had4mvekufu3))/Reader.aspx?p=994206&o=601&u=O3YHieEdjAmC80n%2fEMS%2bcg%3d%3d&t=1462989241&h=FC174CAEF952D0C2EBCFBA75437C941959C4A05E&s=45134199&ut=1828&pg=1&r=img&c=-1&pat=n&cms=-1&sd=2.

Note that there is a period between the entry for the first container (the book) and the second container (in this case, *Ebook Library*).

2.4 Other Contributors

The most important contributor to a work is its author. But depending on the source, and your purposes for using it, you might want to list other kinds of contributors as well. The MLA lists some of these types of contributions and how they would be cited. These include: directed by, edited by, introduction by, translated by, illustrated by, and so on. Flagging these other kinds of contributions is most common in multimedia productions, like film and television, which are highly collaborative works. Obviously, you're not going to list all of these people in every citation. Call out the ones that are relevant to your project.

For example,

> "Pilot." *The Wonder Years,* directed by Steve Miner, season 1, episode 1, 3 April 2016, *YouTube,* uploaded by Darcel Howard, www.youtube.com/watch?v=eme2-Utvu2c&list=PLciWCLt_SjCvbMmcX3z9CAfScTkzEUoj0.

2.5 Version

A book like *The Curious Researcher*, which has been around since 1994, has come out in a number of editions. The one you hold in your hand is the 9th edition. Some books include a date ("2016 edition") or a description ("Expanded edition") or some other indication that this one is different from the one that came before it. This information will be included in a citation so readers know exactly which book you're using. For example,

> Ballenger, Bruce. *The Curious Researcher: A Guide to Research Papers.* 9th ed., Pearson, 2017.

2.6 Number

Academic journals are typically issued in a series using both volume and issue numbers. Television programs might include season and episode numbers (see the "Wonder Years" example in 2.4). Some publications simply number each issue. Include this information in the citation, separated by commas. Use abbreviations like "no." and "vol." and leave them uncapitalized.

Potter, Sharyn J. "Reducing Sexual Assault on Campus: Lessons from the Movement to Prevent Drunk Driving." *American Journal of Public Health*, vol. 106, no. 5, 2016, pp. 822–829.

2.7 Publisher

2.7.1 The Basics Finding the publisher of a work is usually no big deal. For books, publishers are typically listed on the title page or copyright page. This information is listed following the title of the work. Previous editions of the *MLA Handbook* instructed writers to include the city where the work was published, but this is no longer necessary. "University Press" should be abbreviated to "UP," as in the following example.

Bruner, Jerome. *Actual Minds, Possible Worlds*. Harvard UP, 1986.

2.7.2 When the Publisher Is Not Obvious. Things get a little more complicated when a source, like a movie or television program, seems to have multiple publishers, or when it's hard to find the publisher's name, as is often true for a Web site. In the first case, when in doubt the MLA instructs writers to cite TV and films with the publisher that appears to have "the primary overall responsibility for it." Finding the publisher for a Web site might require some hunting. Check the fine print at the bottom of the home page, or if there is one, click on the "About" tab. Information about the publisher of the Web article that follows was listed at the bottom of the page, but it listed three publishers: The Writing Lab, The OWL at Purdue, and Purdue University. It was a judgment call to list only the first. I assumed the Writing Lab was primarily responsible.

"MLA Formatting and Style Guide." *Purdue Online Writing Lab*, The Writing Lab, owl.english.purdue.edu/owl/resource/747/01.

2.8 Publication Date

2.8.1 The Basics Determining the publication date used to be uncomplicated because it was typically published in one format. Now you can read an article online that was published a year—or 15 years—ago in a print magazine. These versions might have different publication dates. Which do you use? The MLA instructs writers to use the date of the version they consulted. If that version was online, cite that date, not the earlier print version. However, it's far more common that the online and print publication dates are the same, as in this example:

Brantley, Susan L., and Anna Meyendorff. "The Facts on Fracking." *The New York Times*, 13 March 2013, www.nytimes.com/2013/03/14/opinion/global/the-facts-on-fracking.html.

When you are citing the publication of a book that is in multiple editions, use the date of the edition you used.

2.8.2 Other Publication Date Information Things can get a little more complicated when you're citing sources that include a range of publication date information. For example, a YouTube clip of an episode of the TV show *The Wonder Years*, which aired in late 1980s, doesn't say when that clip was originally aired. No matter. Include the date the clip was uploaded.

> "Pilot." The Wonder Years, directed by Steve Miner, season 1, episode 1, 3 April 2016, *YouTube*, uploaded by Darcel Howard, www.youtube.com/watch?v=eme2-Utvu2c&list=PLciWCLt_SjCvbMmcX3z9CAfScTkzEUoj0.

Another piece of publication date information you might include is the time the work was posted online. This is the kind of thing you sometimes see in reader comments posted in response to an article or blog post. For example,

> Ross, Emery. Comment on "Sven Birkert's Day." *Creative Nonfiction Workshop*, 21 April 2016, 7:52 a.m., cnfworkshop.blogspot.com/2016/04/sven-birkerts-day.html#comment-form.

2.9 Location

Location is a term that is meant to broaden our notion of where exactly to find a source. Traditionally, location would mean page numbers—and it still does for many sources—but because online sources typically lack page numbers, location might be a URL. Some sources' locations might even be a place, like a museum or gallery. This information, whatever form it takes, appears at the end of a citation. When citing page numbers, use the abbreviation "pp." When citing URLs, copy and paste the address from your browser, but cut the "http://" prefix. These URLs are particularly useful if they are live links in a document that readers can click on. In some cases, you might find an academic article includes something called a *digital object identifier*, or DOI. These are stable locations for online sources, and therefore are always preferable to a URL. For example,

> Stubbersfield, Joseph M. et al. "Serial Killers, Spiders, and Cybersex: Social and Survival Information Bias in the Transmission of Urban Legends." *British Journal of Psychology*, vol. 106, no. 2, 2015, pp. 288–307. *American Search Premier*, doi: 10.1111/bjop.12703.

In this example, you can see that there are actually two locations listed: the page numbers from the print version and the DOI that flags the location of the online version. In rare cases, you might describe the physical location of a source. For example, suppose you were analyzing a painting in the university gallery. The citation might look something like this:

> Young, Richard. *Godzilla's Sister*. 2005, Visual Art Gallery, Boise State University, Boise, Idaho.

Part Three: Preparing the Works Cited Page and Other Formatting

If you're writing a print essay, the Works Cited page ends the paper. If you are presenting your research in another format, like a slide presentation, it might appear in a final slide. On a poster, the Works Cited might appear in fine print at the bottom. If you're presenting in audio or video formats, your instructor may simply want you to submit a Work Cited page separately. No matter what form your research takes, a Works Cited page is key because it helps your audience know how to follow a trail back to sources that influenced your thinking.

A Works Cited list is essentially an alphabetical listing of all the sources you quoted, paraphrased, or summarized in your paper. If you have used MLA format for citing sources, your paper probably has numerous parenthetical references to authors and page numbers. The Works Cited page provides complete information on each source cited in the text for the reader who wants to know. (In APA format, which is typically used in psychology and the social sciences, this page is called "References" and is slightly different in format. See Appendix B for APA guidelines.)

3.1 Format of Works Cited

ALPHABETIZING THE LIST After you've assembled complete information about each source you've cited, put the sources in alphabetical order by the last name of the author. If the work has multiple authors, alphabetize by the last name of the first author listed. If the source has no author, then alphabetize it by the first key word of the title. If you're citing more than one source by a single author, you don't need to repeat the name for each source; simply place three hyphens followed by a period (—.) for the author's name in subsequent listings.

INDENTING AND SPACING Type the first line of each entry flush left, and indent subsequent lines of that entry (if any) a half inch. Double-space between each line and each entry. For example:

Hall 10

Works Cited

Biernacki, Patrick. *Pathways from Heroin Addiction.* Temple UP, 1986.

Brill, Leon. *The De-Addiction Process.* Thomas, 1972.

Collins, Liz. "Too Many Young Lives: The Heroin Addiction Epidemic." *CBS Minnesota*, 11 May 2016, minnesota.cbslocal.com/2016/05/11/heroin-addiction.

Henden, Edmund. "Heroin Addiction and Voluntary Choice: The Case of Informed Consent." *Bioethics*, vol. 27, issue 9, 2013, pp. 395–401. *Academic Search Premier*, doi: 1467-8519.20120.01969.

3.2 The Layout of Print Essays

One of the changes in the 8th edition of the *MLA Handbook* is that there is no longer a chapter devoted to formatting research papers. There's a reason for this, of course. In its commitment to reimagining the many formats that research is published in these days, the MLA chose not to emphasize the most conventional format: the paper. However, student writers will continue writing research essays for some time, and in the interest of helping those of you are writing papers, I've included the basics of formatting, drawing on the *Handbook's* previous editions.

3.2.1 Printing Print your paper on white, $8^1/_2 \times 11$-inch paper. Make sure the printer has sufficient ink or toner.

3.2.2 Margins and Spacing The old high school trick is to have big margins so you can get the length without the information. Don't try that trick with this paper. Leave 1-inch margins at the top, bottom, and sides of your pages. Indent the first line of each paragraph a half-inch, and indent blocked quotes an inch. Double-space all of the text, including blocked quotes and Works Cited.

3.2.3 Title Your paper doesn't need a separate title page; the title will go on your first page of text. On that page, 1 inch from the top on the upper left-hand

Figure A1 The Basic Look of an MLA-Style Paper

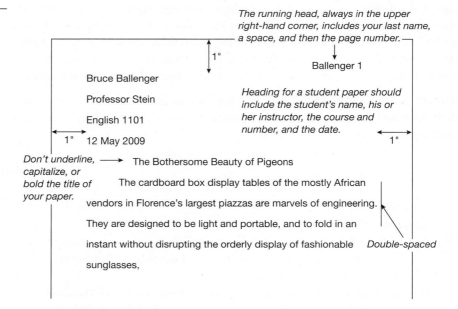

side, type your name, your instructor's name, the course name and number, and the date. Below that, type the title, centered on the page. Begin the text of the paper below the title. For example:

Karoline Ann Fox

Professor Dethier

English 401

15 December 2016

Metamorphosis, the Exorcist, and Oedipus

Ernst Pawel has said that Franz Kafka's *The Metamorphosis*...

Note that everything is double-spaced. The title is not italicized (although italics would be used for the name of a book or other work that should be italicized), underlined, or boldfaced.

3.2.4 Header with Pagination Make sure that every page is numbered. That's especially important with long papers. Type your last name and the page number in the upper right-hand corner, a half inch from the top and flush with the right margin: Ballenger 3. Don't use the abbreviation *p.* or a hyphen between your name and the number.

3.2.5 Placement of Tables, Charts, and Illustrations With MLA format, papers do not have appendixes. Tables, charts, and illustrations are placed in the body of the paper, close to the text that refers to them. Number tables and charts consecutively (Table 1, Table 2, and so on; Fig. 1, Fig. 2, and so on; notice the abbreviation of "Figure"). Place the title of a table above it, flush left. Place the caption for a chart or illustration below it. For tables, charts, and illustrations that are borrowed, give full citations. This information goes at the bottom of a table or at the end of a caption for a chart or illustration. See Figure A2 for an example of a table formatted according to MLA guidelines.

Table 1 Percentage of Students Who Self-Report Acts of Plagiarism

Acts of Plagiarism	Never/Rarely	Sometimes	Often/ Very Freq.
Copy text without citation	71	19	10
Copy paper without citation	91	5	3
Request paper to hand in	90	5	2
Purchase paper to hand in	91	6	3

SOURCE: Scanlon, Patrick M., and David R. Neumann; "Internet Plagiarism among College Students." *Journal of College Student Development*, vol. 43, no. 3, 2002, p. 379.

Figure A2
Example of Format for a Table

3.3 Some Style Considerations

3.3.1 Handling Titles As I noted in the previous section on building citations, the general MLA rule for capitalization of titles is that the writer should capitalize the first letters of all principal words in a title, including any that follow hyphens. Words not capitalized include articles (*a, an,* and *the*), prepositions (*for, of, in, to,* and so on), coordinating conjunctions (*and, or, but, for*), and *to* in infinitives. However, these words are capitalized if they appear at the beginning or end of the title.

The rules for deciding whether to italicize a title or place it in quotation marks (the usual alternative) make this distinction:

1. If the work is "published independently," italicize it. These works are typically books, Web sites, online databases, TV broadcasts, plays, periodicals, and so on.
2. If the title is part of a larger work—say, an article in a periodical or an episode of a TV program—then place it in quotation marks.
   Here are examples:

   The Curious Researcher (book)

   A Streetcar Named Desire (play)

   "Once More to the Lake" (essay in a collection)

   The New York Times (newspaper)

   "Psychotherapy" (encyclopedia article)

   "Funny Talking Animals" (YouTube clip)

3.3.2 Style Related to Sources and Quotations

Names. Though it may seem by the end of your research project as if you're on familiar terms with some of the authors you cite, it's not a good idea to call them by their first names. Give the full names of people you cite when you first mention them, and then give only their last names if you mention them again.

Ellipsis Points. Those are the three dots (or four, if the omitted material comes at the end of a sentence where they join a period) that indicate you've left out a word, phrase, or even whole section of a quoted passage. It's wise to use ellipsis points and omit material when you want to emphasize part of a quotation and don't want to burden your reader with unnecessary information, but be careful to preserve the basic intention and idea of the author's original statement. Ellipsis points can come at the beginning of a quotation, in the middle, or at the end, depending where it is you've omitted material. When using ellipsis in the middle or end, put a space before the first and after the last. For example,

> "After the publication of a controversial picture that shows, for example, either dead or grieving victims..., readers in telephone calls and in letters to the editor, often attack the photographer for being tasteless..." (Lesser 56).

Quotations. Quotations that run more than four lines long should be blocked, or indented 1 inch from the left margin. If your quote is longer than a single paragraph, indent the first sentence of each additional paragraph an additional quarter inch.

The quotation should be double-spaced. Quotation marks should not be used. The parenthetical citation is placed *after* the period at the end of the quotation. A colon is a customary way to introduce a blocked quotation. For example,

> Chris Sherman and Gary Price, in *The Invisible Web*, contend that much of the Internet, possibly most, is beyond the reach of researchers who use conventional search engines:
>
> > The problem is that vast expanses of the Web are completely invisible to general-purpose search engines like AltaVista, HotBot, and Google. Even worse, this "Invisible Web" is in all likelihood growing significantly faster than the visible Web that you're familiar with. It's not that search engines and Web directories are "stupid" or even badly engineered. Rather, they simply can't "see" millions of high-quality resources that are available exclusively on the Invisible Web. So what is this Invisible Web and why aren't search engines doing anything about it to make it visible? (xxi)

Part Four: Student Paper in MLA Style

Rachel Gallina, the daughter of former Christian aid workers in Kosovo, has experienced terrorism firsthand. Her family was targeted by Al-Qaeda for their work, and there were kidnapping threats against her and her siblings. Yet remarkably, Rachel writes in "Seeing Past Fear" that this experience has not made her less sympathetic to the Islamic community but more so. She urges readers to acknowledge their understandable fears of terrorism but not to give into bigotry. In the end, Rachel argues, that will only exacerbate the problem. Combining considerable research with a strong narrative voice, "Seeing Past Fear" is a compelling, readable essay, one that addresses the issue of Islamophobia with directness and honesty. Rachel's essay is an ideal piece to study and discuss. She makes a number of interesting rhetorical moves in the work, and it's a great example of how research can be deployed in the service of an argument.

Gallina 1

Rachel Gallina
Professor Carrie Seymour
English 112
10 May 2016

Seeing Past Fear

Martin Luther King, Jr. once said, "To return hate for hate does nothing but
intensify the existence of evil in the universe" (King). We live in an era of hate.
We see it all around us. Whether it's racially, sexually, or religiously driven much
injustice is committed on a daily basis. In particular, right now we live in the time
of terror. According to the Brookings Institution, the 21st century brought with it
massive technological innovation, the expansion of the Internet, and *terrorism*.
From London to Casablanca to New Delphi to Bali acts of terrorism have ruled
the first decade and a half of this century (Riedel). Spending large
portions of my life in "danger zones," I've seen what terrorism has
the power to do with my own eyes. But if terrorism is the expression of hate and hate fuels only more hate, what is to be done
about it? Martin Luther King goes on to say, "Someone must have
sense enough and religion enough to cut off the chain of hate
and evil, and this can only be done through love" (King). In other
words, someone, or *someones* (you and me) are responsible for
having enough intelligence and strength to see beyond our fear
and put an end to hate-filled thinking. Then, and only then, can
we see a reverse in the escalation of hate driven evils.

But maybe you are *afraid*? Maybe that's what you're thinking?
Guess what? I am afraid sometimes too. People all around the globe
are afraid. You've seen the news. You've heard the stories. You've
maybe experienced some of it firsthand. If nothing else, you likely
remember exactly what you were doing and what you felt on 9/11.
When terrorists bombed Paris in November of 2015 you probably
shuddered. I also watch the news and read the stories. I remember 9/11 and I felt
for Paris. Actually, I have some firsthand experience, too. I grew up in the post-
war Muslim country of Kosovo where fear ran rampant. My family, Christian aid
workers, were targeted by Al-Qaeda; it was rumored there were kidnapping threats
against me and my sisters when I was 5. I *understand* the fear. I want you to realize
this. Fear is okay. Fear is natural. Fear is there. Fear is justified. You *can* be afraid.

Unrestrained fear, though, distorts our reasoning. Trevin Wax, writing for
The Washington Post puts it this way, "Terrorism thrives on fear, and fear—if left
unchecked—can spread in the deepest darkest corners of our hearts and lead
to decisions and choices that, in normal times, would be unthinkable" (Wax).
With the escalation of terrorism around the globe we've seen the emergence of
Islamophobia. We've seen rational fear give way to irrational discrimination and

*In rhetoric, we often talk
about three appeals—logos,
pathos, and ethos. Ethos
is how the writer man-
ages her credibility. Here
Rachel enhances her ethos
by confiding that she has
seen terrorism "with my
own eyes."*

*In another interesting
rhetorical move, Rachel directly addresses the reader.
How effective is this do
you think?*

Gallina 2

prejudice. Living and working cross-culturally my whole life, I am no stranger to prejudice. I'm not claiming that I'm above irrational thinking. It's impossible to entirely eradicate one's prejudices and pre-conceived notions; I am as biased as anyone else. I do try daily, though, to recognize and re-evaluate my own biases. The more aware we are of our own subjective paradigm the more control we have over our ability to act indiscriminately.

The first step to eliminating hatred and unjust discrimination in this world is recognition. A prejudice we've seen escalate in modern times is Islamophobia.

The Center for Race and Gender at UC Berkeley defines Islamophobia as "a contrived fear or prejudice fomented by the existing Eurocentric and Orientalist global power structure. It is directed at a perceived or real Muslim threat through the maintenance and extension of existing disparities in economic, political, social and cultural relations, while rationalizing the necessity to deploy violence as a tool to achieve 'civilizational rehab' of the target communities (Muslim or otherwise). Islamophobia reintroduces and reaffirms a global racial structure through which resource distribution disparities are maintained and extended" ("Defining Islamophobia").

Here Rachel pivots from her opening, where she finds common ground with her readers over fear of terrorism, to billboard her purpose in the essay: "unrestrained fear" makes us all vulnerable to bigotry.

Now, this might sound contrived, distant, or straight up too wordy. Based on this definition maybe you're thinking you've never interacted with an Islamophobe before nor possess any Islamophobic tendencies yourself. Well, let me ask you a few questions:

- Do you think Islam is set in its ways and unable to adapt to new realities?
- Do you think it has no common values with other major world religions, say the Western ones like Christianity and Judaism?
- Have you ever thought Islam is inferior to Western thinking, that it's somehow outdated, barbaric, and irrational?
- Do you think Islam is violent and supportive of terrorism?

If you answered yes to any one of those questions *you're* Islamophobic. I reworded them a bit, but those are the same framework of questions UC Berkeley's Center for Race and Gender uses to determine the manifestation of Islamophobia. Now, rethink whether or not you or someone you know might be Islamophobic. Likely, you know countless people who would fit the definition.

According to a recent survey more than 50% of the US population has an either "somewhat unfavorable" or "very unfavorable" opinion of Islam (Moore). If you think about that it's actually a little bit heartbreaking. We see continued backlashes of anti-Islamic sentiment in response to terrorism. Whether it's hate filled Facebook posts, viral tweets, or actual criminal offenses, the general public seems to respond to its fear of terrorism by lashing out at innocent Muslims. In 2015, thirty-one US governors actively attempted to implement policies that would deny entrance of Syrian refugees into their states, an action directly linked to the widespread pandemonium which seized the west following terrorist attacks in Paris (Brumfield and Fantz).

Unfortunately, this is not the first time fear has driven policy and public thought. Islamophobia may be a phenomenon of the 21st century but fear-fueled hatred is something we've seen countless times in the past. Some of the darkest hours in U.S. history are those where fear palpably blinded society. Most of us are familiar with the anti-Soviet Union sentiment that dominated the post WWII era. McCarthyism and the Red Scare, the famous 300-person blacklist which ruined many Hollywood careers, and widespread paranoia about anything potentially "communist" are things you've likely read about before. In 2010 the *American Sociological Review* published a study examining the unimaginable spillover effects of fear in that era. What they found is that "when a few individuals or organizations are engaged in wrongdoing and publicly targeted, stigma by association can lead to false positives and harm many innocents" (Pontikes et al. 456). The Red Scare is a perfect example of how susceptible society is to acting irrationally in the face of fear and the inability to control the effects of stigma once they've taken root. The study emphasizes the fact that, aside from the famous 300-person blacklist of famous motion picture artists that we are all familiar with, another "graylist" was also published. The 151 actors, writers, musicians, and entertainers who lost their jobs as a result of this list were named as communists simply on the basis of their "Red connections." That's the power of negative stigma and association.

Another horrific instance of fear dominating public action came in the form of FDR's 1942 signing of Executive Order 9066. After the bombing of Pearl Harbor fear of Japanese Americans overcame the general public. Within six months of the issuance of the order, over 100,000 Japanese Americans were forcibly interned in ten "relocation camps" around the country. The terrible conditions of the camps and the involuntary nature of forced "relocation" bespeak a massive violation of civil rights. Years later, Kimi Durham, a Japanese-American who was interred, said in an interview that "everyone felt betrayed. Before the internment, some Japanese-Americans said America wouldn't intern its own citizens. But it didn't matter if you were Japanese-born, American-born, had one-fourth Japanese blood or one half—everyone had to go" (qtd. in Rogers). When we look back on this moment in our nation's history I think most of us cringe at the injustice of what was done in the name of "national security." Thousands of innocent people had their lives turned upside down because policy was implemented based on pubic pandemonium.

Sadly enough, Islamophobia is proving to be a resurgence of similar injustices in the name of "national security." The mayor of Roanoke, Virginia, David A. Bowers, actually drew upon the example of Japanese internment camps as a defense for his stance regarding the treatment of Syrians in a 2015 address: "Thus, today, I'm requesting that all Roanoke Valley governments

Rachel's assertion here opens the door on historical evidence to support her contention that contemporary Islamophobia isn't new. In a sentence like this one, research writers reinforce their role as narrators, guiding the direction of the conversation with readers by always keeping their purpose in mind.

Gallina 4

and non-governmental agencies suspend and delay any further Syrian refugee assistance until these serious hostilities and atrocities end, or at the very least until regarded as under control by U.S. authorities, and normalcy is restored. I'm reminded that President Franklin D. Roosevelt felt compelled to sequester Japanese foreign nationals after the bombing of Pearl Harbor, and it appears that the threat of harm to America from ISIS now is just as real and serious as that from our enemies then" (Bowers).

Just as people managed to lump all Japanese people into one category and associate them with one act of violence so too are people lumping all Muslims with the acts of just a few extremists. Since 9/11 anti-Muslim hate crimes have seen a five-fold increase (Ingraham). Earlier this year three Muslim students were killed execution style in Chapel Hill, NC (Berman, Kaplan, and Sullivan). A 14-year-old Muslim high school student, Ahmed, was arrested in Texas, when his teachers called the police for suspecting his homemade clock was a bomb. Journalists covering the story wrote that "the 14-year-old's day ended not with praise, but punishment, after the school called police and he was arrested" (Almasy, Fantz, and Stapleton). In 2015, Susan Milligan of *US News* reported that in one week, likely in retaliation to the Paris attacks, a mosque in Austin was defiled with feces, a mosque in Nebraska was vandalized with graffiti, a Muslim family in Orlando came home to bullet holes in their walls, and an Uber driver was beaten for being suspected as a Muslim (Milligan).

Again, the narrator guides the discussion by making a connection between the information that came before and the information that comes next. Much of the challenge of writing—at both the sentence and paragraph levels—is connecting old information to new information, which is exactly what Rachel does here.

To make it more personal, I interviewed a fellow student on my college campus. As an Iraqi American Muslim whose spent almost her entire life here in Boise, Idaho, it's horrifying that what she describes here is simply part of her day to day:

One of the most effective ways to make an abstract issue or idea meaningful is to put a face on it. Here Rachel uses an interview to personalize the problem of Islamophobia.

> The worst was high school and junior high. It was just like five boys and two or three girls. I grew up with them all the way through…. When they assassinated Osama (pause) that one year (pause) it was night when we found out. That evening, they (my parents) told me, "Noora, you'll have people say things to you." Then, I go to school the next day. It just all started. People were saying, "I'm sorry for your loss. I'm sorry your cousin died. Etcetera." I was so angry at how little knowledge they knew about it. I couldn't say anything; I would just burst into tears and go sit in the library or in the corner. I'd have friends that would say to just ignore it, but it's hard to ignore. You're just this small person with a whole bunch of people attacking you…. So for the last five years it was just constant: "Oh look! There's that terrorist! Oh look, watch out, there's a bomb in there!" every time I opened my locker. (Muhammad)

Considering recent developments, I think it's hard to deny: Islamophobia has taken hold of the nation, maybe even of the whole globe. But, it's *fear*, you say, it's *fear and* it's *founded.* People will argue that their fear is justified, expected, and appropriate. I already told you: I concur. I'm not asking you to stop being afraid. But did you know that more Muslims around the world are adversely affected every day by extremism than any other group of people? You read about Paris, but did you know more than 150 others were victims of similar attacks this week in Lebanon, Palestine, Nigeria, Iraq, Cameroon, Israel, and Mali? As Anne Barnard, bureau chief for *The New York Times* points out, the attacks in Beirut paralleled those in Paris, took 43 innocent lives, and received next to no coverage (Barnard). In our fear and hatred, in our attempts to lump all Muslims together, we ignore that they, more than anyone else are justified in their fear.

Journalist Yasmine Hafiz reported that in 2014 Muslim countries around the globe are exhibiting increased fear and concern over the rise of extremism. In places such as Lebanon, public concern about extremism has reached 92% (Hafiz). This is a staggering figure, especially when you think about more than nine out of ten inhabitants in a nation living in fear of extremism. And remember, we're talking about the predominantly Islamic nation of Lebanon. The same nation whose terrorist attacks went largely unheralded. A recent UN report states that in the first eight months of 2014 ISIS contributed to the deaths of more than 9,347 Iraqi civilians (Buchanan). ISIS and its extremism is also in large part responsible for the situation in Syria which, according to Amnesty International, has to date displaced more than 10 million and killed over 220,000 ("Syria's Refugee Crisis"). By comparison, in 2014 terrorism was responsible for the death of only 19 Americans (Goodman). So who is *most* affected by extremism, and potentially more justified in a legitimate fear and hatred of it? That's right, Muslims themselves.

Terrorism in the name of Allah is a horrific reality of 21st century existence. It's scary and it needs to be stopped. We all agree on that. But the Western world is actually fueling it. Our Islamophobia is playing right into the hands of extremist groups like Al-Qaeda and ISIS. By perpetuating violence, by preaching a message of discrimination and hatred, by delineating "us" vs. "them," we're making it easier and easier for young people to sign on to campaigns of rage. Put yourself in the shoes of one of the young Muslim males that make up much of Middle Eastern society right now: you're being entirely forgotten by the international community when horror strikes, you're poor, lacking opportunity, and responsible for feeding your family: you're surrounded on all sides by war and conflict, you taste fear daily, and now you're getting messages from the West that say being Muslim makes you just as bad as being a terrorist. How would you feel?

Erin Banco, from *The International Business Times* examined the psychology behind terrorism. After interviewing psychologists who specialize in understanding terrorism, she concluded that a driving force behind why people join such organizations is a need for belonging (Banco). People become terrorists because they want a sense of connection, belonging, and community. In effect, Islamophobia is the antithesis of making people feel that they belong. Is that not exactly

Gallina 6

what presidential candidates Jeb Bush and Ted Cruz said in 2015 in response to allowing Syrians into this country? In wake of the Paris attacks, Cruz and Bush argued that only *Christian* Syrians should be allowed into this country (Becker). Now you tell me, how is that not sending a message to young Muslim Syrians that the West is not welcoming them with open arms and an assured sense of belonging? Isn't such Islamophobia setting the ground work for ISIS recruiters to convince disgruntled youth that the West is full of infidels that hate them?

So what can you do? You're afraid but rational and tracking with my thoughts; you don't *want* to fuel extremism and terrorism around the world. Now you're aware of Islamophobia and you agree with me that it's absurd and unfair. But at this stage you're wondering what can be done about it? Is awareness enough in this case? No. I'll tell you, awareness is *not* enough. Don't you think that during both the "Red Scare" and the era of Japanese internment camps fellow citizens were "aware"? You must believe thousands, if not millions, sat by and watched but patted themselves on the back for not "taking part." What did their awareness without action lead to? Does not silent passivity make you equally as culpable as "taking part?" What if people had stepped up? What if when irrational fear took hold of whole communities a few had been brave enough to speak out and stand in solidarity with those being persecuted? How different history might look.

Let's not create an era to be ashamed of. Let's not repeat past wrongs and lump all Muslims in with terrorists. If we—you and I and the kid next to you—*vocalize* and *mobilize* we've got a chance of being those strong enough and brave enough to cut off the chain of evil and end the cyclical nature of hatred. If we speak up when anti-Islamic slurs are tossed about, if we defend the rights of refugees around the globe, if we actively attempt to make our fellow students of Islamic faith feel that *they belong,* if we pressure our media agencies and local governments to change the way they portray Muslims as a people group, and if we, most importantly, alter our own thinking about what makes a Muslim a Muslim and a terrorist a terrorist, *maybe* we stand a chance of making MLK's legacy proud. Stop sitting silently as hate filled thinking engulfs our nation. Be the one with sense enough and strength enough to speak out and cut chains.

Directly addressing the reader with questions like this can be very effective, assuming, of course, that readers are likely to answer them in a way that furthers the writer's argument.

The purpose of an argumentative essay like this one is to persuade readers to not only think differently but to act—to do something to solve the problem. In her closing act, Rachel issues the call to action.

Works Cited

Almasy, Steve, et al. "Muslim Teen Ahmed Mohamed Creates Clock, Shows Teachers, Gets Arrested." *CNN,* 16 Sep. 2015, www.cnn.com/2015/09/16/us/texas-student-ahmed-muslim-clock-bomb/.

Banco, Erin. "Why Do People Join ISIS? The Psychology of a Terrorist." *International Business Times,* 5 Sep. 2014, www.ibtimes.com/why-do-people-join-isis-psychology-terrorist-1680444.

Gallina 7

Barnard, Anne. "Beirut, Also the Site of Deadly Attacks, Feels Forgotten." *The New York Times,* 15 Nov. 2015, www.nytimes.com/2015/11/16/world/middleeast/beirut-lebanon-attacks-paris.html?_r=0.

Becker, Olivia. "Jeb Bush is Cool with Syrian Refugees Who Can 'Prove' They are Christian." *VICE News,* 18 Nov. 2015, news.vice.com/article/jeb-bush-is-cool-with-syrian-refugees-who-can-prove-they-are-christian.

Berman, Mark, et al. "Three Muslims Killed in Shooting Near UNC; Police, Family Argue Over Motive." *The Washington Post,* 11 February 2015, www.washingtonpost.com/news/post-nation/wp/2015/02/11/three-killed-in-shooting-near-university-of-north-carolina.

Bowers, David. "Statement of Mayor David A. Bowers." *Office of the Mayor, City of Roanoke*, 18 Nov. 2015, assets.documentcloud.org/documents/2515956/statement-from-roanoke-mayor.pdf.

Brumfield, Ben, and Ashley Fantz. "More Than Half the Nation's Governors Say Syrian Refugees Not Welcome." *CNN,* 19 Nov. 2015, www.cnn.com/2015/11/16/world/paris-attacks-syrian-refugees-backlash.

"Defining Islamophobia." *Center for Race and Gender,* University of California at Berkeley, crg.berkeley.edu/content/islamophobia/defining-islamophobia.

Goodman, H. A. "Of the 17,891 Deaths from Terrorism Last Year, 19 Were American. Let Iraqis Fight ISIS." *HuffPost Politics,* 14 Sep. 2014, www.huffingtonpost.com/h-a-goodman/of-the-17891-deaths-from_b_5818082.html.

Hafiz, Yasmine. "Muslims Worldwide Fear the Rise of Islamic Extremism: Pew Survey." *HuffPost Religion,* 23 July 2014, www.huffingtonpost.com/2014/07/02/muslims-against-extremism-pew-survey_n_5551693.html.

King, Martin Luther. "King Quotes on War and Peace." *The Martin Luther King, Jr., Research and Education Institute,* kinginstitute.stanford.edu/liberation-curriculum/classroom-resources/king-quotes-war-and-peace.

Ingraham, Christopher. "Anti-Muslim Hate Crimes Are Still Five Times More Common Today Than Before 9/11." *The Washington Post,* 11 Feb. 2015, www.washingtonpost.com/news/wonk/wp/2015/02/11/anti-muslim-hate-crimes-are-still-five-times-more-common-today-than-before-911.

Milligan, Susan. "No Welcome Mat." *U.S. News and World Report,* 20 Nov. 2015, http://www.usnews.com/news/the-report/articles/2015/11/20/after-paris-islamophobia-is-on-the-rise.

Moore, Peter. "Poll Results: Islam." *YouGovUS,* 9 Mar. 2015, today.yougov.com/news/2015/03/09/poll-results-islam.

Muhammad, Noora. Personal Interview. 11 October 2015.

Pontikes, Elizabeth, et al. "Stained Red: A Study of Stigma by Association to Blacklisted Artists during the 'Red Scare' in Hollywood. *American Sociological Review,* vol. 75, no. 3, June 2010, pp. 456–478. *Academic Search Premier,* doi: 10.1177/0003122410368929.

Gallina 8

Riedel, Bruce. "The Grave New World: Terrorism in the 21st Century." *India Times,* 9 Dec. 2011. *Brookings*, www.brookings.edu/research/articles/2011/12/terrorism-riedel.

Rogers, Kim. "Internment: Japanese-American Recalls Prison Camps." *St. Louis Post Dispatch,* 2 Aug. 1992, p. 4A. *ProQuest*, search.proquest.com/docview/303629742/A0170F57E08148A7PQ/1?accountid=9649.

"Syria's Refugee Crisis in Numbers." *Amnesty International*, 3 Feb. 2016, www.amnesty.org/en/latest/news/2016/02/syrias-refugee-crisis-in-numbers.

Troup Buchanan, Rose. "Paris Attacks: ISIS Responsible for More Muslim Deaths Than Western Victims." *The Independent,* 19 Nov. 2015, www.independent.co.uk/news/world/europe/paris-attacks-isis-responsible-for-more-muslim-victims-than-western-deaths-a6737326.html.

Wax, Trevin. "Should We Really Close the Border to Refugees? Here's Why Fear Drives out Compassion." *The Washington Post,* 15 Nov. 2015, www.washingtonpost.com/news/acts-of-faith/wp/2015/11/15/should-we-really-close-the-border-to-refugees-heres-why-fear-drives-out-compassion.

Appendix B
Guide to APA Style

The American Psychological Association (APA) style is, like MLA style, commonly used for documenting and formatting college papers. APA style is the standard for papers in the social and behavioral sciences as well as in education and business. In those disciplines, the currency of the material cited is often especially important. Therefore, APA style's author/date citation system emphasizes the date of publication, in contrast to MLA's author/page system.

I think you'll find APA style easy to use, especially if you've had some practice with MLA. Converting from one style to the other is easy (for some key differences between the two, see Table 1). This appendix covers what you need to know about APA style, including how and when to cite sources in your essay (Part One) and how to assemble the References page (Part Three). The discussion of conventions for formatting your paper (Part Two) offers guidance on pagination, layout, and specifics of style. Finally, you can see what APA style looks like in a paper like the one you're writing (Part Four).

The *Publication Manual of the American Psychological Association** is the authoritative reference on APA style, and the sixth edition, published in 2010, features some updates, including some new guidelines for referencing electronic sources. The APA Web includes a nifty tutorial on the basics. Though the information in the sections that follow should answer your questions, check the manual when in doubt.

Checklist before Handing in a Paper in APA Style

- My paper is double-spaced throughout, including the References list (see pages 000, 000, and 000).
- I have a running head (see pages 000–000) in the upper left-hand corner on each page, and a page number in the upper right-hand corner.
- I've cited page numbers in my paper whenever I've quoted a source.
- I've "blocked" every quotation that is 40 or more words (see page 000).

- Whenever possible, I've mentioned in my text the names of authors I cite and put the date of the appropriate publication next to their names.
- I've doubled-checked the accuracy of DOIs and URLs of electronic sources that I included in my References.
- The References list begins on a new page and is organized alphabetically by the authors' last names.
- In article and book titles cited, only the first words of titles and subtitles are capitalized; the remaining words are not capitalized unless they would always be capitalized.

---

* *Publication Manual of the American Psychological Association.* 6th ed. Washington, DC: APA, 2010. Print.

Table 1 Key Differences between MLA and APA Formats

MLA	APA
Capitalizes most words in book and article titles on Works Cited page.	Capitalizes only the first word and proper nouns in book and article titles on References page.
Uses author's full first and last names on Works Cited page.	Uses author's last name along with first and middle initials on References page.
Uses the word *and* to combine authors' names in in-text citations and on Works Cited page if there is more than one author for a source.	Uses an ampersand (&) to combine authors' names in in-text citations and on References page if a source has more than one author.
In-text citations use author's last name and pages cited.	In-text citations use author's last name and date; page numbers aren't required except for quotations.
In-text citations use no punctuation between author's name and page number.	In-text citations use a comma between author's last name and date, and between date and page numbers.
Page numbers are listed simply as a number in in-text citations.	Page numbers are denoted with a "p." or "pp." in in-text citations.
There is no separate title page.	There is a title page with running head.
Running head contains author's last name and the page number, in the top right-hand corner.	Running head contains the first words of the paper's title (at left) and the page number (at right).
No subheadings occur within the paper.	Subheadings often occur within the paper. Paper often begins with an abstract.
Tables and figures are integrated into the body of the paper.	Tables and figures can be integrated or appear in an appendix.

Directory of APA Style

Part One: Citing Sources in Your Essay
1.1 The APA Author/Date System

THE BASICS OF USING PARENTHETICAL CITATION   The author/date system is pretty uncomplicated. If you mention the name of the author in your text, simply place the year her work was published in parentheses immediately after her name. For example:

> Herrick (2006) argued that college testing was biased against minorities.

If you mention both the author's name and the year in the text of your essay, then you can omit the parenthetical citation altogether. For example:

> In 2006, Herrick argued that college testing was biased against minorities.

If you don't mention the author's name in the text, then include that information parenthetically. For example:

> A New Hampshire political scientist (Bloom, 2008) studied the state's presidential primary.

Note that the author's name and the year of her work are separated by a comma.

When to Cite Page Numbers. If the information you're citing came from specific pages (or chapters or sections) of a source, that information may also be included in the parenthetical citation, as in the example that follows. Including page numbers is essential when quoting a source.

> The first stage of language acquisition is called *caretaker speech* (Moskowitz, 1985, pp. 50—51), in which children model their parents' language.

Or, if the author's name is mentioned in the text:

> Moskowitz (1985) observed that the first stage of language acquisition is called *caretaker speech* (pp. 50–51), in which children model their parents' language.

1.1.1 A Work By One Author

> Herrick (2006) argued that college testing was biased against minorities.
>
> *or*
>
> One problem with college testing may be bias (Herrick, 2006).

1.1.2 A Work By Two Authors
When a work has two authors, always mention them both whenever you cite their work in your paper. For example:

> Allen and Oliver (1998) observed many cases of child abuse and concluded that maltreatment inhibited language development.

Notice that if the authors' names are given in a parenthetical citation, an ampersand is used:

> Researchers observed many cases of child abuse and concluded that maltreatment inhibited language development (Allen & Oliver, 1998).

1.1.3 A Work By Three To Five Authors
If a source has three to five authors, mention them all the first time you refer to their work. However, in any subsequent references give the name of the first author followed by the abbreviation et al. For example, here's what a first mention of a multiple-author source would look like:

> The study found that medical students sometimes responded to an inquiry-based approach by becoming more superficial in their analyses (Balasoriya, Hughes, & Toohey, 2011).

Subsequent mentions use the abbreviation et al.:

> Though collaboration is supposed to promote learning, in one case it actually hindered it (Balasoriya et al., 2011).

1.1.4 A Work By Six Or More Authors
When citing works with six or more authors, *always* use the first author's name and *et al.*

1.1.5 An Institutional Author   When citing a corporation or agency as a source, simply list the year of the study in parentheses if you mention the institution in the text:

> The Environmental Protection Agency (2007) issued an alarming report on global warming.

If you don't mention the institutional source in the text, spell it out in its entirety, along with the year. In subsequent parenthetical citations, abbreviate the name. For example:

> A study (Environmental Protection Agency [EPA], 2007) predicted dire consequences from continued global warming.

And later:

> Continued ozone depletion may result in widespread skin cancers (EPA, 2007).

1.1.6 A Work With No Author   When a work has no author, cite an abbreviated title and the year. Place article or chapter titles in quotation marks, and italicize book titles. For example:

> The editorial ("Sinking," 2007) concluded that the EPA was mired in bureaucratic muck.

1.1.7 Two or More Works by the Same Author   Works by the same author are usually distinguished by the date; these would rarely be published in the same year. But if they are, distinguish among works by adding an *a* or *b* immediately following the year in the parenthetical citation. The References list will also have these suffixes. For example:

> Douglas's studies (1986a) on the mating habits of lobsters revealed that the females are dominant. He also found that the female lobsters have the uncanny ability to smell a loser (1986b).

These citations alert readers that the information came from two works by Douglas, both published in 1986.

1.1.8 Authors with the Same Last Name   In the rare case that you're using sources from different authors with the same last name, distinguish between them by including the first initials of each author whenever you mention them in your paper, even if the publication dates differ:

> M. Bradford (2010) and L. S. Bradford (2008) both noted that Americans are more narcissistic.

1.1.9 Several Sources in a Single Citation   Occasionally, you'll want to cite several sources at once. Probably the most common instance is when you refer to the findings of several relevant studies, something that is a good idea as you try to establish a context for what has already been said about your research topic. When listing multiple sources within the same parenthetical citation, order them as they appear in the References (that is, alphabetically) and separate them with semicolons. For example:

> A number of researchers have explored the connection between Internet use and depression (Sanders, Field, & Diego, 2000; Waestlund, Norlander, & Archer, 2001).

1.1.10 Indirect Sources If you discover, say, a great quotation or idea from someone who is mentioned in another author's book or article, try to track down the original source. But when you can't find it, signal parenthetically that you're using an indirect source with the phrase *as cited in.*

> De Groot's study on chess expertise (as cited in Kirschner, Sweller, & Clark, 2006) is....

The only source you'll include in your References list is the indirect source you used; you won't include the original source.

1.1.11 New Editions of Old Works For reprints of older works, include both the year of the original publication and that of the reprint edition (or the translation).

> Pragmatism as a philosophy sought connection between scientific study and real people's lives (James, 1906/1978).

1.1.12 Interviews, E-Mail, and Letters Interviews and other personal communications are not listed in the References at the back of the paper because they are not *recoverable data*, but they are parenthetically cited in the text. Provide the initials and last name of the subject (if not mentioned in the text), the nature of the communication, and the complete date, if possible.

> Nancy Diamonti (personal communication, November 12, 1990) disagrees with the critics of *Sesame Street.*

> In a recent e-mail, Michelle Payne (personal communication, January 4, 2011) complained that....

1.1.13 A Web Site When referring to an *entire* Web site, cite the address parenthetically in your essay. Do not include a citation for an entire Web site in your References list.

> The Centers for Disease Control (http://www.cdc.gov) is a reliable source for the latest health information.

If you're quoting from a Web site, you should cite the date of online publication, if available, and the page number, if available. (When simply referring to a part of a Web site, just use the date, if available, not the page number.) However, most Web documents that aren't also available in print do not have page numbers. What do you do in that case? If you can, use a heading or short title from the source to help readers locate the part of the document where they can find the material you cited. Then add a paragraph number using the abbreviation *para.*

According to Cesar Milan (2010), it's essential that dog owners establish themselves as "pack leaders" ("Why Does CDC Teach Wolf Pack Theory?", para. 2).

Part Two: Formatting Your Essay
2.1 Formatting the Essay and Its Parts

2.1.1 Page Format and Header Papers should be double-spaced, with at least 1-inch margins on all sides. Number all pages consecutively, beginning with the title page; using the Header feature of your word processor, put the page number in the upper right-hand corner. In the upper left-hand corner of each page, beginning with the title page, give an abbreviated title of the paper in uppercase letters. As a rule, the first line of all paragraphs of text should be indented five spaces or a half-inch.

2.1.2 Title Page Unlike a paper in MLA style, an APA-style paper usually has a separate title page. The title page includes the title of the paper, the author's name, and the author's affiliation (e.g., what university he or she is from). As Figure B1 shows, this information is double-spaced, and each line is centered. The upper left of the title page has the abbreviated title in uppercase letters, preceded by "Running head" and a colon, and the upper right has the page number.

2.1.3 Abstract Though it's not always required, many APA-style papers include a short abstract (between 150 to 250 words) following the title page. See Figure B2. An abstract is essentially a short summary of the paper's contents.

Figure B1
Title Page in APA Style

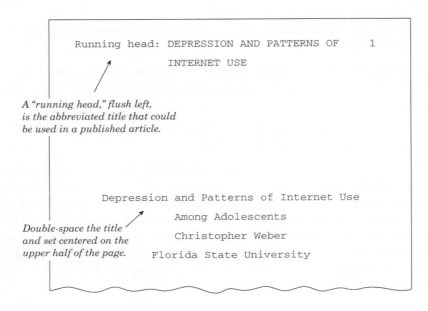

Running head: DEPRESSION AND PATTERNS OF   1
                    INTERNET USE

A "running head," flush left, is the abbreviated title that could be used in a published article.

Depression and Patterns of Internet Use
Among Adolescents
Christopher Weber
Florida State University

Double-space the title and set centered on the upper half of the page.

An abstract usually follows the title page.
This is a concise (no longer than 250 words)
summary of the article and its thesis,
purpose, or findings.

DEPRESSION AND PATTERNS OF INTERNET USE   2

Abstract

With the growth of the Internet as both a
source of information and entertainment,
researchers have turned their attention to
the psychology of Internet use, particularly
focusing on the emotional states of high
Internet users. This project focuses on the
relationship between patterns of Internet
use and depression in adolescent users,
arguing that

Continue the
page header.

Figure B2
The Abstract Page

This is a key feature because it's usually the first thing a reader encounters. The abstract should include statements about what problem or question the paper examines and what approach it follows; the abstract should also cite the thesis and significant findings. Type the title "Abstract" at the top of the page. Type the abstract text in a single block, without indenting.

2.1.4 Body of the Paper The body of the paper begins with the centered title, followed by a double space and then the text. Like all pages, the first page of the body will have an abbreviated title and a page number ("3" if the paper has a title page and abstract). See Figure B3.

```
DEPRESSION AND PATTERNS OF INTERNET USE        3
Depression and Patterns of Internet Use Among
                  Adolescents
       Before Johnny Beale's family got a new
computer in August 2008, the sixteen-year-old
high school student estimated that he spent
about twenty minutes a day online, mostly
checking his e-mail. Within months, however,
Beale's time at the computer tripled, and he
admitted that he spent most of his time
playing games. At first, his family noticed
```

Center the title
of the paper
and double-space
to begin the body
of the text.

Figure B3
The Body of the
Paper in APA Style

If your paper is fairly formal, you might need to divide it into specific sections, each with its own heading—for example, "Introduction," "Method," "Results," and "Discussion." Check with your instructor about whether to follow this format. If you do not need to follow it, you can create your own headings to clarify the organization of your paper.

In the formal structure mentioned, which is typical in academic journals, the sections would include content such as the following:

- Introduction: Why does your research question matter? What has already been said about it? What is the hypothesis you'll be exploring?
- Method: How did you test your hypothesis? What you say here depends on the kind of study you did.
- Results: What did you find?
- Discussion: How do you interpret the findings? To what extent do they support—or fail to support—your initial hypothesis? What are the implications of these discoveries?

2.1.5 Headings

If you use headings, the APA specifies the following hierarchy:

> **Centered, Boldface, Uppercase and Lowercase** (Level 1)
>
> **Flush Left, Boldface, Uppercase and Lowercase** (Level 2)
>
> **Indented, boldface, lowercase, ending with period, running into paragraph.** (Level 3)
>
> ***Indented, boldface, italicized, lowercase, ending with period, running into paragraph.*** (Level 4)
>
> *Indented, italicized, lowercase, ending with a period, running into paragraph.* (Level 5)

Five levels of headings

A paper, particularly a short one, will rarely use all five levels of headings. In fact, it's much more common for a student paper to use just two or possibly three.

2.1.6 Handling Quoted Material When you borrow words, phrases, or passages from another author, typically the material must be contained in quotation marks. Usually, it is smoothly integrated with attribution (*According to Ballenger,...*), and parenthetical citation including page numbers, into your own sentences and paragraphs. For example,

> According to Ellison, Steinfeld, and Lampe (2007), Facebook and other social networking sites offer researchers an "ideal" chance to -investigate "offline and online connection" (p. 12).

But if the quoted material is 40 or more words, it should be "blocked." Indent the entire quoted passage five spaces or a half-inch from the left margin, and omit the quotation marks. For example,

> According to Perfetti's (2003) book on women in the Middle Ages and laughter,

Laughter is both a defense mechanism and a weapon of attack, essential to groups struggling to be taken seriously by the rest of society. But it is perhaps women, more than any other group, who have had the most complicated relationship with humor in Western culture. People of every religion, nationality, ethnicity, class, and occupation have at some time found themselves the butt of an offensive joke and told to lighten up because "it's just a joke." But it is women who have been told that their refusal to laugh at jokes made at their expense shows that they don't have a sense of humor at all. So a woman has to assert her right not to laugh at offensive jokes but simultaneously prove that she is capable of laughter or risk being seen as a humorless spoilsport: a balancing act requiring a quick wit. (p. viii)

Notice that blocked quotations are double-spaced and that the parenthetical reference is placed *after* the period rather than before it.

If you omit material from an original source—a common method of using just the relevant information in a sentence or passage—use *ellipsis points* (…). For example,

The study (Lampe, 2010) noted that "student-athletes in U.S. universities are highly visible…. They are often considered to be representatives of the university, and may be the most visible spokespeople for, in some cases…" (p. 193).

2.1.7 References List All sources cited in the body of the paper are listed alphabetically by author (or title, if the source is anonymous) in the list titled "References," as shown in Figure B4. This list should begin a new page, and it is double-spaced throughout. The first line of each entry is flush left; subsequent lines are indented a half-inch. Explanation of how to cite various types of sources in the References list follows (see "Part Three: Preparing the References List").

Figure B4
The References Page

DEPRESSION AND PATTERNS OF INTERNET USE   10

References

Sanders, C., Tiffany, M., & Diego, M. (2000). The relationship of Internet use to depression and social isolation among adolescents. *Adolescence, 35,* 237–242.

Always start the "References" on a new page.

Waestlund, E., Norlander, T., & Archer, T. (2001). Internet blues revisited: Replication and extension of an Internet paradox study. *CyberPsychology & Behavior, 4,* 385–391.

Create a five-space "hanging indent."

2.1.8 Tables And Figures Should you include a table, chart, or photograph in your paper? Sure, if you're certain that it adds something to your discussion and if the information it presents is clear and understandable. If you use a table (and with programs like Excel and Word, tables are incredibly easy to generate), place it in the manuscript as close as you can to where you mention it. Alternatively, you can put your tables and figures in an appendix. Tables should all be double-spaced. Type a table number at the top, flush left. Number tables "Table 1," "Table 2," and so on, corresponding to the order in which they are mentioned in the text. The title, in italics, should be placed on the line below the number. Tables that you put in an appendix should be labeled accordingly. For example, Table 1 in Figure B2 in this appendix would be numbered Table B1.

Figures (graphs, charts, photographs, and drawings) are handled similarly to tables. They are numbered consecutively beginning with "Figure 1." This figure number, below the figure itself, is followed by a title and, if needed, a caption (see Figure B5) . Captions are often helpful in explaining a chart, photograph, drawing, or other figure. As with tables, insert figures in your paper as close as you can to where you refer to them or, alternatively, put them in an appendix.

2.1.9 Appendix This is a seldom-used feature of an APA-style paper, though you might find it helpful for presenting specific material that isn't central to the discussion in the body of your paper: a detailed description of a device mentioned in the paper, a copy of a blank survey, a table, or the like. Each item, placed at the end of the paper following the References page, should begin on a separate page and be labeled "Appendix" (followed by "A," "B," and so on, consecutively, if you have more than one Appendix in your paper).

2.1.10 Notes Several kinds of notes might be included in a paper. The most common are *content notes*, or brief commentaries by the writer keyed to superscript numbers in the body of the text. These notes are useful for discussion of key points that are relevant but might be distracting if explored in the text of your paper. Present all notes, numbered consecutively, on a page titled "Footnotes" (placed after the References page but before any appendixes) or at the bottom of the relevant page. Notes should be double-spaced. Begin each note with the

Figure B5
Example of Format for a Figure

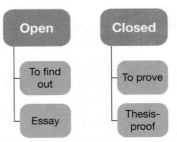

Figure 1. Two broad categories of writing assignments. Open-ended and more closed writing assignments each are characterized by a different motive and result in a different genre.

appropriate superscript number, indented like the first line of a paragraph; subsequent lines of a note are not indented.

2.2 Some Style Considerations

2.2.1 Use of Italics The APA guidelines for *italicizing* call for its use when:

- Giving the titles of books, periodicals, films, and publications that appear on microfilm.
- Using new or specialized terms, but only the first time you use them (e.g., "the authors' *paradox study* of Internet users…").
- Citing a phrase, letter, or word as an example (e.g., "the second *a* in *separate* can be remembered by remembering the word *rat*").

Use quotation marks around the titles of articles or book chapters mentioned in your essay.

2.2.2 Treatment Of Numbers Numbers 9 and less that don't represent precise measurements should be spelled out, and numbers 10 and higher should be expressed as numerals. Any numbers that begin a sentence or represent a commonly used fraction (e.g., "one-quarter of the sample") should be spelled out.

Part Three: Preparing the References List

Each parenthetical citation in the body of the paper should correspond to a complete source listing in the References list. The format for this section was described previously in this appendix (see "References List" in Part Two).

3.1 Order of Sources and Information

ORDER OF SOURCES List the references alphabetically by author's last name or by the first key word of the title if there is no author. This alphabetical principle has a few complications:

- You may have several sources by the same author. If these sources weren't published in the same year, list them in chronological order, the earliest first. If the sources were published in the same year, include a lowercase letter to distinguish them. For example:

  Lane, B. (2007a). Verbal medicine…
  Lane, B. (2007b). Writing…

- Because scholars and writers often collaborate, you may have several references in which an author is listed with several *different* collaborators. List these sources alphabetically using the second author's last name. For example,

  Brown, M., Nelson, A. (2002)

  Brown, M., Payne, M. (1999)

ORDER OF INFORMATION   A References list entry for a periodical or book includes this information, in order: author; date of publication; book title or, for articles, article title followed by periodical title; and publication information. Here are some basics about each of these entry parts; details and examples follow. Remember that all entries should be double-spaced and that the first line of each should begin flush left and all subsequent lines should be indented.

Author or Authors. List up to six authors—last name, comma, and then initials. Invert all authors' names. Use commas to separate authors' names; add an *ampersand* (&) before the last author's name. End the list of names with a period. When citing an edited book, list the editor(s) in the author's place, and add the abbreviation *Ed.* or *Eds.* in parentheses after the last editor's name. If more than six authors, then after sixth author, use an ellipsis and then last author name inverted followed by a period.

Date. After the last author's name, in parentheses list the year the work was published. If the source is a magazine or newspaper, also include the month and day; for example, "(2011, April 4)." If a source doesn't list a date, use the abbreviation *n.d.* in parentheses. Add a period after the closing parenthesis.

Book Title or Article Title. Use a period at the end of each title, and style titles as follows:

- *Book titles* are italicized. Only the first word of titles and subtitles is capitalized; all other words are lowercase unless ordinarily capitalized. For example:

  The curious researcher: A guide to writing research papers.

  Sound reporting.

- *Article titles* are given without italics or quotation marks. As with book titles, capitalize only the first word of the title and any subtitle.

  Student athletes on Facebook.

  Oyster apocalypse? Truth about bivalve obliteration.

Periodical Title and Publication Information. Periodical titles are italicized, like book titles; unlike book and article titles, periodical titles use both uppercase and lowercase letters. Add the volume number (if any), also italicized and separated from the title with a comma. If each issue of the periodical starts with page 1, then also include the issue number in parentheses immediately after the volume number. End the entry, following a comma, with the page numbers of the article.

For example, you might have *Journal of Mass Communication, 10,* 138–150. Use the abbreviation *p.* (for one page) or *pp.* (for more than one page) only if you are citing a newspaper.

Publication Information for Books. List the city and state or country of publication (use postal abbreviations for states) and then, following a colon, the name of the publisher, followed by a period.

Bringing these elements together, a print book citation would look like this in APA style:

> Blakeswell, S. (2010). *How to live or a life of Montaigne.* New York, NY: Other Press.

And a print periodical citation would look like this:

> Alegre, A. (2011). Parenting styles and children's emotional intelligence. What do we know? *The Family Journal, 19,* 56–62.

Digital Sources. In many ways, citing an electronic source is the same as citing a print one—you'll include author, title, and publication information. But there are also significant differences. Online material may appear in different versions—say, as a talk and as an article based on that talk—and because electronic sources may come and go, it's hard to be certain that readers will be able to find a particular source. APA has been making changes in an effort to meet the special challenges posed by online material. Basically, the organization recommends that you identify where the article or document is located using one of two methods:

1. Cite the DOI (digital object identifier).

Or, if you can find no DOI,

2. Include the URL of the home page (Web address).

The digital object identifier is a unique number that is assigned to an electronic document. Almost all journal articles these days have a DOI, which is often listed on the first page of a document. Because these numbers are stable and unique to each source, they are the preferred method of citing the location of an electronic source.

A journal article with a DOI would be cited like this:

> O'Neil, J. (2011). The privatization of public schools in New Zealand. *Journal of Education Policy, 26,* 17–31. doi: 10.1080/02680939.2010.493227

For example, here's a typical citation of an online document that has no DOI:

> Perina, K., Flora, P., & Marano, H. P. (2011, January 1). Who are you? (And what do you think of me?). *Psychology Today.* Retrieved from http://www.psychologytoday.com/articles/201012/who-are-you-and-what-do-you-think-of-me

3.2 Citing Books in Print and Online

3.2.1 A Book With One Author Cite a print book like this:

> Barry, J. M. (2004). *The great influenza: The epic story of the deadliest plague in history*. New York, NY: Viking.

In-Text Citation: (Barry, 2004) *or* According to Barry (2004), . . .

Cite a book that appears only electronically like this:

> Burnheim, J. (2006). *Is democracy possible? The alternative to electoral politics*. Retrieved from http://setis.library.usyd.edu.au/democracy/index.html

In-Text Citation: (Burnheim, 2006) *or* According to Burnheim (2006), . . .

For an electronic book that is also available in print, include information in brackets about how it appeared digitally. For example,

> Gwynne, S. C. (2010). *Empire of the summer moon* [iBook version]. Retrieved from http://www.apple.com/us/ibooks

In-Text Citation: (Gwynne, 2010) *or* According to Gwynne (2010), . . .

3.2.2 A Book with Two Authors

> Glenn, J., & Hayes, C. (2007). *Taking things seriously*. New York, NY: Princeton Architectural Press.

In-Text Citation: (Glenn & Hayes, 2007) *or* According to Glenn and Hayes (2007), . . .

3.2.3 A Book with Three to Seven Authors

> Belenky, M., Clinchy, B. M., Goldberger, N. R., & Tarule, J. M. (1986). *Women's ways of knowing: The development of self, voice, and mind*. New York, NY: Basic Books.

In-Text Citation: (Belenky, Clinchy, Goldberger, & Tarule, 1986) when mentioned first, and (Belenky et al., 1986) thereafter.

3.2.4 A Book With Eight Or More Authors For a work with eight or more authors, give the first six authors followed by an ellipsis (. . .) and the final author. For example,

> Jones, B., Doverman, L. S., Shanke S., Forman, P., Witte, L. S., Firestone, F. J., . . . Smith, L. A. (2011). *Too many -authors spoil the soup*. New York, NY: Oyster Press.

In-Text Citation: (Jones et al., 2011)

3.2.5 A Book with an Institutional Author

> American Red Cross. (2007). *Advanced first aid and emergency care*. New York, NY: Doubleday.

In-Text Citation: (American Red Cross, 2007)

3.2.6 A Book with No Author

> *The Chicago manual of style* (16th ed.). (2010). Chicago, IL: University of
> Chicago Press.

In-Text Citation: (*Chicago Manual of Style,* 2010) *or* According to the *Chicago
Manual of Style* (2010),...

3.2.7 An Encyclopedia Entry Cite an article from a print encyclopedia like this:

> Hansen, T. S. (2003). Depression. In *The new encyclopaedia Britannica* (Vol.
> 12, pp. 408–412). Chicago, IL: Encyclopaedia Britannica.

In-Text Citation: (Hansen, 2003) *or* Hansen (2003) defines depression as....
Cite an article from an online encyclopedia like this:

> Diarrhea. (2008). In *Columbia encyclopedia* (6th ed.). Retrieved from http://
> www.encyclopedia.com/doc/1E1-diarrhea.html

In-Text Citation: ("Diarrhea," 2008) *or* According to the *Columbia Encyclopedia*
(2008), diarrhea....

3.2.8 A Chapter in a Book

> Kuhn, T. S. (1996). The route to normal science. In *The structure of scientific
> revolutions* (pp. 23–34). Chicago, IL: University of Chicago Press.

In-Text Citation: (Kuhn, 2006) *or* Kuhn (2006) argues that....

3.2.9 A Book with an Editor

> Crane, R. S. (Ed.). (1952). *Critics and criticism.* Chicago, IL: University of
> Chicago Press.

In-Text Citation: (Crane, 1952) *or* In his preface, Crane (1952) observed that....

3.2.10 A Selection in a Book with an Editor

> McKeon, R. (1952). Rhetoric in the Middle Ages. In R. S. Crane (Ed.), *Crit-
> ics and criticism* (pp. 260–289). Chicago, IL: University of Chicago Press.

In-Text Citation: (McKeon, 1952) *or* McKeon (1952) argued that....

3.2.11 A Republished Work

> James, W. (1978). *Pragmatism.* Cambridge, MA: Harvard University Press.
> (Original work published 1907)

In-Text Citation: (James, 1907/1978) *or* According to William James (1907/1978),...

3.2.12 A Government Document

> U.S. Bureau of the Census. (1991). *Statistical abstract of the United States*
> (111th ed.). Washington, DC: Government Printing Office.

In-Text Citation: (U.S. Bureau, 1991) *or* According to the U.S. Census Bureau
(1991),...

3.3 Citing Articles, in Print and Online

3.3.1 A Journal Article Cite a print journal article like this:

> Blager, F. B. (1979). The effect of intervention on the speech and language of children. *Child Abuse and Neglect, 5,* 91–96.

In-Text Citation: (Blager, 1979) or Blager (1979) stated that....
Include the DOI, if available:

> Wang, F., McGuire, P., & Pan, E. (2010). Applying technology to inquiry-based learning in early childhood education. *Early Childhood Education Journal, 37,* 381–389. doi:10.1007/s10643-009-0634-6

In-Text Citation: When first mentioned cite all three (Wang, McGuire, & Pan, 2010) or Wang, McGuire, and Pan (2010) argue that.... Subsequent mentions can use *et al.*: (Wang et al., 2010).

For a journal article with no DOI, include the URL of the database or the online journal's home page:

> Kaveshar, J. (2008). Kicking the rock and the hard place to the curb: An alternative and integrated approach to suicidal students in higher education. *Emory Law Journal, 57*(3), 651–693. Retrieved from http://find.galegroup.com/itx/start.do?prodId=AONE

In-Text Citation: (Kaveshar, 2008) or According to Kaveshar (2008),...

3.3.2 A Journal Article Not Paginated Continuously Most journals begin on page 1 with the first issue of the year and continue paginating consecutively for subsequent issues. A few journals, however, start on page 1 with each issue. For these, include the issue number in parentheses following the italicized volume number:

> Williams, J., Post, A. T., & Strunk, F. (1991). The rhetoric of inequality. *Attwanata, 12*(3), 54–67.

In-Text Citation: (Williams, Post, & Strunk, 1991) or Williams, Post, and Strunk (1991) argue that.... When first mentioned, cite all three authors; subsequently you can use et al.: (Williams et al., 1991).

3.3.3 A Magazine Article To cite print articles, include the year, month, and (if present) day published.

> Moore, Peter. (2003, August). Your heart will stop. *Men's Health.* 142–151.

In-Text Citation: (Moore, 2003) or Moore (2003) observed that....
Cite online articles like this:

> O'Hehir, A. (2008). Beyond the multiplex. Salon.com. Retrieved from http://www.salon.com/ent/movies/btm/

In-Text Citation: (O'Hehir, 2008) or According to O'Hehir (2008),...

3.3.4 A Newspaper Article Cite print articles like this:

> Honan, W. (1991, January 24). The war affects Broadway. *The New York Times*, pp. C15–C16.

In-Text Citation: (Honan, 1991) *or* Honan (1991) said that "Broadway is a battleground" (p. C15).

Cite online articles like this:

> Englund, W., DeYoung, K., & Willgoren, D. (2011, February 4). Huge protests continue for 11th day as Obama administration weighs Egypt options. *The Washington Post.* Retrieved from http://www.washingtonpost.com

In-Text Citation: (Englund, DeYoung, & Willgoren, 2011) *or* According to Englund et al . . . . .

3.3.5 An Article with No Author If there is no author, a common situation with newspaper articles, alphabetize using the first significant word in the article title. For example:

> New Hampshire loud and clear. (1998, February 19). *The Boston Globe*, p. 22.

In-Text Citation: ("New Hampshire," 1998) *or* In the article "New Hampshire loud and clear" (1998), . . .

3.3.6 An Article on A Web Site Note that this citation includes the abbreviation *n.d.* because the article did not include a date.

> Lopez, M. (n.d.). Intellectual development of toddlers. *National Network for Childcare.* Retrieved from http://www.nncc.org/Child.Dev/intel.dev.todd.html

In-Text Citation: (Lopez, n.d.) *or* According to Lopez (n.d.), . . .

3.3.7 An Abstract The growth of online databases for articles has increased the availability of full-text versions and abstracts of articles. Although it is almost always better to use the full article, sometimes an abstract itself contains useful information. Typically, there are two situations in which you might choose to cite just an abstract: when you're working with an original print article or when you've culled the abstract from a database like *Biological Abstracts.* In the first case, include the term *Abstract* in brackets following the title and before the period.

For example,

> Renninger, A. K. (2009). Interest and identity development in instruction: An inductive model [Abstract]. *Educational Psychologist, 44,* 105–118.

In-Text Citation: (Renninger, 2009) *or* Renninger (2009) claims that . . . .

If the abstract was from a database or some other secondary source, include the name of that source. The term *Abstract* in brackets isn't necessary in this case. For example,

> Garcia, R. G. (2002). Evolutionary speed of species invasions. *Evolution, 56,* 661–668. Abstract retrieved from *Biological Abstracts.*

In-Text Citation: (Garcia, 2002) *or* Garcia (2002) argues that....

3.3.8 A Book Review Cite a review that's in print like this:

> Dentan, R. K. (1989). A new look at the brain [Review of the book *The dreaming brain,* by J. A. Hobsen]. *Psychiatric Journal, 13,* 51.

In-Text Citation: (Dentan, 1989) *or* Dentan (1989) argued that....
Cite an online review like this:

> Benfey, C. (2008). Why implausibility sells [Review of the book *Painter in a savage land,* by M. Harvey]. *Slate.* Retrieved from http://www.slate.com/id/2193254/

In-Text Citation: (Benfey, 2008) *or* Benfey (2008) argued that....

3.3.9 An Editorial

> Egypt's agonies [Editorial]. (2011, February 2). *The New York Times.* Retrieved from http://www.nytimes.com/2011/02/04/opinion/04fr1.htm

In-Text Citation: ("Egypt's Agonies," 2011) *or The New York Times* (2011) argued....

3.3.10 A Letter to the Editor

> Hill, A. C. (1992, February 19). A flawed history of blacks in Boston [Letter to the editor]. *The Boston Globe,* p. 22.

In-Text Citation: (Hill, 1992) *or* Hill (1992) complained that....

3.3.11 A Published Interview Personal interviews are usually not cited in an APA-style References list even though they are cited in your text. Published interviews are cited as follows:

> Cotton, P. (1982, April). [Interview with J. Tule, psychic]. *Chronicles Magazine,* pp. 24–28.

In-Text Citation: (Cotton, 1982) *or* Cotton (1982) noted that....

3.4 Citing Other Sources

3.4.1 An Entire Web Site If you're referring to an entire Web site in the text of your essay, include the Web address parenthetically. However, there is no need to include an entry for it in the References list. For example:

> The Google Scholar search engine (http://scholar.google.com) is considered excellent for academic research.

3.4.2 A Film, Dvd, or Online Video

> Hitchcock, A. (Producer & Director). (1954). *Rear window* [Film]. United
> States: MGM.

In-Text Citation: (Hitchcock, 1954) *or* In *Rear Window,* Hitchcock (1954) . . . .
Here's how to cite an online video:

> Price, P. (Writer). (2008, April 4). *Researching online: Five easy steps* [Video
> file]. Retrieved from http://www.youtube.com/watch?v=Ylp9nJpGa
> k4&feature=related

In-Text Citation: (Price, 2008) *or* In *Researching Online*, Price (2008) . . . .

3.4.3 A Television Program

> Burns, K. (Executive producer). (1996). *The West* [Television broadcast].
> New York, NY: Public Broadcasting Service.

In-Text Citation: (Burns, 1996) *or* In Ken Burns's (1996) film, . . .

3.4.4 An Audio Podcast

> Kermode, M. (2008, June 20). The edge of love. *Mark Kermode and Simon
> Mayo's movie reviews* [Audio podcast]. Retrieved from http://www.
> bbc.co.uk/fivelive/entertainment/kermode.shtml

In-Text Citation: (Kermode, 2008) *or* In his latest review, Kermode (2008)
decried . . . .

3.4.5 A Blog

> Shen, H. (2008, June 4). Does your password meet the test? [Web log
> post]. Retrieved from http://googleblog.blogspot.com/2008/06/
> does-your-password-pass-test.html

In-Text Citation: (Shen, 2008) *or* Our passwords are vulnerable, says Shen
(2008), because . . . .

3.4.6 A Wiki

> How to use Audacity for podcasting. (n.d.). Retrieved from http://sites
> .google.com/a/biosestate.edu/podcasting-team/Home

In-Text Citation: ("Audacity," n.d.)

3.4.7 Online Discussion Lists These include listservs, electronic mailing lists,
newsgroups, and online forums, with the method of citation varying slightly
depending on the specific type of source. For example,

> Hord, J. (2002, July 11). Re: Why do pigeons lift one wing up in the air?
> [Online forum comment]. Retrieved from rec://pets.birds.pigeons

In-Text Citation: (Hord, 2002) *or* Hord asks (2002)....

Note that the citation includes the subject line of the message as the title and bracketed information about the source, in this case an online forum comment. For listservs, use "[Electronic mailing list message]."

3.4.8 A Musical Recording

Wolf, K. (1986). Muddy roads [Recorded by E. Clapton]. On *Gold in California* [CD]. Santa Monica, CA: Rhino Records. (1990).

In-Text Citation: (Wolf, 1986, track 5) *or* In Wolf's (1986) song, . . .

Part Four: Student Paper in APA Style

Laura Burns' fascinating look at the 1978 mass suicide among followers of Jim Jones's People's Temple does what good writing should do: It challenges us to take a look at something we may have seen before and consider seeing it differently. She does not dispute that this was a tragedy or that Jones was, in the end, a madman. But Laura argues that to see only these things is to miss the admirable idealism that was once behind the People's Temple, an idealism that makes the tragedy even worse.

Looking for Utopia: The Men and Women

of the People's Temple

Laura Burns

State University

Looking for Utopia: The Men and Women of the People's Temple

Even in mid-November, the air in the Guyanese jungle was thick with heat. The screams of spider monkeys pierced the silence over the corrugated tin roof of a pavilion. Fields of cassava, eddoes, and pineapple lay abandoned, trailing off into the vast green jungle (Hatfield, 1998). And on the soft, spongy ground, circled by plastic barrels dripping with red, lay the bodies of over 900 people. Above the muddy road leading into the settlement, a sign: "Welcome to Jonestown."

The rise and fall of the People's Temple, the Reverend Jim Jones, and the cataclysmic mass murder/suicide at Jonestown, Guyana, on November 18, 1978, still haunt the American consciousness. However, the further removed we are from the devastating events of that day, the less clearly we are able to see the humanity of its victims. The tragedy at Jonestown was not caused only by brainwashing or coercion, but rather by a more complex formula—it was the product of the dream of a new group of liberal idealists who, frustrated with their disaffected society, came together to find solace in the hope of utopian possibility, no matter what the cost.

In most argumentative essays, the thesis is parked right up front in the piece, as it is here.

James Warren Jones, the man who was to become the Reverend Jim Jones, was born on May 13, 1931, in rural Crete, Indiana, and developed an interest in religion early on. At the young age of 21, Jones accepted a position as a pastor at the Somerset Southside Methodist Church in Indianapolis. He had a unique vision for a church, though—one that didn't mesh with what was happening in Indianapolis in the 1950s. Infuriated by the congregation's refusal to desegregate, Jones left and purchased a small building he called the Wings of Deliverance Church (Lattin, 2003). Later that year, the name of the church was changed to the People's Temple.

In developing a doctrine, Jim Jones focused his vision on racial equality and civil rights. This immediately appealed to the black community in Indianapolis, who flocked to the church to hear Jones's sermons: "What is God anyway?" he would ask the congregation, and then answer, "God is perfect justice, freedom, and equality" (Weston, 1981, p. 56). And Jones practiced what he preached.

In 1953, he and his wife, Marceline, went to a local adoption agency, where they witnessed a wealthy black doctor refuse to take home a child, claiming the boy was "too black." Furious, Jones retorted, "Well, in that case, I'll take him" ("Messiah," 1978). This was to be the first of seven ethnically diverse children the family would adopt. For many black congregants, Jones was the first white man who had ever showed kinship to them and compassion for their struggle. Through tithing and other support, they could be a part of Jones's social movement. In religious terms, Jones's style of preaching and practice of healings and psychic magic were aligned with traditional Pentecostalism, a familiar faith for many black congregants. They felt right at home.

In the early 1960s, Jones, like many other Americans, became caught up in nuclear paranoia. He decided a permanent location change for the Church was needed, and selected Ukiah, in Redwood Valley, California. In 1963, Jones

Looking for Utopia 3

and his family, along with over 70 members of the Indianapolis People's Temple, relocated to rural Ukiah. In California, the Temple recruited a new group of converts: white, middle-class intellectuals and idealists. The political landscape in America was in upheaval, and in California, the alienation experienced by many budding idealists led them to fringe religious groups, such as Hare Krishna, Scientology, and the People's Temple. Jones provided an opportunity for recruits of all races—his "rainbow family"—to join hands and work to make a utopia of equality and freedom.

Notice how Laura loops back to her thesis with the reference to the "utopian" dreams of early members of the Church. Imagine that a thesis statement is a tack that the writer drives into the material to keep it anchored to the controlling idea.

Jones preached *apostolic socialism,* which combines Christian doctrine with socialist goals. He quoted Bible verses, such as Acts 4:31–32, which advocates for common finances, and Acts 4:35, which speaks of the distribution of resources according to need (Wessinger, 2000). The People's Temple was engaged in a new kind of civil rights activism, pairing the Christian stance of Martin Luther King Jr. with the militarism of Marcus Garvey (Hall, 1987). Jones was vibrant and well-loved, and the Temple community was tight-knit and warm, and successfully broke down barriers of race, age, and gender (nearly all Temple leaders were women). This meant that even when the doctrine got darker and their leader grew more and more paranoid, the congregants stayed put. Everything the People's Temple was fighting against lurked right outside the Church doors; if they wanted to realize their dream of utopia, they had to stick with Jones.

Laura hammers in another tack, building support for her thesis.

By the early 1970s, the Church was already functioning as a standalone socialist community, financially supported by members' donations of Social Security checks, paychecks, and the funds from the sale of their private homes. However, as his paranoia increased, Jones was tightening the reins. He forced members to prove their loyalty by signing blank power-of-attorney forms and false confessions of murder and child molestation, stating that should they leave the Church, he would turn these in to the police (Maaga, 1998, p. 13). The Diversions Committee, a group comprised of Jones's most loyal confidantes, was organized to push forth the principles of the Temple and undermine opposition in the public arena. He also began to lay the groundwork for an exodus from "capitalist America,-racist America, fascist America" (Chidester, 1988, p. 72) to Guyana, a small nation in South America that had granted Jones a lease in October 1973 (Weston, 1981). He preached the danger of radioactive fallout and the threat of the government and media, asserting that he had "seen, by divine revelation, the total annihilation of this country and other parts of the world" (Appel, 1983, pp. 28–29).

In 1977, *New West Magazine* published an article by Marshall Kilduff that was harshly critical of Jones and the People's Temple. It was a public relations nightmare, and Jones panicked and moved immediately to Guyana, enacting an emergency six-week egression. Most Temple members followed him. A planned exodus of this kind is not out of line with the actions of similar groups, such as Marcus Garvey's Back-to-Africa movement, and Guyana provided an opportunity to start fresh. "I wanted my son to grow up in a better place," remembered Vernon

Gosney. "I wanted to help create this utopia that Jim Jones had talked about, where people would live in harmony and peace" (Vandecarr, 2003, p. 38). Guyana was the promised land, and Jones was going to lead them there (Hall, 1987).

Once the members arrived in Georgetown, the capital of Guyana, they were transported by small passenger plane to Port Kaituma. From there, they were driven by truck for seven miles on muddy, unpaved roads to the Jonestown Agricultural Commune. In the beginning, there was little to see—merely a large, open-air pavilion framed by fields of cassava, eddoes, and pineapple. Eventually, thanks to the ceaseless hard work of the Temple members, the commune would house a sawmill, a 10,000-book library, a nursery, a hospital, a dispensary, ammunition and equipment storage, a repair shop, and a playground. On the walls of the buildings hung signs painted with hopeful quotes: "Where the spirit of the Lord is, there is liberty," "All that believed were together, and had all things in common" ("What I Saw," 1978, p. 43). "It was a harmonious, supportive community," recalled Vernon Gosney. "Everyone was building beautiful buildings. Jim Jones was a benevolent figure" (Vandecarr, 2003, p. 38).

One sign of authoritative research writing is a paragraph like this one, which uses three different sources rather than relying on one.

Despite that early sense of harmony, the move to Jonestown only increased the intensity of the control Jones wielded over Temple members, and his paranoia was significantly worsened by his descent into prescription drug addiction. Jones enacted frequent emergency drills, or *white nights,* announced with sirens. Some white nights concluded with suicide drills. Members were given wine, which they were told was poisoned. If they didn't drink it immediately, they were berated until they did. They were told that in death, they would be transformed and live with Jones in a better world (Long, 1994). Although extreme, suicide drills were not unheard of in other radical movements. Jones's white nights followed the example of Black Panther Minister of Defense Huey Newton, who stated, "By having no family, I inherited the family of humanity. By having no possessions, I have possessed all . . . . By surrendering my life to the revolution, I have found eternal life" (Chidester, 1988, p. 14). "The white nights didn't seem real," recalled Vernon Gosney. "I should have seen it coming, but I didn't" (Vandecarr, 2003, p. 38).

Gosney was not the only one who didn't seem to see the warning signs. While in the United States, Temple members didn't defect mostly for ideological reasons, but in Guyana, miles away from civilization, the reasons became more mortal. In Jonestown, Temple members were mentally and emotionally exhausted from constant fear of punishment, excessive work, and malnourishment. For many, despite the conditions, the community they were creating in Guyana was still the closest they had ever come to their idea of a societal utopia. The problem was that the "People's Temple at some point lost its ability to look self-critically at itself and to challenge the decisions of the leadership—not just Jim Jones," states the Rev. Mary McCormick Maaga, a Jonestown scholar. "And Jones lost his ability to lead because of drug addiction and mental illness" (Hatfield, 1998).

Looking for Utopia 5

Shortly after Jones's exodus to Guyana, on November 17, 1978, a delegation of reporters, photographers, and concerned relatives of Jonestown residents, led by California Congressman Leo Ryan, arrived in Port Kaituma. The junket spent that evening in Jonestown interviewing Temple members, who were effusive about their love for Jonestown, and enjoying entertainment and freshly prepared food. Impressed, Ryan announced, "From what I've seen there are a lot of people here who think this is the best thing that has happened in their whole lives" (Neff, 1978, p. 41). However, before the party left for the evening, a small note was slipped to reporter Don Harris, who later showed it to Ryan. It read: "Vernon Gosney and Monica Bagby. Please help us get out of Jonestown." The next day, Ryan extended an open invitation to any Temple members who wanted to leave with him, and at around 11:00 in the morning, 16 defectors, including Vernon Gosney, Monica Bagby, and last-minute addition Larry Layton, departed for the airstrip in Port Kaituma, where two planes waited to take them back to the United States. The smaller plane was boarded by Monica Bagby, Vernon Gosney, Dale Parks, and Larry Layton, who, upon the closing of the doors, pulled out a gun, wounding Bagby and Gosney. Simultaneously, a tractor and two trailers belonging to the People's Temple arrived on the airstrip and opened fire. Congressman Ryan, defector Patricia Parks, and reporters Greg Robinson, Don Harris, and Bob Brown were shot dead within seconds. Brown's camera, which was on, kept rolling even after he fell to the ground (Stephenson, 2005).

Further evidence supporting the thesis: Despite the incredible hardship, the utopian dream was powerful enough that the residents of Jonestown endured.

Meanwhile, Jones was preparing for the end of his own movement. As night fell, the familiar siren rang out over Jonestown: "This is a white night. Everyone to the pavilion." Jones instructed Dr. Laurence Schacht and others in his inner circle to prepare the concoction of Fla-V-or Aid, liquid cyanide, and Valium (which Dr. Schacht believed would cause painless death) in large white buckets. Slowly, carefully, Jones explained the drastic action. "Some months I've tried to keep this thing from happening," he said breathily into his microphone. "But now I see . . . it's the will of the Sovereign Being that this happen to us. That we lay down our lives in protest against what's being done." One woman, 60-year-old Christine Miller, interrupted Jones: "As long as there's life," she said, "there's hope." Kindly, Jones responded: "Well, someday, everybody dies . . . . And I'd like to choose my own kind of death for a change" (Stephenson, 2005, pp. 131–136). Miller relented and joined the others, who walked willingly to the poison. Certainly, they had been prepared for this moment by the suicide drills and Jones's recent apocalyptic sermons, but more importantly, the Temple members didn't see their deaths as senseless. Their suicides fit in with the doctrine of the Temple, enacting a release from a corrupt society, revenge against capitalism and inequality, and a revolution against the degradation that they believed existed in American society (Chidester, 1988).

With the organization of Temple leaders, the children were lined up before the vats of Fla-V-or Aid, and with syringes, squirts of the red liquid were pressed into their mouths. Adults were given plastic cups with the poison, and after drinking,

Looking for Utopia 6

were told to lie down in the grass with their children. However, the mixture wasn't quite right, and the Valium didn't adequately dull the pain of the cyanide's work. Within minutes, Temple members began to convulse and sob, blood flowing out of their noses and mouths. Jones and his inner circle escaped this brutal fate, and moved to Jones's private cabin, where they shot themselves (Hall, 1987). Within about an hour, 914 people, blood covering their faces, tears staining their cheeks, arms tightened about each other, lay dead.

This is an ending that not only echoes the thesis but also poignantly adds to it. The last lines remind readers through the voice of a sister of Jonestown victims that the aftermath of the tragedy led to yet another: The idealistic motives of the victims were ignored and misunderstood.

"The people who died in Jonestown were sweet, altruistic people," stated survivor Timothy Stoen. "One of the tragedies of Jonestown is that people haven't paid enough attention to that" (Hatfield, 1998). It was not only Jones's sweet talking that convinced the Temple members to "drink the Kool-Aid." The people of Jonestown were idealists building a utopia, following a man they thought would lead them there. They loved their children, and feared for their futures. They cared for each other, and stayed together, even in death. They believed in a better world, and dedicated their lives, and deaths, to making it a reality. "As a society we fail to take seriously the very strong and powerful desire, or hunger, for community, a community of people working for social change," stated Rebecca Moore, whose sisters, Carolyn Layton and Annie Moore, died in Jonestown. "At times I despair we've learned nothing" (Hatfield, 1998).

Always begin the References on a new page.

References

Appel, W. (1983). *Cults in America*. New York, NY: Holt, Rinehart and Winston.

Chidester, D. (1988). *Salvation and suicide*. Indianapolis, IN: Indiana University.

Hall, J. R. (1987). *Gone from the promised land*. Somerset, NJ: Transaction.

Hatfield, L. (1998, November 8). Utopian nightmare. *San Francisco Chronicle*.

Kilduff, M., & Tracy, P. (1977, August 1). Inside people's temple. *New West*.

Lattin, D. (2003, November 18). Jonestown: 25 years later. *San Francisco Chronicle*.

Long, R. E. (Ed.). (1994). *Religious cults in America*. New York, NY: H. W. Wilson.

Maaga, M. M. (1998). *Hearing the voices of Jonestown*. Syracuse, NY: Syracuse University.

Messiah from the midwest. (1978, December 4). *Time*.

Neff, D. (1978, December 4). Nightmare in Jonestown. *Time*.

Stephenson, D. (Ed.). (2005). *Dear people: Remembering Jonestown*. Berkeley, CA: Heyday.

Vandecarr, P. (2003, November 25). He lived to tell. *The Advocate,* pp. 37–39.

Wessinger, C. (2000). *How the millennium comes violently*. New York, NY: Seven Bridges.

Weston, J., Jr. (1981). *Our father who art in hell*. New York, NY: Times Books.

What I saw. (1978, December 4). *Newsweek*.

Credits

All photos not otherwise credited appear courtesy of the author.

Image credits

Cover: Visitors in the Museum of Modern Art, Manhattan, New York, USA, America© Daniel Schoenen/Glow Images

FM: Bruce Ballenger portrait

Intro: Small graphic to be repeated in each Presenting Research in Alternative Genres box © TongRo Images/Corbis Images

p. 01: Long shot of a school

p. 01: Shot of steps with shadow

p. 01: View of business people standing in conference room from outdoors Echo/Cultura/Getty Images

p. 02: Looking for Pattern

p. 03: Illustration of a tree Maribom/Fotolia

p. 04: knotted strings Jorg Greuel/Photodisc/Getty Images

Text credits

p. 21: Figure 1.1 Interest Inventory: A Student Example Reprinted with permission of Amanda Stewart.

p. 22: List of Opening Questions Reprinted with permission of Amanda Stewart.

p. 22: List of Ending Questions Reprinted with permission of Amanda Stewart.

p. 45: Screenshot of Library of Congress Authorities Library of Congress.

p. 65: Google Scholar settings page Google, Inc.

p. 65: Google Scholar search results page Google, Inc.

p. 66: Google Scholar Boolean search page Google, Inc.

p. 73: Figure 2.11 (Screenshot) A Sample Online Survey Source: Survey Monkey, LLC.

p. 83: Online Daters by Age Group Source: Based on Aaron Smith and Monica Anderson 5 facts about online dating. Retrieved from: http://www.pewresearch.org/facttank/2016/02/29/5factsaboutonlinedating/.

p. 83: Attitudes Toward Online Dating Source: Based on 5 facts about online dating by Aaron Smith and Monica Anderson Feb 29, 2016.

p. 83: Opinions of Online Dating, 20042013Source: Based on Online Dating & Relationships By Aaron Smith and Maeve Duggan Oct 21, 2013. Retrieved from http://www.pewinternet.org/2013/10/21/online datingrelationships/.

p. 100: Figure 3.4 Amanda's Double Entry Journal Reprinted with permission of Amanda Stewart.

p. 101: Figure 3.5 Double Entry Journal Reprinted with permission of Amanda Stewart.

p. 103: Figure 3.6 Research Log Reprinted with permission of Amanda Stewart.

p. 105: Figure 3.7 Amanda's Narrative Notes Reprinted with permission of Amanda Stewart.

p. 150: Figure 5.2 Amanda Wins the Wrestling Match Reprinted by permission from Amanda Stewart.

p. 196: Student essay: Seeing Past Fear Reprinted with permission from Rachel Gallina.

p. 210: Figure Title Page in APA Style Title Page in APA Style, Source: Christopher Weber, Florida State University.

p. 211: Figure The Abstract Page The Abstract Page, Source: Christopher Weber, Florida State University.

p. 211: Figure The Body of the Paper in APA Style The Body of the Paper in APA Style, Source: Christopher Weber, Florida State University.

p. 213: Figure The References Page The References Page, Source: Christopher Weber, Florida State University.

p. 225: Essay: "Looking for Utopia: The Men and Women of the People's Temple."Reprinted with permission from Becca Ballenger.

Index